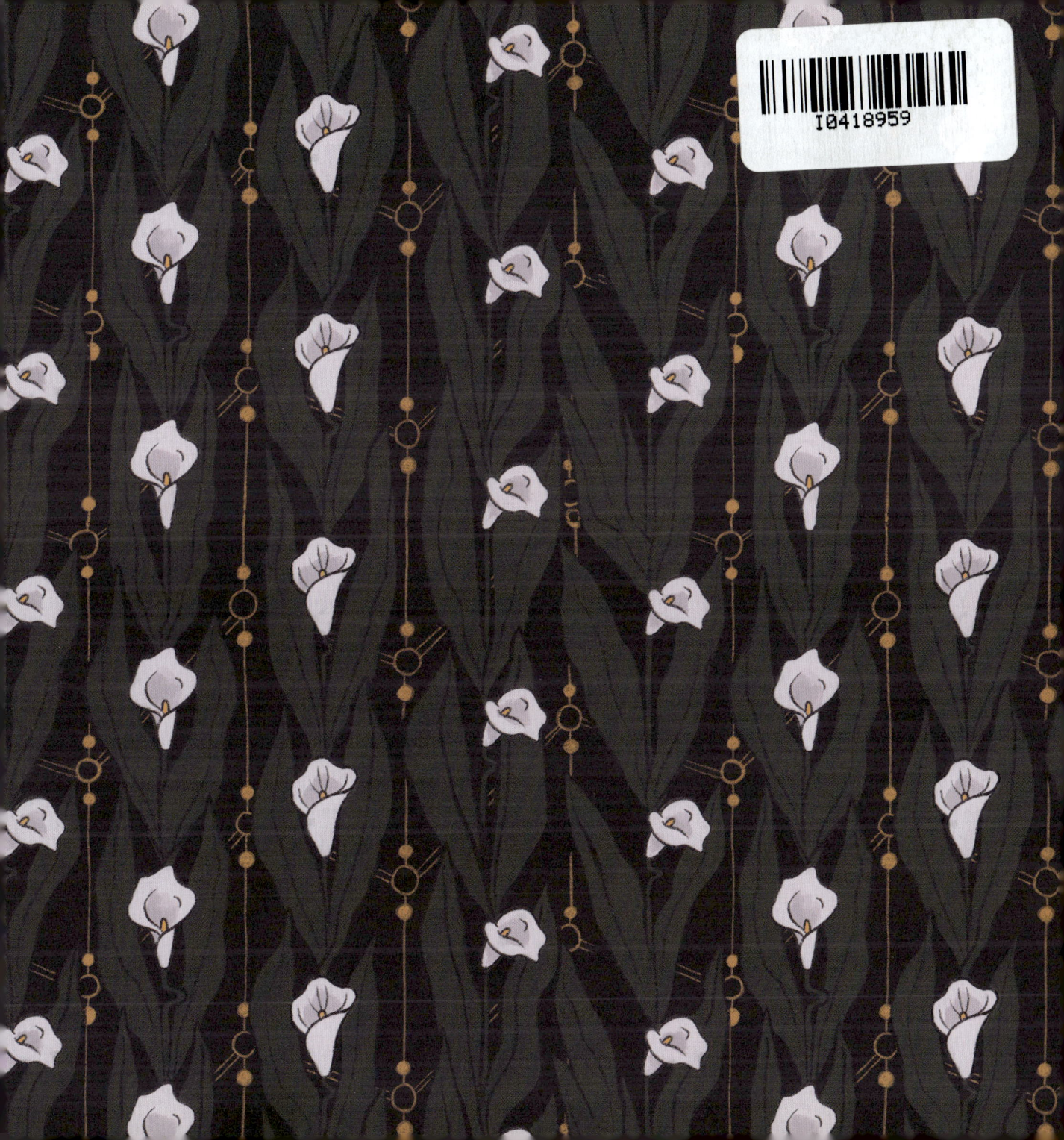
I0418959

I'M NOT YOUR
MUSE

I'M NOT YOUR
MUSE

UNCOVERING THE OVERSHADOWED BRILLIANCE OF

WOMEN ARTISTS
& VISIONARIES

BY LORI ZIMMER
ILLUSTRATED BY MARIA KRASINSKI

RUNNING PRESS

PHILADELPHIA

Text copyright © 2025 by Lori Zimmer
Interior and cover illustrations copyright © 2025 by Maria Krasinski
Cover copyright © 2025 by Hachette Book Group, Inc.

Hachette Book Group supports the right to free expression and the value
of copyright. The purpose of copyright is to encourage writers and artists to produce
the creative works that enrich our culture.

The scanning, uploading, and distribution of this book without permission is a
theft of the author's intellectual property. If you would like permission to use material from
the book (other than for review purposes), please contact permissions@hbgusa.com.
Thank you for your support of the author's rights.

Running Press
Hachette Book Group
1290 Avenue of the Americas, New York, NY 10104
www.runningpress.com
@Running_Press

First Edition: February 2025

Published by Running Press, an imprint of Hachette Book Group, Inc.
The Running Press name and logo are trademarks of Hachette Book Group, Inc.

The Hachette Speakers Bureau provides a wide range of authors for speaking events.
To find out more, go to www.hachettespeakersbureau.com or email HachetteSpeakers@hbgusa.com.

Running Press books may be purchased in bulk for business, educational, or promotional use.
For more information, please contact your local bookseller or the Hachette Book Group
Special Markets Department at Special.Markets@hbgusa.com.

The publisher is not responsible for websites (or their content) that are not owned by the publisher.

Print book cover and interior design by Amanda Richmond

Library of Congress Cataloging-in-Publication Data
Names: Zimmer, Lori, author. | Krasinski, Maria, illustrator.
Title: I'm not your muse : uncovering the overshadowed brilliance of women artists & visionaries /
by Lori Zimmer ; illustrated by Maria Krasinski.
Description: First edition. | Philadelphia : Running Press, 2025. | Includes bibliographical references and index.
Identifiers: LCCN 2024028792 | ISBN 9780762485383 (hardcover) | ISBN 9780762485390 (ebook)
Subjects: LCSH: Women artists. | Creation (Literary, artistic, etc.)
Classification: LCC NX164.W65 Z56 2025 | DDC 700.92/52--dc23/eng/20240701
LC record available at https://lccn.loc.gov/2024028792

ISBNs: 978-0-7624-8538-3 (hardcover), 978-0-7624-8539-0 (ebook)

Printed in China

TLF

10 9 8 7 6 5 4 3 2 1

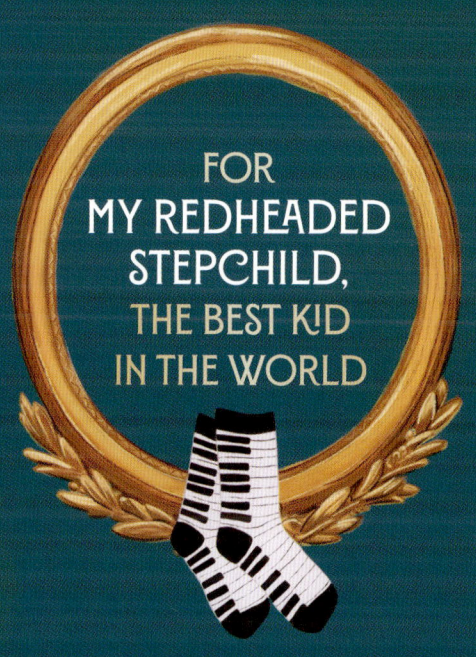

FOR
MY REDHEADED
STEPCHILD,
THE BEST KID
IN THE WORLD

CONTENTS

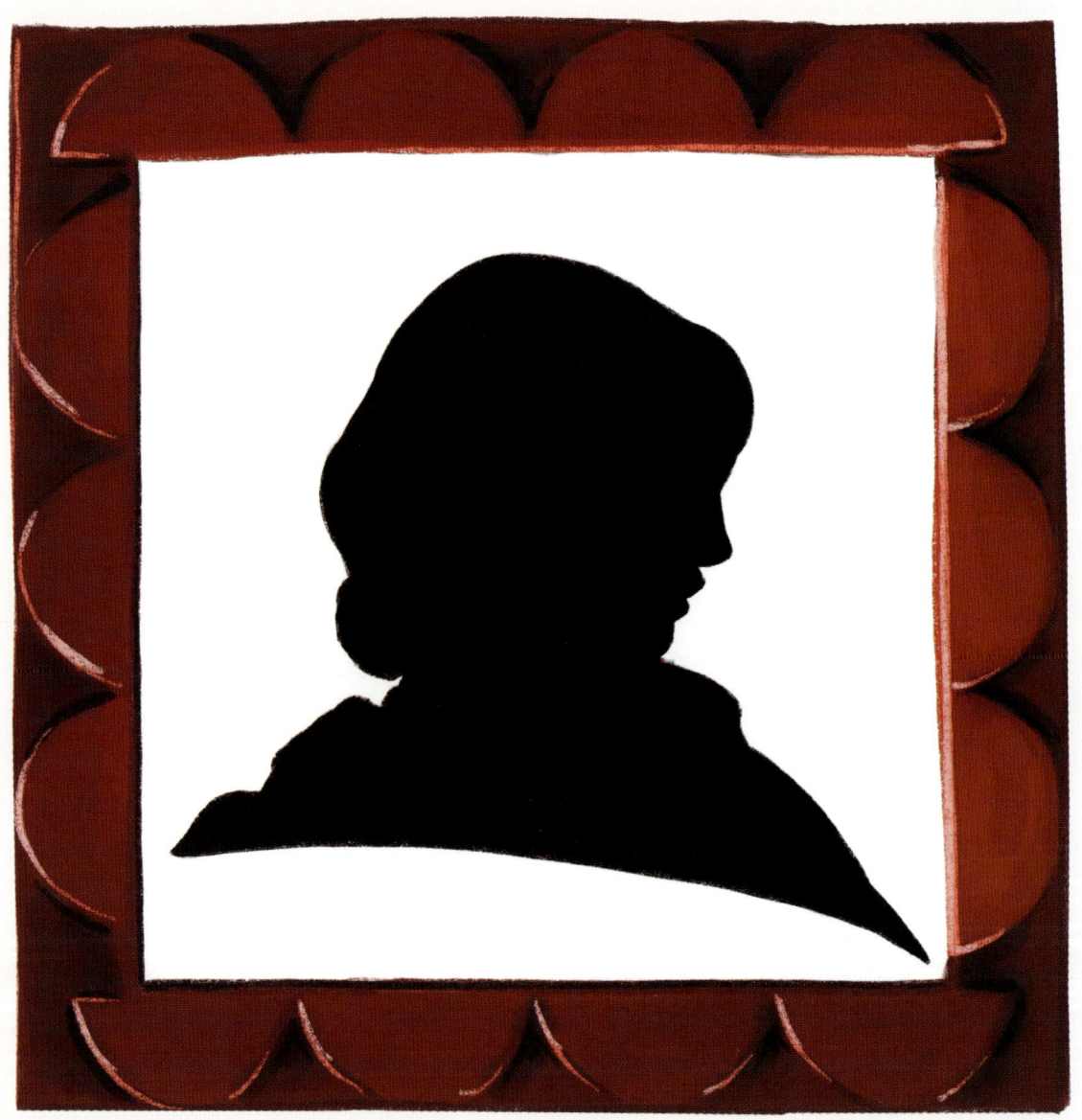

AUTHOR'S NOTE

Writing this book changed me. Truthfully, at times, writing it made me really, really angry. During one particularly long research period, I was basically pissed off or seething for weeks. The injustices repeated over and over again with every woman's story really affected me. Once I punched through the initial membrane of anger, though, I started to form an attachment to these women. I suddenly felt protective of them, responsible for them. I ordered a low-end version of Eileen Gray's E-1027 table for my living room. I resurrected an old H&M dress printed with Morris & Co's Pimpernel pattern from deep in my closet when I read that May Morris had been its true designer. I felt pangs of pride when I'd read about one of their wins. I screamed when Clara Rockmore finally got to tell Lev Termen that it was unfair that he got all the credit for their work in the documentary *Theremin: An Electronic Odyssey*—which is a great film. It didn't matter that he was ninety-seven and hard of hearing. I yelled at a Manhattan gallerist who left Clara Driscoll's name out of an extensive exhibition of Tiffany lamps that included a majority of her designs.

I started to cringe when I'd read clichéd terms like *unsung*, *forgotten*, and *in her own right*. Even *her-story* sounds like a consolation prize to me now. I began to notice that the articles about these women always included several biographical paragraphs about their male spouses or partners. Rarely did articles or biographies about their male counterparts include anything about the women, other than that they were married or how they were otherwise entwined. I became especially disappointed and defensive when this sort of slanted writing was the work of a contemporary writer. I started to notice the comments by women on social media tearing down other women, picking on celebrities and each other. It made me hyperconscious of how I treat and talk to and about women—online and in real life—and I now try my best to fight the cultural urge to go negative. (We all have our moments. The world is angering.)

As I was nearing the finish line for this book, a movie about a plastic doll was being treated like a controversy instead of a mainstream Hollywood blockbuster. We feign progress, but there is much work left to do—and it is more important than ever. A start is to recognize the scores and scores of incredible women whom the writers of history have tried to keep from us. We need to be their champions.

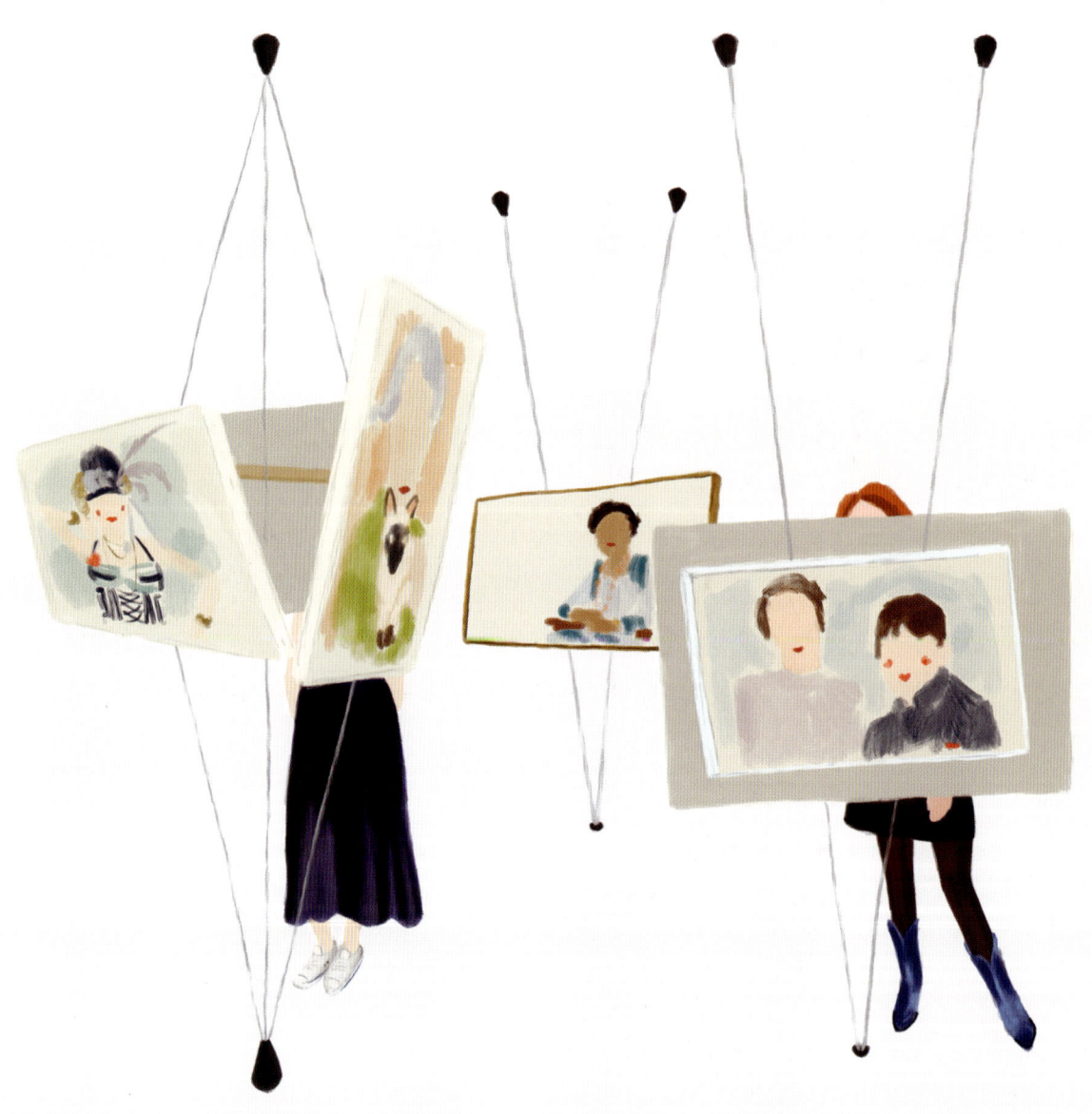

INTRODUCTION

On January 5, 1943, *Exhibition by 31 Women* opened at Peggy Guggenheim's gallery, Art of This Century, in New York City. The show, which is considered the first exhibition to solely feature work by female artists, was controversial simply for its roster. Most critics wrote of the exhibition with patronizing condescension, calling it "radical," "revolutionary," and "notorious"—that is, if they wrote about it at all. One writer from *Time* magazine simply refused to review it, based on his opinion that "there were *no* worthy women artists." Many of the women who participated in the exhibition were widely known in artistic circles around the world. But on paper, the writers of history would only acknowledge their existence if they were playing one role: the muse.

In recognition of that seminal exhibition, I have chosen to spotlight thirty-one incredibly talented women whose creative contributions have, at one time or another, been dismissed and whose professional titles have been ignored, in lieu of the label "muse." Historically, to be called a muse among artistic circles has been marketed as a flattering title. It is a commendation that most often refers to a woman whose vivacity and beauty are the source of inspiration for a usually male artist or creator. She is most likely a lover of this "great man," and her relationship with the inspired one is a catalyst for his artistic success. As a muse, she is a model, a companion, and a collaborator, whose immortalization in the man's resulting artworks is meant to be reward enough for her efforts. But the very concept of a muse underestimates these women and their abilities. At its root, muse is a supporting role, the title a consolation prize that claims to recognize a woman's greatness—but only in how she feeds the energy of another. A muse is like an unpaid intern. It is of no consequence if she has achieved anything on her own. No, no. It is by her contributions to a man's genius that the writers of history have chosen to define her. It is dismissive, reductive, and, frankly, very frustrating.

I speak from experience. As a creative person, I have circulated in the New York art world for nearly two decades. Given that, it is no surprise that I chose a romantic partner within this world, one who shares my passion for art and art history. And as the partner of a professional artist, I've had the word *muse* tossed at me often during the decade we have been together. Yes, I have posed for his paintings, written his artist bios, and helped with his career—just as he has supported mine. Being characterized as his muse is not untrue. But, like the women in this book, I have found most people assume that is *all* I am. When they find out I have written books, penned articles, and curated exhibitions, they are quite often in shock. Even today, many people assume that I work for my partner in some sort of administrative role, rather than as a creative professional on my own. That, too, is dismissive, reductive, and—you guessed it—very frustrating. I cannot imagine having to face this same erasure in the eras in which the women in this book lived.

I am obviously not the only person to feel this way. Martha Gellhorn, the prolific author and war correspondent whose work spanned six decades, famously said, "I will not be a footnote in another's life." Though she tried her damnedest, she is mostly remembered for the few years she spent as Ernest Hemingway's third wife, rather than for her incredible bravery reporting from the front lines of every major international conflict into her eighties. Leonora Carrington, who was one of the thirty-one artists in Guggenheim's seminal exhibition, plainly declared, "I didn't have time to be anyone's muse," yet the Surrealists pigeonholed the young beauty as a femme-enfant. Though she eventually redefined herself in Mexico City and established a Surrealist sect of her own, her work has only recently been celebrated as part of the Surrealist movement.

I think the women in this book are not household names for a plethora of reasons. Art Deco designer Hildreth Meière, illustrator and Algonquin Round Table member Neysa McMein, and Louise Blanchard Bethune, the first American woman to work as a professional architect, were all wildly successful and known in their lifetimes. They had clients and received accolades, were written about in newspapers, and attracted professional recognition. It was not their contemporaries, but the writers of history who omitted their names from books and encyclopedias, gradually phasing them out of cultural memory. Some of the women recognized they would never get their due. Tiffany Studios designer Clara Driscoll and Jane and May Morris, the wife and daughter of William Morris of Morris & Co, knowingly worked under someone else's name for their whole careers, with the truth of their contributions only coming to light decades after their deaths. Still others had their endeavors actively erased from their own timelines by jealous men in their lives. For years, Bauhaus founder Walter Gropius passed off hundreds of photographs documenting the original work of the movement taken by Lucia Moholy as his own. The inventor of narrative film and the first known female film director, Alice Guy-Blaché, spent decades attempting to prove that dozens of films credited to others—from her ex-boss to her ex-husband—were, in fact, her creations. Irish designer Eileen Gray, who *taught herself* architecture and built a modernist villa in the South of France, spent years watching her design be attributed to the famous male architect Le Corbusier.

In all cases, to simply be acknowledged was an uphill battle. It was a fight made even more difficult by societal norms and gender roles that confined women to the home or in the realm of domesticity. To break out of this role, a woman had to be one of two things: a bohemian, who was truly defiant of society's expectations, or sublimely rich. Each made a creative life more possible, though in different ways. And this book represents a collection of both.

It is true that a muse can be anyone. But this book is about a handful of the incredible women whose life's work has been slighted by being reduced to one seemingly innocent yet completely destructive label. *Muse* is a four-letter word, after all.

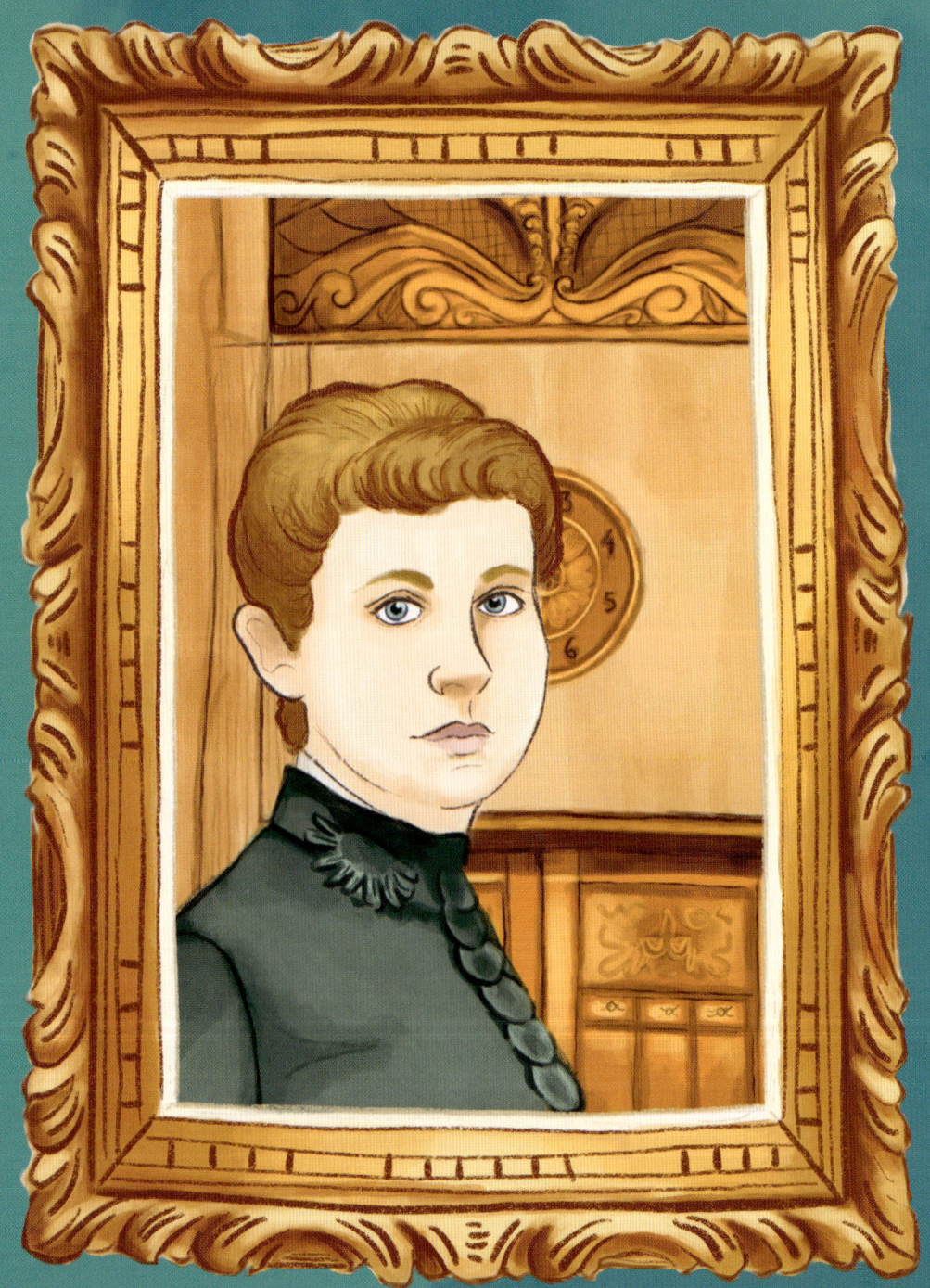

LOUISE BLANCHARD BETHUNE

ARCHITECT AND BICYCLIST

JULY 21, 1856–DECEMBER 18, 1913

For generations, architecture has been consistently, seemingly interminably, dominated by men. Although female students now make up roughly half the enrollment in architecture programs across the United States, they comprise only 23.3 percent of the country's registered architects. Dozens of recent articles explain why: women continue to be discouraged by wage disparity, workplace prejudice, the lack of mentors, and a slew of other factors. In other words, while design continues to soar into the future, this aspect of architecture as a profession is slow to change. While it is still hard to be a woman in architecture in the twenty-first century, I can't imagine having the fortitude to be the first.

I grew up in Buffalo, New York, where Louise Blanchard Bethune became the first registered female architect in the United States in 1881. As a teen in the mid-1990s, I was mesmerized by the beautiful, though decaying and sometimes abandoned, buildings that spoke of a thriving past, particularly the Hotel Lafayette, a French Renaissance beauty that Bethune designed at the turn of the twentieth century. By my time, the hotel had long been used as a single-room occupancy building. Its formerly gleaming Art Deco lobby was a massive pawnshop for its residents, and the crumbling basement was the venue for illegal raves where I'd dance until dawn as a teenager. (Sorry,

Mom!) The gorgeous redbrick and terra-cotta exterior recalled better days, but Bethune's most famous project had largely fallen into horrific disrepair. It was all the more heartbreaking because this striking building should have been a landmark and a beacon to American feminism.

When Buffalo's Hotel Lafayette opened its doors in 1904, the *New York Times* lauded it as "one of the most perfectly appointed and magnificent hotels in the country." Though it was originally designed to accommodate the thousands of visitors who flocked to Buffalo for the Pan-American Exposition of 1901, the delay did not detract from the hotel's success. The seven-story edifice catered to well-to-do tourists and offered "modern" amenities for the first time, like elevators, a telephone in each room, and hot and cold water in each bathroom. It was Bethune's crowning professional achievement, a project that meshed elegance with technological advancement.

The *New York Times* article (from the June 1, 1904, issue), though just a small paragraph, was a triumph for a hotel 400 miles from New York City. After declaring it the "Handsomest Hotel in the Country," the article strangely goes on to credit nearly every man loosely associated with the project: the hotel's investor Walter B. Duffy,

the president of the Hotel Men's Association George W. Sweeney, the businessmen Charles J. Spalding and Joseph Oakes who were to lease the hotel, and the Transportation Club of Buffalo, which vowed to rent the entire seventh floor for club rooms. Glaringly absent is a mention of the architect or architectural firm that had designed said triumph. At first, I assumed this was accidental negligence—surely the *Times* wouldn't shy away from giving credit where credit was due? However, the last line in the article leaves me feeling suspicious when it notes, "Many well-known *men* participated in the opening of the hotel." This seemingly arbitrary statement begs the question: Was the *New York Times* really *that* hesitant to give credit to a *woman*? Perhaps. Despite Bethune having her hand in more than 150 architectural projects over the course of her career, the *New York Times* did not mention her name once in her lifetime.

Luckily for Bethune, Buffalo was not the *New York Times*. By the time the Hotel Lafayette opened, Bethune had been working in the field of architecture for twenty-eight years. She learned the trade as a respected draftsperson at the firm of Waite & Caulkins, which was an accepted practice equal to studying architecture at school in the nineteenth century. When she left Waite

& Caulkins after five years to open an independent firm with her husband and fellow architect Robert Bethune in 1881, she officially became the country's first professional female architect. Her work was so respected that in 1885 she became the only female member elected to the Western Association of Architects. In 1888, she became the first female associate of the American Institute of Architects (AIA). She was later awarded an AIA fellowship in 1889 (also the first woman to receive such a distinction). All the while, she was also a mother to a young son born in 1883.

Raised in Buffalo, Bethune was influenced by the work of the suffragists and abolitionists that had swept the region, including at the nearby Seneca Falls Women's Rights Convention in 1848. In the second half of the nineteenth century and into the early twentieth, Buffalo was experiencing a cultural and technological heyday. Thanks to increased trading, made possible by the opening of the Erie Canal in 1825 and the construction of the Niagara Falls hydroelectric power plant in 1895, Buffalo became the first American municipality to have widespread electric lights. The flourishing city saw a rise in both population and business, becoming one of the richest of the Gilded Age with more millionaires per capita than anywhere else in the country. This cultural and financial affluence, coupled with the influence of the women's suffrage movement, set up the headstrong and independent Louise Blanchard Bethune for success.

The firm—headed by Bethune, her husband, and later a third partner named William Fuchs who had started as the Bethunes' draftsman—focused mostly on industrial and public buildings. Not wanting to be pigeonholed by her gender, Bethune refused to take on residential projects because of their association with domesticity as well as their lower rates of compensation. Instead, she preferred to design diverse projects that showed her varied architectural strengths—largely steel-framed factories, storefronts, and public schools. Her designs utilized advanced features like sanitation, fireproofing, and improved ventilation, which raised the safety standard for public schools and are still used today.

Bethune was a natural feminist before the word had even reached U.S. shores. She was the first in Buffalo to buy a "woman's" bicycle, which became an accidental symbol of feminism by giving women the independence to go wherever they pleased. Like the suffragists, she believed in equality between the genders, though she expressed this by fighting gender prejudice through example rather than protest. As such, she understood the responsibilities she had to her gender as a trailblazer in the field of architecture. One area where she made strides, not just for architects but for all women, was in pay advocacy. Wage parity for all workers performing the same job was not a priority in the late 1800s, as married women were not expected to work. Instead, they were expected to contribute only domestic labor, because the employment of women could take jobs away from men. Bethune was unbothered by this societal norm, insisting on equal pay for her work. She famously turned down an invitation to compete in the 1893 World's Columbian Exposition in Chicago on these grounds, refusing to participate because women were to be paid $1,000, while men would receive $10,000 for the same amount of work. And though she claimed her success *was* activism, she also supported the burgeoning women's rights movements, often speaking at conventions to encourage other women to go into architecture. When Bethune died in 1913, at just fifty-seven years old, there were nearly 200 women working as licensed architects in the United States—many thanks to her encouragement and influence.

Of the 150 buildings Bethune had a hand in across Western New York, only a few remain, including the Iroquois Door Plant Company warehouse (now a textile factory), Witkop and Holmes Headquarters (ironically now apartments given that she didn't design domestic buildings), and the Hotel Lafayette in downtown Buffalo, which she would be pleased to know has regained its status as a crown jewel of the city. In 2010 the hotel was listed on the National Register of Historic Places, and in 2012 it was reopened after a $35 million rehabilitation project, which restored much of the interior to Bethune's original vision—apart from the gorgeous lobby, which itself was reimagined as an Art Deco masterpiece in 1942.

While all the women in this book have stories worth exploring, I know not all of them would have become household names—even without the tangle of patriarchy. Louise Blanchard Bethune, however, is a woman whose name and accomplishments should be taught in school. Becoming the first professional woman in a field that has been, and continues to be, profoundly male-dominated is incredibly consequential. To find professional success while also being a loving wife and mother is a testament to the often dismissed notion that women can have it all. To do so years before women had even won the right to vote is mind-boggling. And to excel at it is the most feminist thing I can think of.

Mending their past omissions, the *New York Times* included Bethune in their wonderful Overlooked No More obituary series on November 4, 2021.

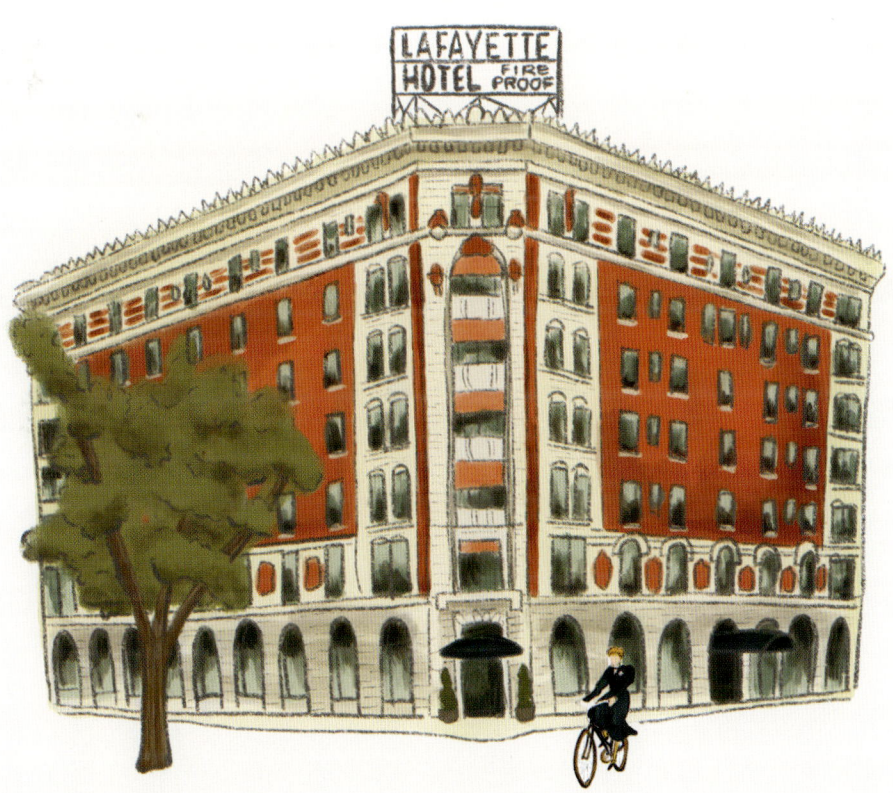

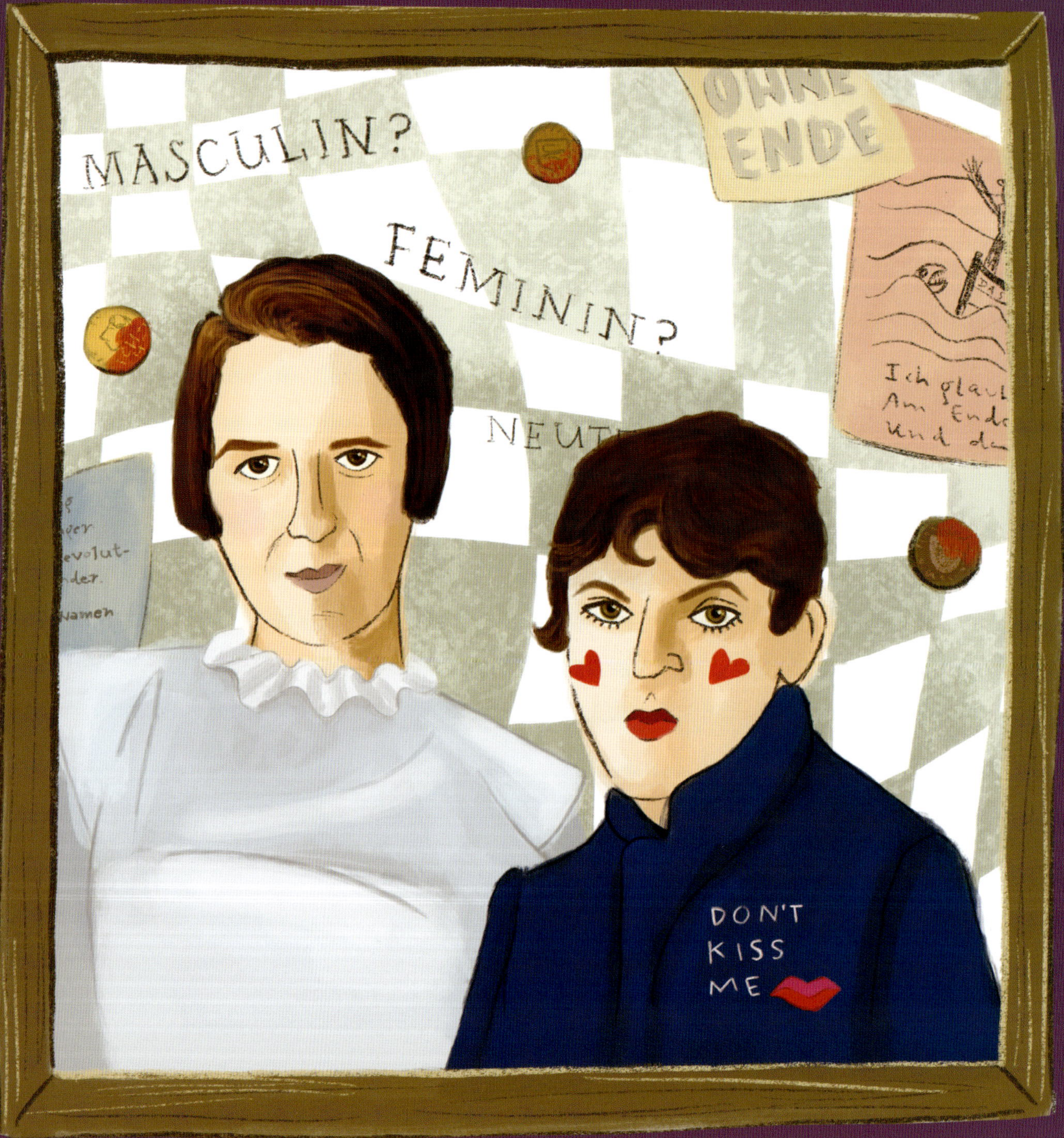
MASCULIN?
FEMININ?
OHNE ENDE
DON'T KISS ME

CLAUDE CAHUN
& MARCEL MOORE

MAKE ART, FIGHT NAZIS

CLAUDE CAHUN | OCTOBER 25, 1894–DECEMBER 8, 1954
MARCEL MOORE | JULY 19, 1892–FEBRUARY 19, 1972

Before today's lexicon of gender-inclusive and nonbinary terms blossomed, Claude Cahun and Marcel Moore sought to investigate and refine their ideas of gender identity through a series of incredible Surrealist photographs. From 1912 through the 1930s, the pair explored gender nonconformity and expression, with Cahun as model and Moore as photographer. Although they were largely unknown to the public at the time, they have since been recognized as beloved and important pioneers of genderqueer exploration and identity. As partners in both love and art, the revolutionary couple spent the second half of their lives quietly, yet forcefully, fighting Nazis by causing a wave of doubt and confusion among soldiers on the British isle of Jersey.

Cahun and Moore were deeply connected on multiple levels. They were lovers, collaborators, soulmates, and oddly, eight years after meeting, they became stepsisters. When the two were first introduced as teenagers in 1909, at school in Nantes, France, Cahun described it in her diaries as a lightning strike—an electric energy she felt to her core. From that moment on they felt complete, like two halves of a whole. Cahun was fifteen, born Lucy Renee Mathilde Schwob, to a Christian mother and an affluent, intellectual Jewish father. Moore, seventeen at their meeting, was born Suzanne Alberte Malherbe to a well-to-do family in Nantes. Their inseparability, which began right away, would last until Cahun's death in 1954.

While they were certainly teenage lovers, the women presented themselves as best friends, shielding the nature of their relationship from outsiders. Then, when Cahun's divorced father married Moore's widowed mother in 1917, the pair officially became "family," giving them an easier cover when traveling together or when they just wished to keep their love private. After school, they moved into a flat in Nantes so Moore could study art. In 1919, they headed to Paris, enticed by the avant-garde Dada and Surrealist movements, as well as the literary Left Bank. By this time, they had already taken up androgynous pseudonyms, which they felt would shroud the origin of their writings, artworks, and performances in mystery. Cahun chose the sexually ambiguous name Claude, which meshed well with "Cahun," a family name she adopted after a brief stint writing under the name Claude Courlis. Her partner chose Marcel, which could be perceived as male

or female, as her first name and Moore, in the spirit of alliteration, for her surname.

In Paris, Cahun and Moore quickly became part of the avant-garde scene, where their work and sexuality were both encouraged. They fell in with the lesbian literary set, including Djuna Barnes, Natalie Barney, and the bookshop-owning couple Sylvia Beach, of Shakespeare and Company, and Adrienne Monnier, who ran a shop called La Maison des Amis des Livres. Cahun and Moore's flat became a sanctuary in which they regularly hosted salons where everyone could freely talk about social justice, sexuality, communism, art, and the rise of fascism elsewhere in Europe. Inspired, supported, and floating merrily along on family money, Cahun and Moore were free, romantically and financially, to create art that did not have to be judged or sold to feed their bellies. The art they made was important, but it was only possible because of the freedom of privilege.

Publicly, the pair participated in the Surrealist scene by making collaborative photomontages. Cahun also became a writer of intense, philosophical prose that pensively questioned gender identity, as well as a novel (*Heroines*, published in 1925) and a mixed-media memoir that combined essays, musings, poems, and photomontages, which she published as *Aveux Non Avenus* in 1930. Moore made illustrations, both for fashion magazines and to accompany Cahun's essays and poems.

Surrealism was a movement that embraced the absurd, examined fantasy and dreams, broke from the confines of tradition, and moved away from social norms to accept a more liberated attitude toward sex and sexuality. Despite being ensconced in this forward-thinking enclave, Cahun and Moore chose to make some artworks for their eyes only. Cahun's personal writing questioned gender identity, but the visual art she shared did not.

Privately, the pair shot revolutionary portraits that would still provide a provocative reconsideration of gender norms nearly seventy years later. The detailed black-and-white tableaux star Cahun, who had been experimenting with self-portraiture since her teens, cast in myriad roles blurring the line between masculine and feminine. In one photograph, she posed as a beautifully androgynous boxer, her short hair oiled and parted, with red hearts painted on her cheeks to match her cupid's bow lips. Cahun's white bodysuit—emblazoned with the phrase I AM IN TRAINING, DON'T KISS ME—is dotted with two faux nipples, while a faux barbell rests on her lap. In other self-portraits, she is a dandy, a doll, a vamp, and an angel. Cahun is covered in masks, dressed as a puppet, shown in a double exposure with her head shaved, appearing to whisper into her own ear, with the text "What do you want from me?" written in French. Moore, who stood behind the camera, was a collaborator in these images, even though she did not star in them herself.

Others in their circle were also experimenting with gender identity. Marcel Duchamp photographed himself as his female alter ego, Rrose Sélavy, and several female writers like George Sand and the Brontë sisters chose masculine pen names to allow their work to be engaged with without the specter of preconceived sexist notions. But none of these contemporaries explored their own gender identities like Cahun and Moore did with their photographs.

These images take on even more meaning today as a reflection of the ongoing social dialogue around gender identity. But they were also remarkable at the time of their creation, when the vocabulary to discuss gender fluidity, nonbinary gender, and transgender identity did not yet exist. Cahun and Moore kept their work mostly private during their lifetimes, and so they did not become the leaders of gender liberation they may have otherwise. Scholars believe that, had the term been available, Cahun would have identified as nonbinary. There is a lot of debate over which pronouns to use for Cahun and Moore—they both referred to themselves as *elle* (she) in writings—but as I feel gender identity is personal, I did not want to make that judgment for them.

However they may have chosen to identify themselves, had they been able to at the time, it is hard to imagine from our modern vantage point two artists working so prolifically for their eyes only. There is an innocence to work meant to impress no one but its creators. Photos of Cahun were only "discovered" by French historian François Leperlier in the 1990s, and for years was thought to be decidedly her own, even though Moore's signature appears on some of their work.

In 1937, as the Nazis advanced across Europe, Cahun and Moore decided it would be best to seclude themselves in a safer place, effectively ending their affiliation with the Parisian art world. Between their sexuality and Cahun's Jewish heritage, it was simply too dangerous for them to stay put. Both women had spent childhood vacations on the idyllic British island of Jersey, off the coast of Brittany. There, they bought a beautiful house, La Rocquiase, and prepared to buckle in for the duration of the war, supposing the tiny island would not be of interest to the Nazis. Their assumption was gravely incorrect. In 1940, Hitler set his sights on the Channel Islands, which he thought would be a strategic base against the British. By June of that year, German soldiers had occupied Jersey. Cahun and Moore, both now in middle age, decided to weather the storm—but not without a fight.

For three years, the women waged a quietly revolutionary campaign against the Nazis. Hitler's soldiers had woven themselves into every facet of the island, occupying hotels, businesses, and homes. (At one point, Cahun and Moore had to share La Rocquiase with four soldiers.) Given this proximity, the artists' attack was not overt. They did not try to convince the German soldiers of the evils of antisemitism and the unfairness of blind hatred. They did not appeal to them with their friendship, either. Instead, they quietly chipped away at their morale, casting a cloud of doubt over them through messages typed anonymously on their Nazi-forbidden Underwood typewriter. Cahun and Moore assumed the role of a disillusioned German soldier, signing their notes simply, "The Soldier With No Name," in an act of both political resistance and gender provocation. Their messages highlighted doubts about the war and painted Hitler as a weak and selfish leader. By crafting these under the guise of a fellow soldier, they hoped to convince the Nazis they encountered that the war was unending and pointless. "Ohne Ende"—without end—became their slogan of protest. Their typed notes often included fake codes that meant nothing, snippets of fake conversations between soldiers, overt mocking of Nazi phrases and propaganda, and nonsensical color coding meant to look important and, more important, confuse the soldiers. They ended each missive with the words "please distribute," implying the notes were the work of a larger network rather than two middle-aged women.

Cahun and Moore delivered these messages themselves by hand, armed with nothing more than a few sleeping pills kept in a Milk of Magnesia bottle, which they planned to swallow if they got caught. They spent months placing the fragile papers in mailboxes, on car windshields and tables at cafés, pinned to doors, and even directly into soldiers' pockets as they passed them around town. They painted coins with nail polish and scratched anti-Nazi messages on them before dropping them on the ground or into the collection plate at church. They grew brazen, slipping photo collages and faux advertisements into magazines at newsstands, and even snuck into the soldiers' church to hang a banner that read "Jesus is great but Hitler is greater, because Jesus died for people, but people die for Hitler!"

Though these messages were wildly subversive, Cahun and Moore didn't know if anyone was receiving them or regarding them with any seriousness. But in 1944, Cahun and Moore found out just how successful their quiet rebellion had been. They were arrested, and a thick folder of their typewritten notes, collected by Nazi officials, was produced. Their captors were shocked to learn the sophisticated spy network they had been chasing was instead two women in their fifties. Cahun and Moore remained defiant throughout their trials and were sentenced to six years' imprisonment and death. Cahun asked which she would serve first.

Liberation came before their execution, but the nearly yearlong stint in prison was hard on Cahun's health. She died at age sixty, nine years later in 1954, having never quite recovered from the illness and malnourishment she experienced under the Nazis. Moore, devastated and depressed, moved to a smaller home on Jersey and died by suicide in 1972. They share a grave, marked with their birth names—together in death as they were in life in their final quiet rebellion.

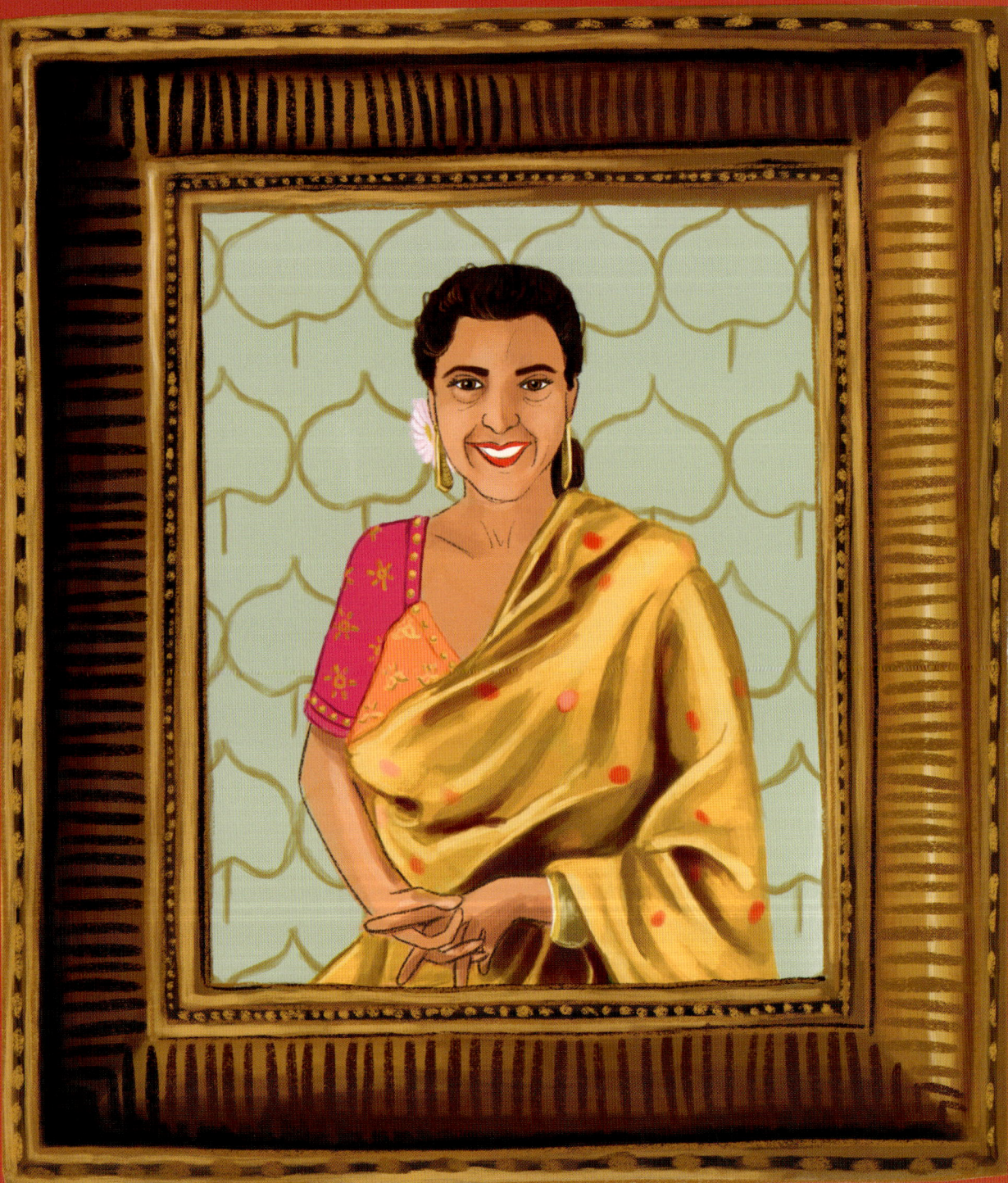

MINNETTE DE SILVA

MOTHER OF SRI LANKAN MODERNISM

FEBRUARY 1, 1918–NOVEMBER 24, 1998

In September 1947, as the dust from World War II was beginning to settle, the leading minds of modernist architecture gathered for the first CIAM Conference (Congrès Internationaux d'Architecture Moderne, or International Conference of Modern Architecture in English) in a decade. Held in Bridgwater, a quaint historic town in Somerset, England, the conference brought together ninety-seven leading architects, urban designers, and writers from around the globe to discuss the latest in modernist design, with a focus on the reconstruction of postwar Europe. After engaging in a weekend of presentations, the conference's participants posed for a massive group photo, creating a veritable who's who of architecture. In this photograph, seated in the front row next to keynote speaker and Bauhaus founder Walter Gropius, is a woman draped in an elegant sari, with a flower in her hair. She sits in sharp contrast to the sea of drab postwar fashions behind her. At just twenty-eight years old, Minnette de Silva was the first Asian member of the CIAM, representing India and her native Ceylon (renamed Sri Lanka in 1972). Behind the traditional clothing was a modern woman and pioneer of modernist architecture, whose work melded the old and new to create a novel style for a freshly independent island nation.

Though de Silva was one of the only students at the CIAM Conference, she was not without experience. She had studied at schools in Bombay (now Mumbai) and Colombo, and also had spent time working in the Bombay offices of Mistri & Bhedwar, as well as for expat German architect Otto Königsberger in Bangalore. At the time of the conference, she was in her second year of study at the Architectural Association in London and was serving as an editor for *Marg*, a quarterly magazine focused on Indian art and architecture that had been founded the year before by her friend Mulk Raj Anand and her sister Anil de Silva. One of de Silva's aims at the conference was to promote the publication among the stars of architecture she met there. De Silva, whose social circle already included figures both important and avant-garde, like Henri Cartier-Bresson, Aldous Huxley, Constantin Brâncuşi, and Pablo Picasso, had met the star of the modernist movement, Le Corbusier, the year before in his Paris studio. The conference was her opportunity to reconnect and learn from him.

Following the conference, Le Corbusier and de Silva stayed in touch. He acted as a mentor, sounding board for her design ideas, and participant in a yearslong exchange of vaguely flirtatious correspondence. When de Silva became the first Asian woman associate of the Royal Institute of British Architects (RIBA) in 1948, Le Corbusier was supportive. (Quite the contrast from his treatment of Eileen Gray, see page 47.)

Though the modernist movement swept across North America and Europe in the early 1930s, it didn't reach Sri Lanka until 1949, just as that nation was finding its voice after 130 years of British occupation and colonization. Nearly twenty years after Eileen Gray built the modernist masterpiece that had filled Le Corbusier with jealous rage, de Silva returned to her birthplace of Sri Lanka to translate that style in a region with a very different climate and socioeconomic environment than Europe. In the large Sri Lankan city of Kandy, de Silva opened her own firm, which she called simply Studio of Modern Architecture. She was only the second woman to establish her own firm, and the first woman to work as an architect in Sri Lanka. What began as a few home designs for friends of the family turned into a successful practice that changed the face of postcolonial Sri Lankan architecture. From 1950 until 1962, de Silva designed forty buildings, thirty-seven of which were residential.

While the cantilevered levels and open verandas of modernism worked well in the tropical climate of Sri Lanka, flat roofs would not. Neither would the expensive materials associated with modernism, as clients in the developing country did not have budgets for glass curtain walls and steel. De Silva's solution was to recontextualize modernism by placing it within a geographical and cultural framework, which she called Regional Modernism. (It has since been redubbed Critical Regionalism.) The movement was essentially a modernist compromise that swapped out elements of the International Style with local materials and influences that also benefited the local community. De Silva's designs traded modernism's lack of ornamentation for carvings, weavings, and other decorative elements made by local artisans, who had been left impoverished after British occupation ended. She especially supported the women who worked as traditional Kandy weavers, as well as Sri Lankan Cubist George Keyt, whom she commissioned to paint murals for several projects.

Unlike other modernist architects, whose singular vision extended to every element of a building inside and out, de Silva believed in the practice of "community architecture," in which future tenants, many of whom were part of the rising middle class, could give input on her designs. In one instance, in the village of Watapuluwa, the tenants hailed from vastly different religious and socioeconomic backgrounds. So, instead of offering one design, de Silva created five variations for different budgets and preferences. More interestingly, she created a rent-to-own model so that tenants would slowly take possession of their chosen properties over a twenty-five-year period—with many of the dwellings greatly appreciating in value and leaving the tenants with valuable holdings. Her large apartment blocks and private homes featured the modernist elements of open-plan living, an emphasis on outdoor space and nature, and modular, adaptive elements, combined with richly lacquered balustrades, metalwork with bodhi-leaf motifs, terra-cotta roof tiles decorated by local artists, highly polished fine woods, and plenty of local limestone. It was a marriage of Sri Lanka and the West.

This was probably why Le Corbusier was not intimidated by her. Throughout their relationship, whatever it was—some suspect the flirtations led to more, though there is no proof—Le Corbusier openly exoticized de Silva. His nickname for her—l'Inde (literally "India")—was reductive at best and emphasized his view of her as a novelty. She introduced him to Indian art, which would greatly influence his later projects, especially in Chandigarh. Yet, when asked, Le Corbusier would not refer to de Silva as an influence, just as a friend. Because her work deviated from the International Style, he felt it did not look like his and therefore did not pose any competition.

Le Corbusier—and most of the West—judged de Silva on appearance rather than her work. She was fetishized for her habit of wearing colorful saris and fresh flowers. Though she claimed to use this to her advantage, most press focused on her saris over her success with Critical Regionalism in Sri Lanka. Even the RIBA website refers to de Silva as "the architect in a sari" in one of the two articles about her. (Can you imagine someone referring to Frank Lloyd Wright as "the architect with the hat"?)

Despite her continuous success throughout the 1950s, de Silva constantly faced distrust from contractors, clients, government officials, and others related to the building process, who were suspicious that she neither worked for nor was married to a man. (She had no interest in marriage and once told a friend that husbands were only good for carrying one's bags.) This doubt hardened de Silva and made her more assertive in business practices. In turn, she became marked as a "difficult woman," and business dried up. Ten years after she had introduced modernism to Sri Lanka, rising architect Geoffrey Bawa would begin his career. Soon after, he would be lauded as the pioneer of modern Sri Lankan architecture instead of her.

After traveling extensively in the 1960s, de Silva designed a few tourist hotels before moving to London in 1973, where she wrote the section on South Asian architecture for Banister Fletcher's textbook *A History of Architecture*. She then joined the Architecture Department at the University of Hong Kong and taught there from 1975 to 1979.

But de Silva missed Sri Lanka. She moved back in 1979 with the hope of restarting her architectural career, but only completed three more buildings during her lifetime, including an expansion of the Kandyan Art Association in her hometown.

In 1996, two years before her death, de Silva became the first woman to be awarded the Sri Lanka Institute of Architects gold medal. (Bawa, meanwhile, had already received the award in 1982.) She died in 1998 at the age of eighty. Her memoir, *The Life and Work of an Asian Woman Architect*, was published a year after her death. With exhibition flyers, plans, personal notes, and diary-like narrative, the book feels like a final attempt to assure her place in history. In some of the photographs of her completed designs, de Silva herself appears, standing proudly as if to say, "This is mine, I was here."

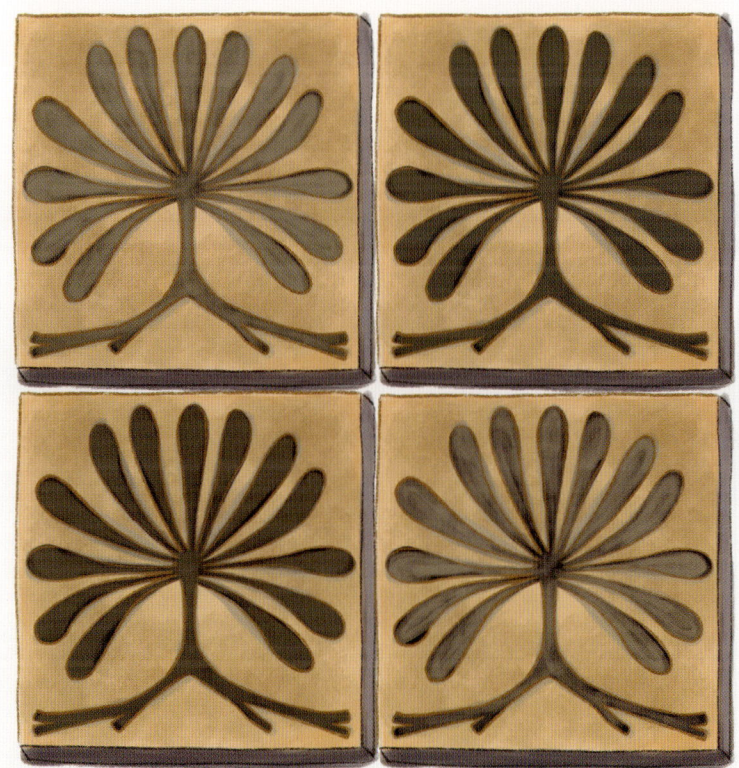

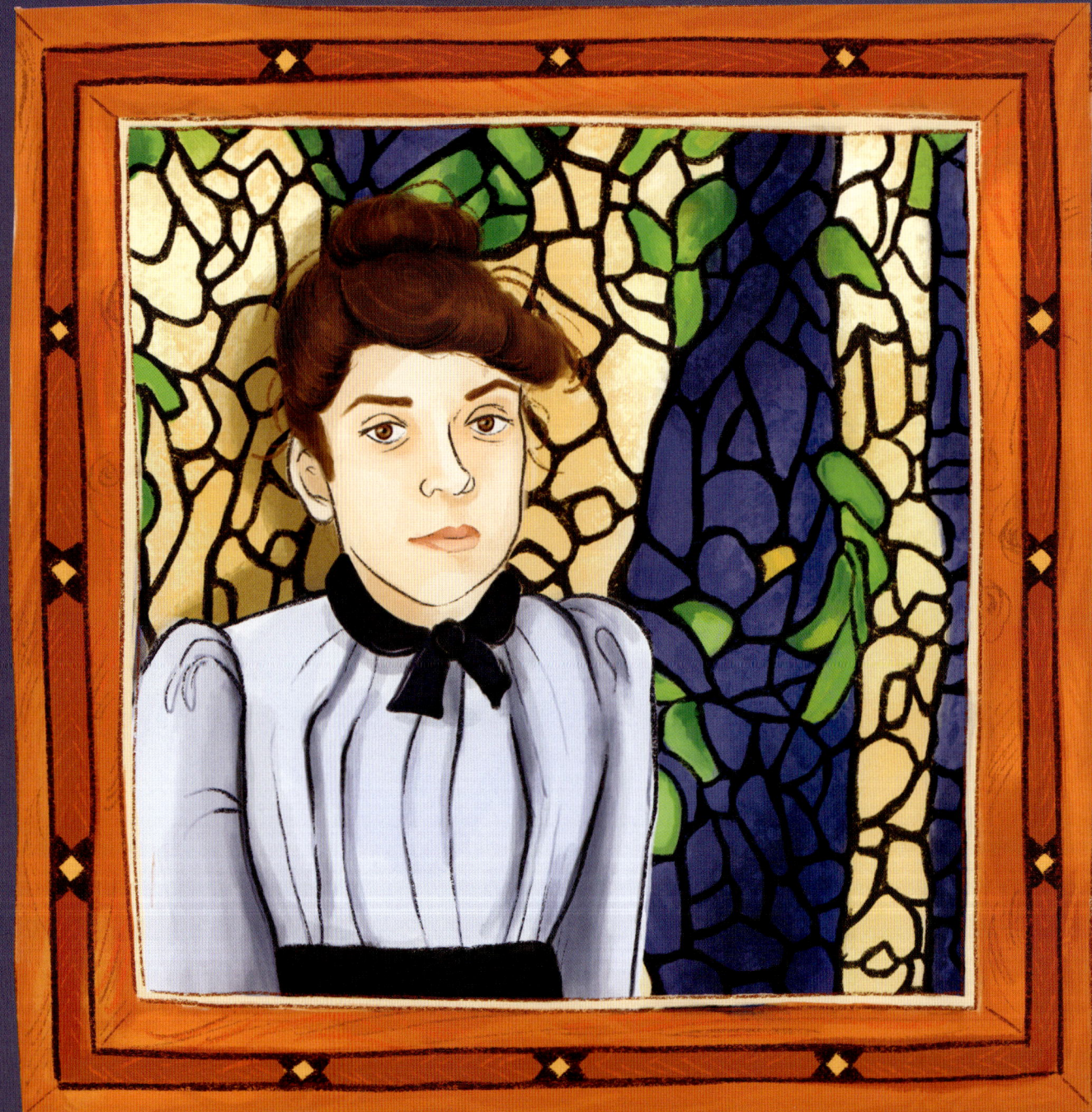

CLARA DRISCOLL

THE TiFFANY WOMAN

DECEMBER 15, 1861–NOVEMBER 6, 1944

The Tiffany lamp, an exquisite jewel of design since its debut in 1893, has long been a coveted collector's item. The lamp's creator, Louis Comfort Tiffany, was a visionary glass artist and artisan, designing beautiful objects and works of art that were then produced with his new glass methods. For more than a century, the Tiffany glass oeuvre—from the iconic lamps to decorative design objects and monumental stained glass installations—was assumed to be designed entirely by Tiffany himself (an assumption he neglected to challenge). In 2007, the truth was revealed. Clara Driscoll, previously known only as the beloved manager of the "Tiffany Girls," the talented Women's Glass Cutting Department that helped the company thrive, was also an incredible artist. During her tenure, she designed at least thirty lamps, as well as decorative desk objects, including some of Tiffany's bestsellers. Driscoll's name may be absent from her pieces, but her visionary designs continue to capture attention in museums, galleries, and at auction.

It was no surprise that Driscoll became an artist, and a successful one at that. As a teen, she was sent from her small town of Tallmadge, Ohio, to the city of Cleveland to attend a special art program at Central High School. She stayed in Cleveland to further her art studies at the Western Reserve School of Design for Women (now the Cleveland Institute of Art) and, after graduation, began working as a designer of Moorish-style furniture at the successful C.S. Ransom company. By 1888, though, she had grown bored of the furniture company (and of Ohio), so she and her sister Josephine moved to New York City to attend the Metropolitan Museum Art School. The sisters lived together in a boardinghouse while they went to school, and later that year both were hired to work in the Women's Glass Cutting Department at Tiffany Studios' Park Avenue workshop.

Working at Tiffany Studios had its perks. With a $20 a week starting salary, they were paid better than they would have been at other jobs generally offered to women, which were mostly limited to harder labor like laundry, sewing, and service jobs. The company even paid unmarried women and unmarried men the same salary. Tiffany also hired only the very best artisans, so he respected his employees for their skill. Despite the great working conditions, though, both sisters lasted only a year. Josephine became homesick and returned to Cleveland, while Clara became engaged to a man named Francis Driscoll, who was thirty years her senior, which complicated her employment. Tiffany, as generous as he was, had adopted a popular business practice of the time of terminating women's employment contracts if they became

engaged and not hiring any married women. The new Mrs. Driscoll's time at Tiffany had come to an end—but not for long.

Three years later in 1892, Francis Driscoll passed away at the age of sixty-one. His death meant that thirty-year-old Driscoll could be welcomed back to Tiffany Studios. She began another four-year stint in the Women's Glass Cutting Department, quit briefly in 1896 for an engagement to a man who would disappear from her life, and then, undaunted, returned to Tiffany again in 1897, this time for a twelve-year stretch. Driscoll soon rose to the top of her department, managing a team of six women, which would later bloom to a staff of thirty-five at the peak of Tiffany's success. She and her team were responsible for the artistic selection and assembling of lamps and objects—they were tasked with putting it all together. Using design blueprints, the women would expertly choose thousands of pieces of house-made glass, bringing together the perfect combination of color and texture to make each piece extraordinary.

The men's department would then solder the pieces together with copper. The men belonged to a union—which the women were not permitted to join—and would occasionally strike if they felt their female coworkers were being treated too well. These misguided male workers believed that women should not compete for the "family wage." In 1903, the insecure men called a strike to demand that the women's department be taken off stained glass work. Tiffany saw the value in his female workers and initially held firm, though he eventually partially caved to the demands of the men's union and agreed to cap Driscoll's team at twenty-seven women. Despite the efforts of the union, Driscoll would always remain in a position of power at Tiffany Studios, outranking many of them.

In time, researchers learned that her era of leadership was also when she designed her most compelling floral lamps—creations that captured the beauty of nature with the flourishes of Art Nouveau. The truth came out in 2005, not long after curator Nina Gray and art historian Martin Eidelberg uncovered boxes of Driscoll's correspondence in the archives of the Queens Historical Society and the Kent State University Library. Soon, the world would know a secret— Louis Comfort Tiffany was not the designer of *all* of his famed lamps. Driscoll's letters reveal that she was among thirty artists who designed and made many of Tiffany's goods in the name of the company.

Driscoll's letters, which spanned most of her adult life, told of her role in Tiffany Studios in great detail. These letters were sent between her mother and sisters, who often replied back in a chain letter style called "round-robins." Driscoll wrote excitedly whenever inspiration struck, like when she designed an entire lamp during her lunch break (the Daffodil). She shared the sketches of her designs with her sisters and mused about watching clients buy her ideas for a small fortune. (In 1903 the Dragonfly Lamp sold for $250, or almost $9,000 in today's dollars.) Through her letters, we can both understand her artistry and discover astonishing revelations, like that two of Tiffany's most popular lamps are hers. Wisteria, a wave of blooms in blue hues spilling from a knot of brown branches, and Dragonfly, which she designed with Alice Gouvy as a daisy chain of insects hanging upside down wing to wing, their heads dropped below the edge as if to spy on one another, are shining examples of Driscoll's talent. So are the other classic designs we can now attribute to her—Cobweb, Butterfly, Poppy, Laburnum, Geranium, and Peony, to name a few. When lit, Driscoll's lamp designs became otherworldly. Her treatment of glass and copper, made to look organic and ethereal, shows a superior understanding of color and material. When the Wisteria Lamp debuted in 1901, Tiffany received so many orders for it that he had to divert some of the work to an unhappy men's department. At $400 (almost $14,000 today), it was the most expensive lamp Tiffany sold, and also the most popular. It is no wonder Driscoll's designs, including Wisteria, are still being copied and manufactured today.

Driscoll never received credit for her overall artistic career, but Tiffany was not entirely dismissive of her contributions to his success. When the Dragonfly Lamp won a bronze prize at the Universal Exposition in Paris in 1900, Tiffany submitted her name for the award. He supported her in an article from 1904 in the *New York Daily News* about women who made salaries of more than $10,000 a year, of which Driscoll was one. He took her and a handful of other artists on trips abroad to find inspiration. Tiffany paid well and created an environment of comradery. He was simply accustomed to leaving the artists on his team unnamed to the wider world. But, looking back, it is important to assign credit where credit is due.

In addition to being an amazing artist and professional leader, Driscoll led the incredible life of a New Woman, breaking with Victorian traditions. Like many feminists of the time, she was an avid bicyclist and even designed her own riding outfit, complete with harem-like pants that would not get stuck in her pedals like a dress would. She loved her life at the boardinghouse on Irving Place, where she rented a room for more than a decade. It had the air of an artist colony, with fellow boarders who were writers, actors, industrial designers, artists, and one businessman, whom she would one day marry. As a group, they'd have rousing conversations over cocktails at home or wander together to art galleries, museums, the theater, and parties. They were always together and even pooled their money to rent a summer home in Point Pleasant, New Jersey, for several summers.

By 1909, Driscoll had became particularly close with one of her housemates. Edward Booth, the lone businessman of the group, had lived down the hall for ten years and had often helped Driscoll with the work she brought home from Tiffany Studios. He was sweet and funny, and over time he became her intellectual confidant. She knew when Booth asked her to marry him that she would have to quit working at Tiffany Studios once and for all. At forty-eight, she felt ready. Her eyes bothered her, and she often suffered from headaches. But beyond that, she was in love. She and Booth retired, traveled extensively, and kept a vacation home in Florida, where Driscoll hand painted silk scarves, which I like to imagine were in the style of her lamps with thick black outlines and jewel-tone colors.

Martin Eidelberg said in a 2007 interview with the *New York Times* that he firmly believed, based on his extensive research, that Tiffany would "have died" if the public had found out that his most famous lamps were designed by Driscoll. During the writing of this book, I visited a comprehensive exhibition of Tiffany lamps at a gallery in Manhattan. I did not find Driscoll's name on any of the wall labels, the price list, or the press release. It seems sellers are still reluctant to give Driscoll her due. Luckily, across town at the wonderful New-York Historical Society, the gallery of Tiffany lamps in the permanent collection features a model of every lamp Driscoll ever designed—with her name on the placard.

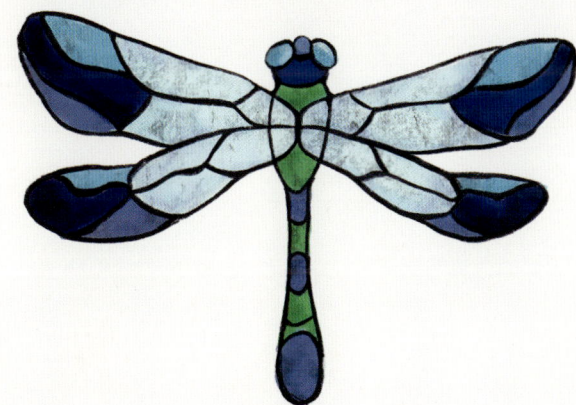

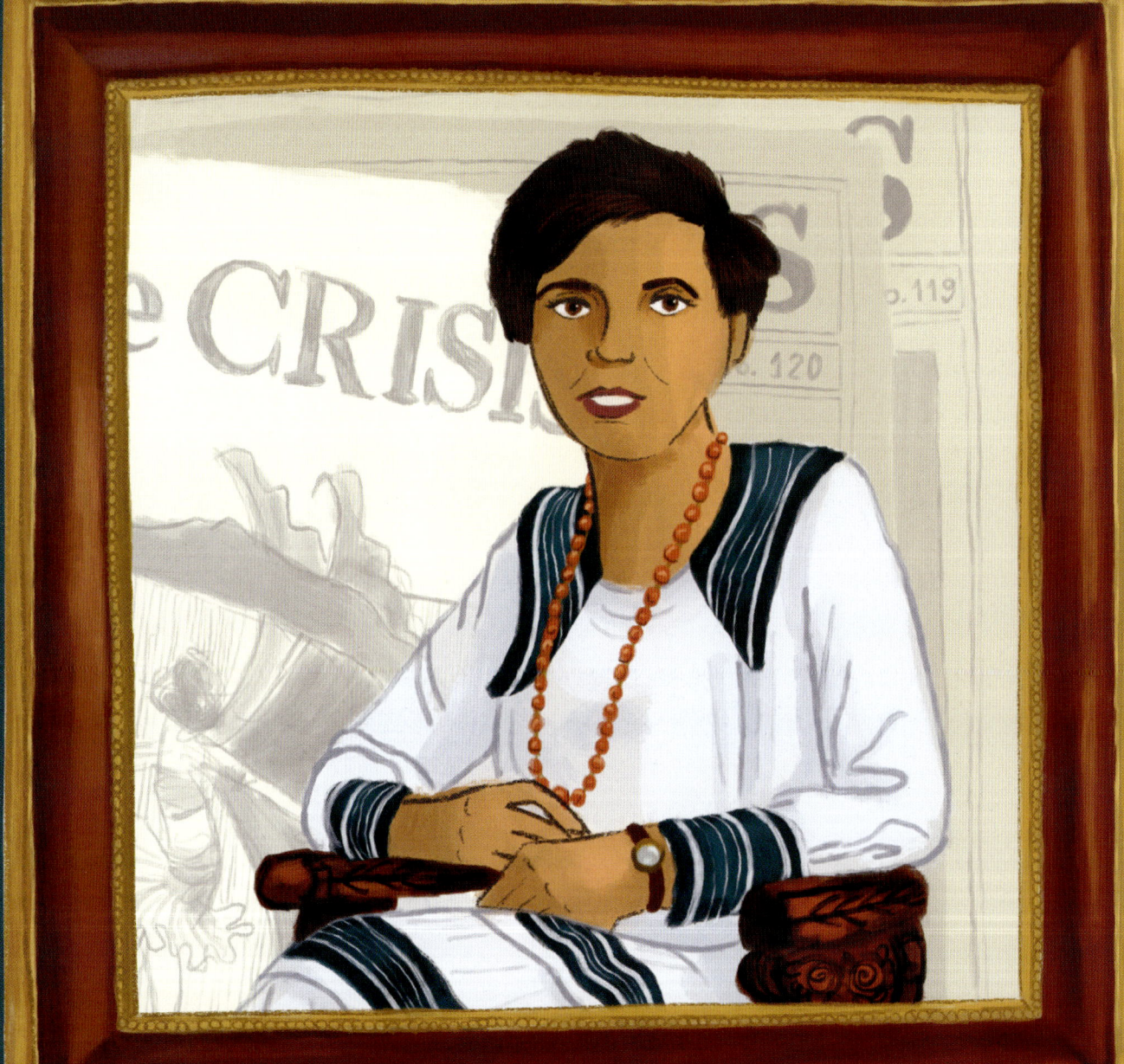

JESSIE REDMON FAUSET

EDITOR OF THE HARLEM RENAISSANCE

APRIL 27, 1882–APRIL 30, 1961

The Harlem Renaissance of the 1920s and '30s changed the nation's general perception of African Americans and African American culture. The period represented an explosion of creativity and intellectualism that sharply contradicted the racist stereotypes perpetuated among white audiences in the decades after the abolition of slavery and pervading white society. For the first time, joyful music, theater, literature, and art from an African American perspective found widespread influence in Western popular culture. Writers of this era put out articles, essays, poems, plays, and novels that celebrated the beauty of Black talent, joy, and ways of life, while sharing honest experiences of discrimination, hardships, and the lasting influence of slavery in their daily lives. In the early 1920s *The Crisis*, the magazine founded by W.E.B. Du Bois and published by the NAACP, was the conduit through which Harlem Renaissance writers could share their perspectives with a broad American audience. Helming the magazine was Jessie Redmon Fauset, a talented editor, writer, translator, and educator who helped shape the voice of a new America.

The Crisis was first published in 1910 as the in-house magazine of the burgeoning NAACP and has been continuously published since, making it the oldest magazine in the world dedicated to African American issues. Under the leadership of Du Bois and a cadre of journalists and writers, the magazine acted as a news and political lifeline for African Americans. Early on, the magazine focused mostly on civil rights and discrimination in articles that aligned with Du Bois's beliefs and opinions on the subjects. It grew to include a smattering of pieces about African American art, theater, and literature by African American writers.

Fauset first contributed poems, short stories, and essays to *The Crisis* in 1912, at age thirty, while working as a French and Latin teacher at schools in Philadelphia and Washington, DC. As nonpolitical features in *The Crisis* gained more traction, Du Bois asked Fauset to take on an editorial role for the literary arm of the magazine, shaping the new voices that were coming out of Harlem. In 1919, she quit her teaching job to focus on her role as literary editor in the magazine's New York office. She and her sister arrived in Harlem just as the Renaissance was beginning to bloom, and soon they were flourishing alongside it. Life in Harlem for the Fauset sisters was charmed. They became active in the bustling artistic scene unfolding in the neighborhood, regularly attending performances, art openings, parties, and readings. Fauset became known for her own social salons, which she dubbed "literary soirées," where Harlem poets and writers gave readings

and the refreshments were notoriously skimpy on the alcohol.

At *The Crisis*, Fauset became the premier tastemaker for African American literature, ushering in new voices who wrote about the Black experience honestly, but also optimistically. She believed that the way to fight discrimination and gain control over the Black narrative was through prosperity, honesty, and positivity. (As the old saying goes, "Success is the best revenge.") Under her discerning eye, literary careers flourished, including those of a dozen or so top writers who defined the Harlem Renaissance, like Jean Toomer, Claude McKay, Gwendolyn Bennett, Zora Neale Hurston, and Langston Hughes. Fauset was the first to publish Hughes's poetry. It appeared in *The Brownies' Book*, a forward-thinking children's magazine that the NAACP produced from 1920 to 1921.

In Hughes's 1940 memoir *The Big Sea*, he wrote that Fauset was one of the "midwives" who brought the literature of the Harlem Renaissance into being and her work was vital to the advancement of African American literature.

During her tenure at *The Crisis*, Fauset wrote fifty-eight of her own pieces, including poems and short stories, while editing hundreds of pieces for others. She also translated from French the work of Black authors from Europe and Africa, bringing new perspectives on the Black experience to Americans. *The Crisis* became an incubator of Black literary talent under the watchful guidance of a strong and capable leader.

In 1924, five years into Fauset's tenure at *The Crisis*, Charles Spurgeon Johnson of the journal *Opportunity* set up a lunch in her honor at the Civic Club on the occasion of her acclaimed debut novel, *There Is Confusion*, about a middle-class African American family and their struggle with discrimination. At the last minute, though, the event turned into an occasion to celebrate a handful of writers, including Langston Hughes, Countee Cullen, and W.E.B. Du Bois. Instead of the planned reading from *There Is Confusion* by the author, several men gave presentations and speeches, and Fauset was introduced briefly at the end.

That dinner began a slow decline in Fauset's relationship with Du Bois and *The Crisis*. By 1927, Fauset felt Du Bois was steering the magazine away from literature at an increasing speed. Uninspired by the new direction, she quit. During her reign, readership of *The Crisis* went from 1,000 to 100,000. Her curation of compelling and inspirational voices bolstered the magazine's popularity.

After Fauset's exit, the quality of the magazine's literary features declined drastically and pieces were rife with errors. Sometimes an old poem would mistakenly be reprinted, or an essay meant as a first draft found its way onto the page. As its focus on Black literature diminished, so did an important group of the magazine's readership.

After she left *The Crisis*, Fauset hoped to get a job in publishing through her NAACP contacts, but instead ended up teaching French in a Bronx high school until 1944. She published three more books—*Plum Bun* (1928), *The Chinaberry Tree* (1931), and *Comedy, American Style* (1933)—which made her the most published writer of the Harlem Renaissance. Each work deals with issues of racial passing, interracial antagonism, self-hatred, misogyny, and identity from the viewpoint of an educated, working-class Black professional—a perspective most of white America had no idea existed.

In 1929, at forty-seven, she married Herbert Harris, an insurance broker. They moved to New Jersey and lived a quiet, happy life until Harris's death in 1958. Fauset died in 1961. During her lifetime, she wrote seventy-seven published works, fifty-eight of which first appeared in *The Crisis*, which she edited for eight years. Faucet's life was full of groundbreaking accomplishments. She graduated as valedictorian from the prestigious Philadelphia High School for Girls (and was likely the first Black graduate) and won a scholarship to Cornell University. (Traditionally, valedictorians from her school went to Bryn Mawr, but the college's president, Carey Thomas, did not want Black or Jewish students at the school and so raised money for Fauset to go to Cornell instead.) She held a master's degree in French from the Ivy League University of Pennsylvania and studied at the Sorbonne. Faucet published four novels, one of which was nationally acclaimed, and ushered in the careers of many important writers. Yet here we are. There's a theory that Fauset is not widely known because the Great Depression and the lead-up to

World War II changed the social trajectory in the United States and effectively ended the Harlem Renaissance. There's another that says she was downplayed in the overall narrative of the Harlem Renaissance because she was not the typical participant, who lived an outrageous, bohemian lifestyle. (She was quite the opposite—she had a steady job, was reserved in demeanor, did well for herself financially, and, as a person in her forties, was older than the typical bohemians.) But the overwhelming evidence of her contributions that has been presented in recent years by scholars, along with the pointed, forgotten mentions of her work, questions if the absence of Fauset in the Harlem Renaissance repertoire was intentional. Nevertheless, without Fauset it may never have been what it was.

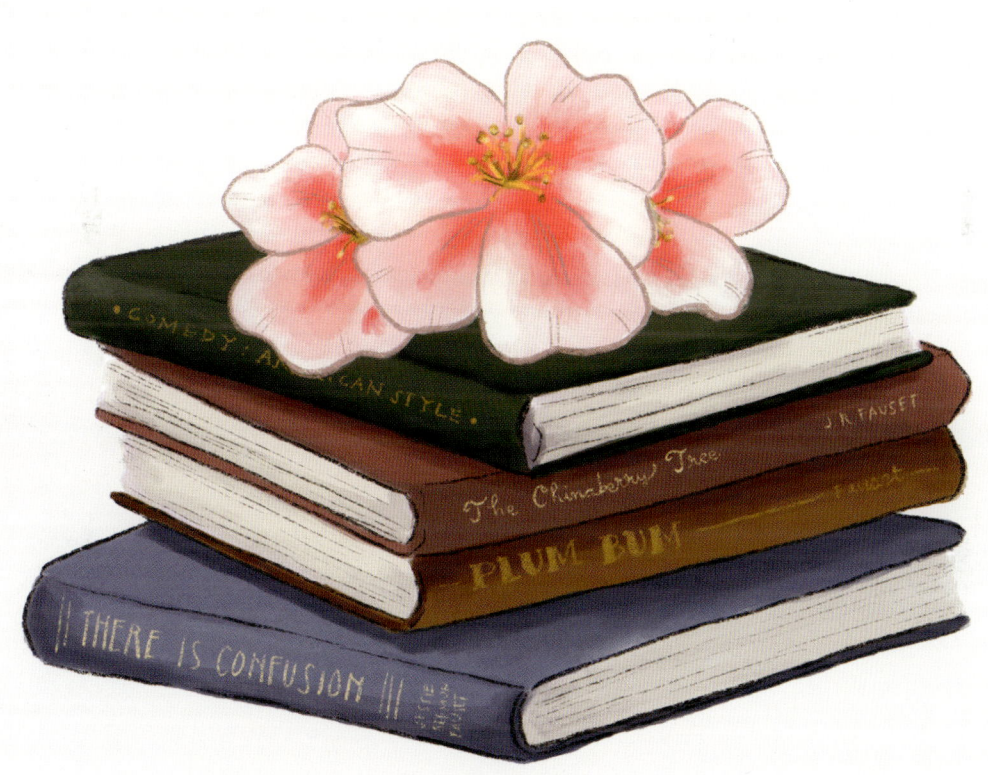

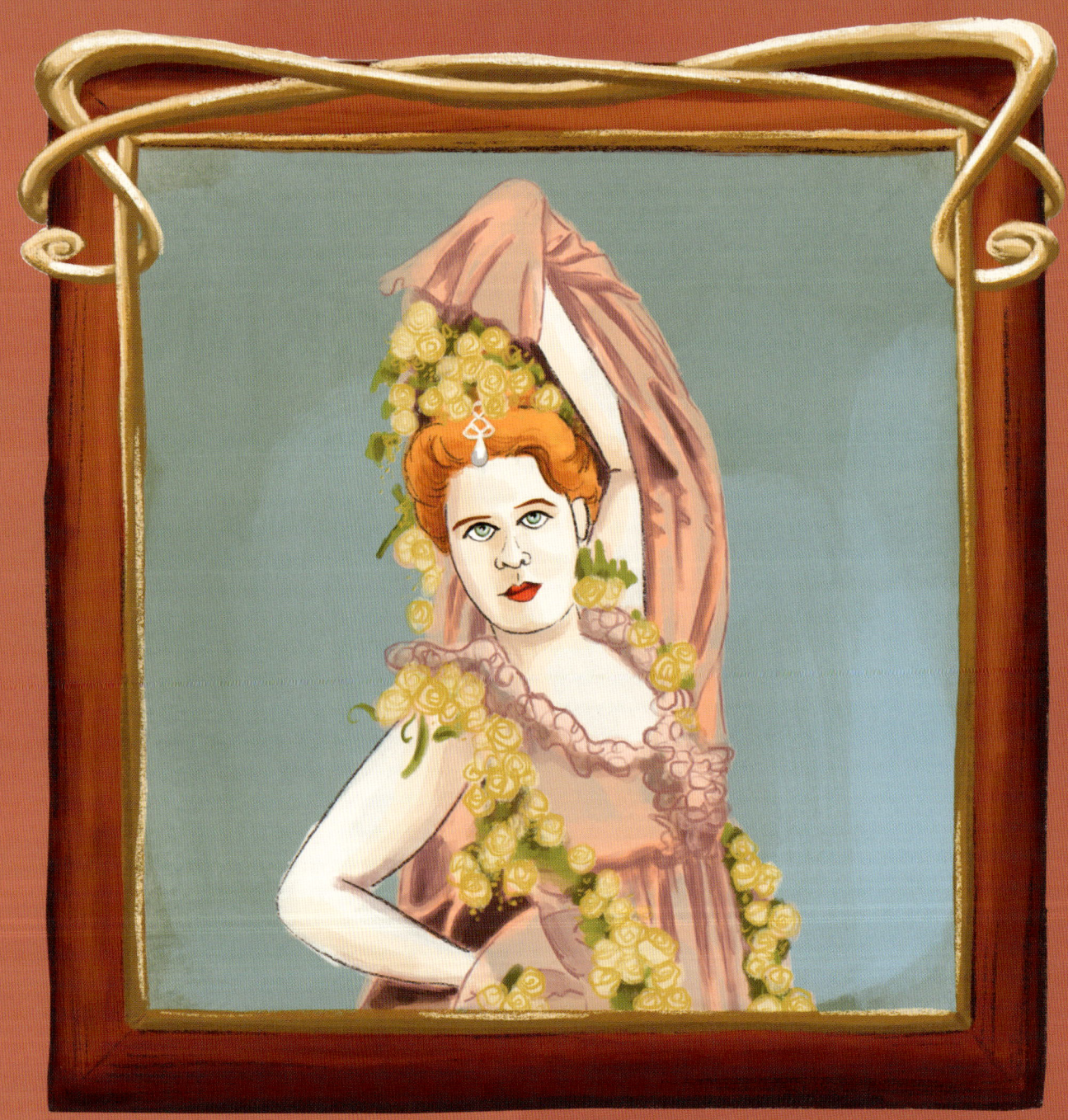

LOIE FULLER

THE EMBODIMENT OF ART NOUVEAU

JANUARY 15, 1862–JANUARY 1, 1928

On the evening of November 5, 1892, the immense velvet curtains that guarded the nether regions of the stage at Paris's famous Folies Bergère parted to reveal a sight quite unlike the music hall's usual bawdy chorus girls and circus acts. In the center of the stage stood Loie Fuller, swathed in a nearly endless cloud of white silk, which cascaded from just below her chin down to the floor in great folds, starkly contrasting the scantily clad performers who usually took to the limelight. The audience was silent, unsure of what to expect from this dancer in an oversize shroud. With each of her hands gripping the ten-foot rods sewn into her sleeves, Fuller took a breath and began to twirl, swinging the rods in undulating patterns that contorted the fabric. Suddenly, her body was consumed by the diaphanous haze of transforming silk, which began to glow with rich hues projected by multicolored stage lights. With a swoop of her arm, Fuller arched her back and vanished into a surreal landscape of rolling hills, her face barely visible behind a swirl of mountain, like a setting sun. As she vigorously cut through the air with twirls and swoops, the vast expanse of silk morphed from one fantastical shape and color to another. She became a butterfly in flight, a rose with unfurling petals, a ghostly apparition, an ephemeral sculpture with the sinuous curves of Art Nouveau. The tumble of white Chinese silk obeyed her every command. After forty-five minutes of intense physical performance, Fuller, now breathless, lowered her arms, brought the billow of fabric to a calm, and took a bow. Stunned silence gave way to an eruption of wild applause. Paris was immediately enamored with the American and her Serpentine Dance.

Even though Fuller had created the Serpentine Dance, her performance was not the first the audience at Folies Bergère had seen that week. (Scandal!) Fuller had arrived in Paris with her sickly mother a few days before her magical debut, after touring the Serpentine Dance up and down the U.S. East Coast, followed by a successful run in New York City. She had conceived of the event in its entirety, from the amorphous costume to the chemical salts used for the colored lights. It was an ingenious piece of performance art, completely outside the realm of dance at the time. American audiences liked the piece, but they didn't give her the artistic recognition she thought Parisians might—and she was probably right. And so, when Fuller arrived at the Folies Bergère early in the week of her debut, she was horrified to find a placard out front advertising the very dance she had come to perform—and had invented herself! Shaking with anger, she agreed to meet with the theater's visionary manager, Édouard Marchand, after a matinee performance of the fraudulent

Serpentine Dance. Fuller immediately recognized the imposter as she took the stage. The thief was an acquaintance in New York who had come to see her perform, clearly stole her act, and hopped the next steamship to Paris to claim it as her own. Luckily, the thief's rendition paled in comparison to the real thing, and Marchand agreed to fire her on the spot. Fuller was booked for an unprecedented 300 performances in a row. She became the toast of Paris.

Fuller's visionary work was like nothing that had preceded it. At the time, dance was a structured art form with careful choreography—whether in traditional ballet theaters or the seductive revues of the music halls. The Serpentine Dance, like the other works Fuller would become famous for, relied on intuitive, spontaneous movements that worked in conjunction with atypical costumes that served as an extension of her body as opposed to mere decoration. The costumes were an integral part of the fantasy, and they were painted with phosphorescent dyes to work with the multicolored stage lights Fuller invented and later patented. (She also attempted to copyright her choreography to deter the many copycats, but Federal Copyright Law would not catch up to her aspirations until 1976.) The combination of Fuller's body movements, costumes, and lighting inventions allowed the audience to experience theater in entirely new ways.

The Folies Bergère had long been frequented by a largely working-class crowd, but the audience began to change as Fuller's popularity grew. The aristocracy descended on the theater and, with them, invitations for Fuller to enter into the upper echelons of society. Along with this social strata came the artists, who saw Fuller as an equal—something she had not experienced with artists in North America. As a result of these connections, some of the leading artists of the day crafted dozens of incredible works inspired by Fuller. Auguste Rodin sculpted her hands. Henri de Toulouse-Lautrec painted her in motion. François-Raoul Larche cast her for a gilt-bronze lamp. Louis Comfort Tiffany and René Lalique captured her in glass, and countless poster artists, including the famed Jules Chéret, drew her in the gorgeous Art Nouveau style she embodied. But each artist took considerable license in their portrayals of Fuller. In the posters, paintings, and sculptures, she was graceful, glamorous, and lithe, while the real Fuller was not. In fact, she didn't look like a typical nineteenth-century dancer at all. At thirty years old, she was already closing in on the age when most showgirls would typically retire. She was also very short and considered rather plump, at least as compared to the stereotypical dancer's build at the time. Luckily, there are many gorgeous photos of Fuller in waves of fabric, showing her as she really was.

Fuller was also a sartorial mess offstage. She had no interest in fashion and wore her hair in a messy bun, in complete opposition to the ruffly, over-the-top style that defined the Belle Époque. She was unbothered by what the public thought of her looks when she wasn't performing, nor did she care what the public thought about her sexuality. Fuller was openly and unapologetically lesbian, which was practically unheard of at the time, even in avant-garde Paris. Her lover of thirty years, banking heiress Gabrielle Bloch (later known as Gab Sorère), was known for only wearing men's suits. Together, they were probably seen as a fashion disaster, but the press left their relationship alone. And neither Fuller's attire nor her love life impeded her fame.

Sorère helped Fuller with her scientific developments and patents, of which she had over a dozen, including for costumes, projectors, colored gels for lights, and chemical salts. In 1898, Fuller read about Pierre and Marie Curie's discovery of radium and wrote to them asking for a sample to paint onto fabric for a luminous costume idea. The Curies quickly squashed the radioactive request, but became friends and scientific advisers, championing Fuller's induction into the French Astronomical Society. The Louvre mounted a show about her accomplishments in light and dance in 1924, which included many of her innovative costumes and lighting techniques.

Sorère also pushed Fuller to open a school and company in Paris, not only to establish a continuing legacy for her developments in dance, but also to compete directly with Isadora Duncan, who had established her own school. Fuller had taken the young Duncan under her wing in 1902 and introduced her to Parisian audiences before the two had a falling out and became bitter rivals. With Sorère's support, Fuller opened her school in 1908, teaching natural movement and improvisational techniques to her students for nearly twenty years. Fuller's deconstructed, interpretive technique was unlike anything found in traditional dance schools and would inspire a new generation to develop modern dance.

When Fuller died of pneumonia in 1928, Sorère continued to run the dance school and laboratory, while also preserving her late partner's legacy as both a dancer and a pioneer of performance art. Sorère had a part in producing films and productions that honored Fuller's choreography and scientific lighting techniques, and she continued Fuller's research and experiments after her death.

The Serpentine Dance is rarely performed anymore, but its otherworldly furls can be experienced in a handful of historic silent films on YouTube, with hand-coloring mimicking Fuller's patented stage lighting effects. (One film was even taken by the famed Lumière brothers in 1896.) Though Fuller herself is not believed to star in any of these choppy black-and-white films, her vision of a swathe of fabric transformed into an Art Nouveau apparition can be experienced in perpetuity.

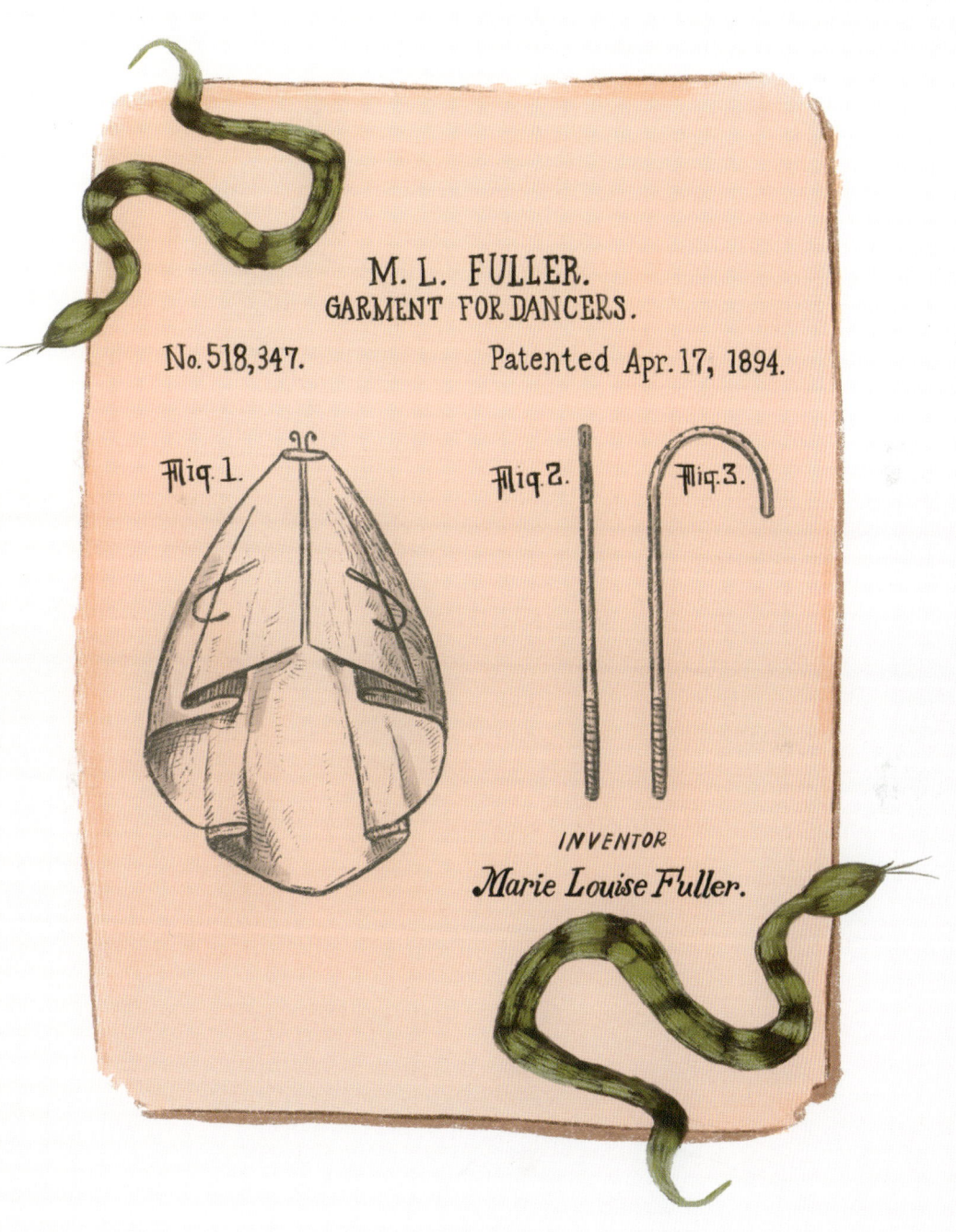

M. L. FULLER.
GARMENT FOR DANCERS.

No. 518,347.   Patented Apr. 17, 1894.

Fig. 1.   Fig. 2.   Fig. 3.

INVENTOR

Marie Louise Fuller.

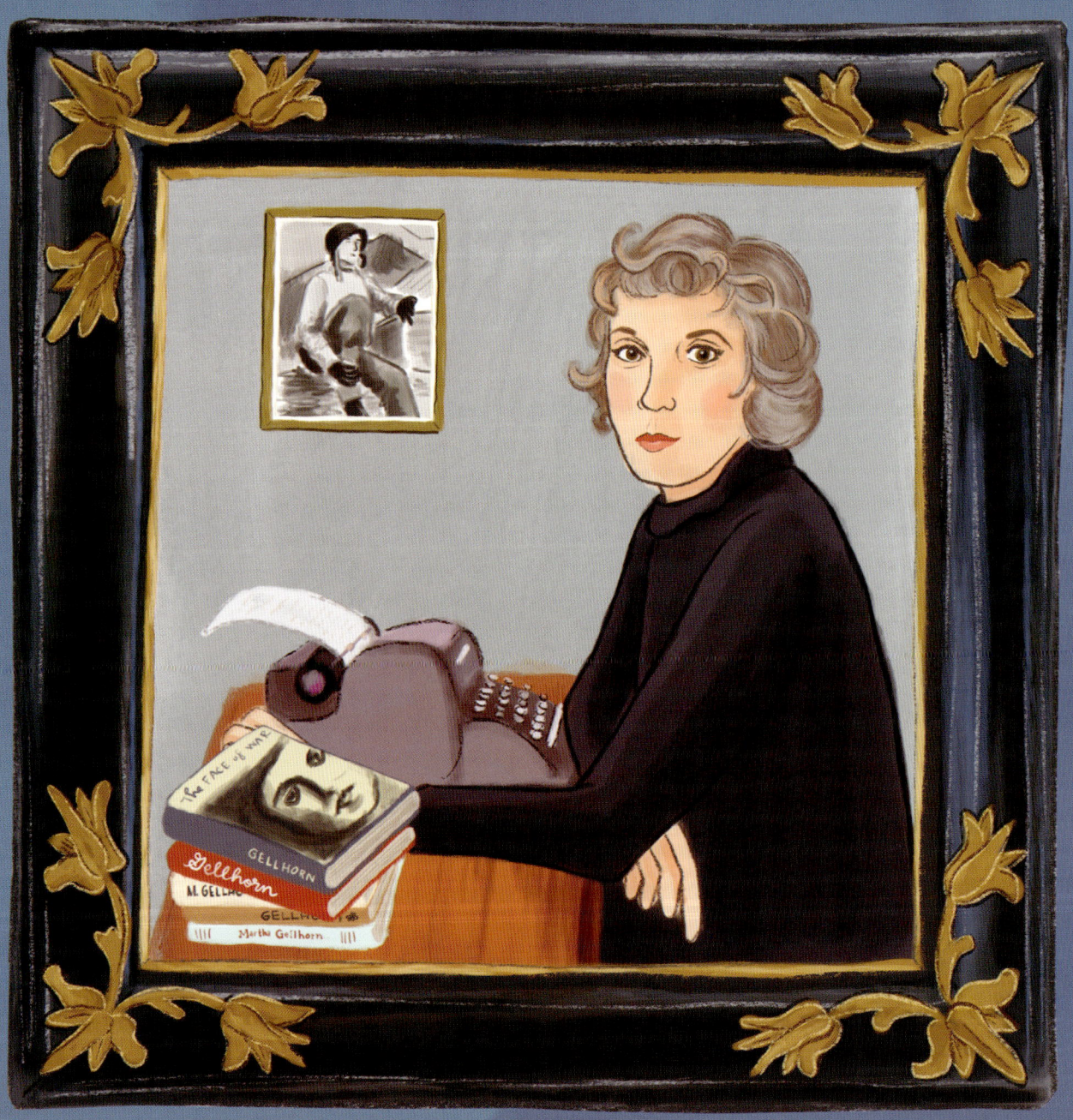

MARTHA GELLHORN

NOVELIST, JOURNALIST, FEARLESS WAR CORRESPONDENT

NOVEMBER 8, 1908–FEBRUARY 15, 1998

On the morning of June 6, 1944, on what would become known as D-Day, writer Martha Gellhorn boarded a water ambulance headed toward the beaches of Normandy to join the Allied troops. When her request for press accreditation to cover the front was denied—along with every other female journalist who had applied—Gellhorn had decided to sneak onto a hospital ship bound for the invasion from London. She stowed away in the ship's bathroom, risking her career and her life for the chance to report from the ground. Once ashore, she was swept up in the chaos and helped medics move the wounded as a stretcher-bearer. Gellhorn was one of only a handful of journalists who made it to land to witness the carnage of D-Day firsthand. She was also the only woman present on D-Day, and the article she wrote about her experience on the front lines for *Collier's Magazine* gave those at home the only direct account of the action.

Gellhorn was afraid of very little. She marched onto virtually every battlefield or conflict zone she could, from the 1930s up to the United States' invasion of Panama in 1989 when she was in her eighties. She wrote frank, honest articles that humanized war and gave dignity to affected communities during the Great Depression, alongside photographer Dorothea Lange. She is the author of five novels, fourteen novellas, and two collections of short stories. Yet, cruelly, a brief relationship has dominated Gellhorn's story. Gellhorn married literary titan Ernest Hemingway in 1940. She was his third wife and the only one to leave him, after a spotty four years of marriage. Her relatively short encounter would haunt her for the rest of her life, with her accomplishments dwarfed by the overblown romanticism of Hemingway.

Gellhorn was encouraged to follow her own path from a young age. Born in St. Louis to George, a progressive doctor, and Edna, a leader of the local women's suffrage movement, she was raised to be independent and curious. Edna and Gellhorn were on Christmas vacation when, by chance, they met Hemingway at a bar called Sloppy Joe's in Key West, Florida, in 1936. Twenty-eight at the time, Gellhorn had already published two novels, spent two years as a freelance foreign correspondent in Europe, and traveled from impoverished towns in New England to North Carolina writing gut-wrenching stories that gave a voice to the American families grappling with the Great Depression. She had most recently spent several months staying at the White House to help Eleanor Roosevelt with her "My Day" column in *Woman's Home Companion*. Like most

writers at the time, Gellhorn had admired Hemingway, who was eleven years her senior, since college, and the two struck up a friendship that night at the bar. Hemingway was immediately attracted to the writer, who was as effortlessly glamorous as she was self-assured, and he began to praise her writing. They hatched a plan to meet in Madrid to cover the Spanish Civil War, and soon Hemingway divorced his second wife Pauline to make Gellhorn his third in 1940.

Yet Gellhorn was not like Hemingway's other wives. Instead, she was very much like him. Writing was the most important thing in her life. She was bold and brash, daring and adventurous. He admired these qualities that he saw in himself.

As soon as they were married, however, Gellhorn noticed things change. She was immediately shocked by how quickly she was addressed as Mrs. Hemingway, even though she had retained her own surname. Hemingway was living in near-squalor across two rustic hotel rooms in Cuba, so her first act as his wife was to find the couple a suitable place to live. She discovered and rented an old villa outside of Havana called Finca La Vigía, and the couple moved in together. She would persuade Hemingway to buy the villa with money from a book advance, and it is now a museum dedicated to *his* life and work. Gellhorn is only mentioned on the museum website as Hemingway's ex-wife.

They spent some happy days at Finca La Vigía, but Hemingway expected Gellhorn to dial back her career and become a submissive wife. It seemed that Hemingway did not want his equal after all. When Gellhorn was covering the Italian Front of World War II in 1943, he sent her a haughty telegram: "Are you a war correspondent, or wife in my bed?" The ultimatum didn't have the effect Hemingway had hoped. While he thought he would guilt her into coming home to be a "good wife" once and for all, Gellhorn instead became disgusted that her husband was at home drinking and partying when there was a war going on that needed to be witnessed and written about. When he thwarted her plans to travel to London to cover the bombings shortly thereafter (he lied and said women weren't allowed on the flight), she decided she was done. And to reinforce her incredible dedication to reporting, as well as her resourcefulness, she arrived in London anyway, finding passage on a freight ship carrying explosives, of course.

Gellhorn was the only one of Hemingway's four wives to leave him. He retaliated against her by scooping her job at *Collier's*. He was a famous, coveted writer at this point, so when he offered up his services for Gellhorn's exact assignments, she was quickly replaced. She got her revenge, though, when *Collier's* published her firsthand account of D-Day right alongside Hemingway's, who was not on the shore like she was. The magazine had found her article so compelling that it decided to publish both, rather than following the initial plan to simply share Hemingway's take. Whether he liked it or not, they *would* be equals. It absolutely infuriated him.

Because of Gellhorn's incredible D-Day stunt, her traveling papers were revoked, but the cunning journalist managed to lie her way into any front she wished for the rest of the war. She was one of the first journalists to go to Dachau in 1945. The atrocities of the camp were unlike anything she had seen in her extensive war reporting. From the piles of victims' bodies to the harrowing condition of the survivors, the horror haunted her deeply. She carried that trauma with her for years, becoming increasingly unsettled in her personal life.

Gellhorn moved from Portugal to London to the United States to Mexico, looking for purpose in her writing. She bought a house in Mexico, finished a novel, and at forty decided to adopt an orphaned Italian boy, only to realize a child would make her lose her independence just as being Hemingway's wife nearly had. Her son Sandro, known as George Alexander Gellhorn, was often left with family in New Jersey when Gellhorn traveled. Eventually, he was enrolled in boarding school so that she could move around freely. Their relationship was contentious until George was an adult. Meanwhile, Gellhorn continued to float in a haze of PTSD into the arms of Tom Matthews, a former editor of *Time* magazine who was extraordinarily wealthy. They were married in 1954, and Gellhorn lost herself in her new life of luxury, with servants and social events to occupy her time. Eventually, she found herself again by taking long solo trips to Africa. She and Matthews divorced in 1963.

Though approaching sixty, Gellhorn was still most comfortable in a war zone. She wrote vivid, honest observations of the Arab-Israeli Conflict and the Vietnam War, for which she openly criticized the U.S. government. Gellhorn's articles got her banned from the front, leading to a terrible period of writer's block that lasted months. In her seventies, she went to South America to write about civil wars. Then, in 1989, and after being on the ground during the U.S. invasion of Panama when she was eighty-one years old, she decided she was finally too old for war.

Gellhorn's eagerness for adventure never dimmed, even as her body declined with age. At eighty-five, she wrote a forty-two-page investigation of the killing of street children in Brazil, but she was so dissatisfied with the finished product that she never wrote again. On February 15, 1998, after becoming nearly blind from a botched cataract surgery, suffering bouts of dementia, and dealing with painful ovarian cancer that had spread to the liver, Martha Gellhorn exited this world as she lived in it—on her own terms, and by cheating a little. She put a vase of her favorite flowers, white tulips, on her nightstand, then took a cyanide pill that ended her life at age eighty-nine.

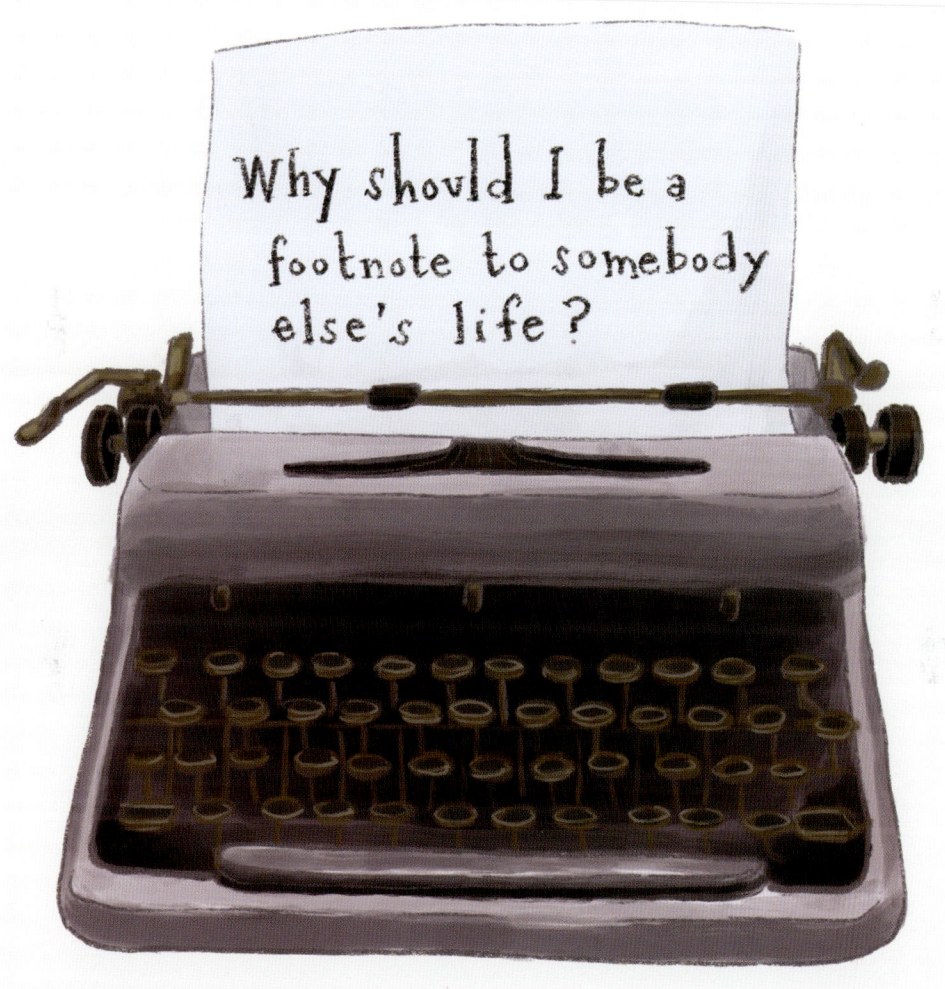

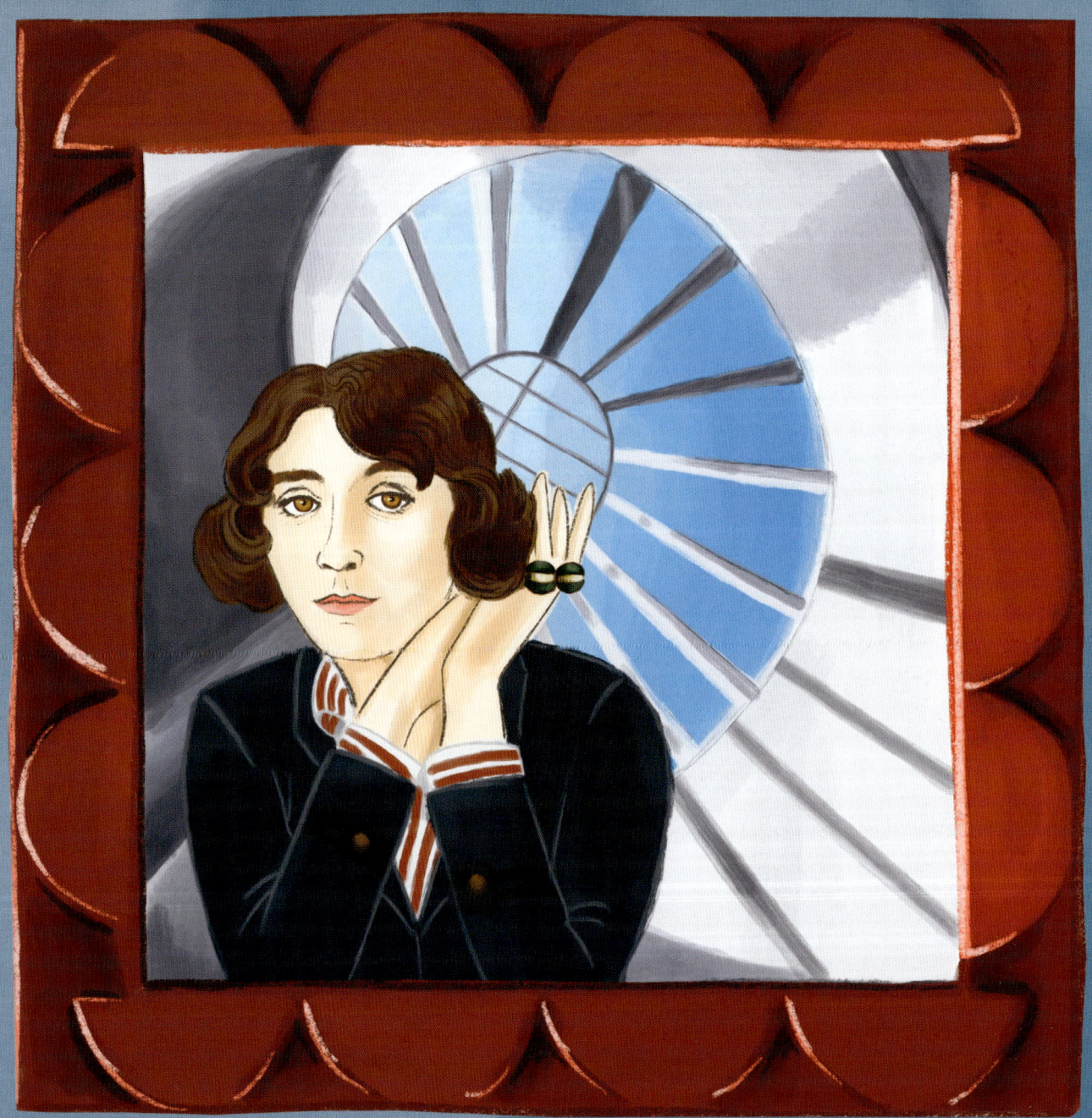

EILEEN GRAY

MAVEN OF MODERNIST DESIGN

AUGUST 9, 1878–OCTOBER 31, 1976

The summer villa Eileen Gray designed for herself and her lover, architect Jean Badovici, became an instant icon of modernist architecture upon its completion. Perched on a remote cliff overlooking the Mediterranean Sea in the South of France, E-1027 was an architectural marvel that reflected the burgeoning modern movement. The pioneering structure was enhanced by Gray's striking interiors, which included her own inventive multifunctional furniture and smart design. The modernists, led by the famously egotistical architect Le Corbusier, claimed to be innovative and forward-thinking in their beliefs. Unfortunately, those beliefs only pertained to design. While the group praised the oddly named villa, they were quick to leave Gray's name out of its discussion whenever they could, going so far as to falsely identify Badovici as its sole architect and even allowing some to think Le Corbusier designed it himself. (Even worse, Le Corbusier would completely deface Gray's masterpiece ten years later in 1939.)

In their social attitudes, the modernists weren't so modern after all. They believed women had no place in architecture, asserting that they were better suited for mere domestic decoration. (Le Corbusier once told young Charlotte Perriand, "We don't need embroidered pillows," when she applied to be an architect at his studio.) Gray experienced this hostile sexism from Le

Corbusier and others like him for much of her life, but her creativity remained undimmed. During her career, which began in the early 1900s and extended until her death in 1976, she reinvented herself over and over again. She was a fine art painter, made exquisite lacquer pieces alongside Seizo Sugawara, transformed jewel box Parisian apartments into stark modern masterpieces for wealthy clients, opened a workshop that produced her abstract carpets and wall hangings, established one of the first female-run art and design galleries, and created incredible modern furniture that remains popular today. After teaching herself architecture, Gray designed and built two dream homes that were harmonious inside and out. (Yes, Eileen Gray taught herself how to be an architect, then actually built homes that became important to architectural history. It's easy to see why the boys' club raged with jealousy.)

Gray was a nonchalant trailblazer for most of her life. She was born Kathleen Eileen Moray Smith, though her family name changed to Gray when her mother, Eveleen Pounden, inherited the title of the nineteenth Baroness Gray in 1895. Her father, a minor Scottish landscape painter named James McLaren Smith, encouraged her to study art. Once Gray did, her remarkable gifts became

evident. She was one of the first women admitted to the Slade School of Fine Art in London, where she studied painting. After Slade, she became the first Western master of Japanese lacquer and, in 1910, opened a studio in Paris with Japanese master Sugawara. Paris allowed Gray to be herself, away from the strict structure of the British aristocracy that her mother's title brought her into. And the bohemian culture of Paris allowed Gray to be open about her bisexuality. She quickly fell in with the legendary lesbian cultural circle that included artist Romaine Brooks, writer Natalie Barney, dancer Loie Fuller, and the popular French singer Damia, with whom Gray had an affair.

She continued to be remarkable. Gray was one of the first Parisians to get a driver's license in 1905, became one of the first women to fly in an airplane in 1909, and later learned to fly a plane herself. Women at the turn of the twentieth century did not behave this way. Gray did not care.

Her lacquer studio with Sugawara was a great success, garnering commissions for decorative screens and wall pieces for some of the wealthiest collectors in Paris. After World War I, she made the leap from lacquer screens to complete Art Deco–inspired interior design, including rugs, wall hangings, and the innovative furniture that reveals Gray's true genius. Her furniture is futuristic and intuitive, often employing clever features that save time, provide storage space, eliminate discomfort, or all three. She focused on fine and modern materials, like hardwoods, tubular steel, glass, fine leathers, and textiles in muted colors. Many of her designs are as popular now as they were 100 years ago. The Bibendum Chair, a stack of three tire-like shapes that was modeled and named after the Michelin Man, and the Transat Chair, an armchair based on a cruise ship's deck chair, are essential pieces for the high-end collector of modernism.

Whether you knew Gray's name before reading this book or not, you likely know the glass table she designed for E-1027 in 1927. The glass and metal adjustable side table has an arm that allows the circular glass tabletop to be raised or lowered. Gray was a very serious person in life, but part of what drove her design was love or warmth. She designed the E-1027 table because her sister loved to eat toast in bed. Gray made the tabletop adjustable to catch her sister's crumbs so they wouldn't fall into the sheets. This table is her most popular design, and today cheap replicas can be found for $150 at online retailers, while high-end versions can fetch up to $1,500 at fancy furniture stores.

By 1922, Gray's rugs and furniture were selling so well that she decided to open a gallery to showcase them, becoming one of the first women to own and run an art gallery. She cleverly avoided the sexism she anticipated facing as a female gallery owner by naming that establishment after an imaginary man. Jean Désert sold Gray's furniture and abstract rugs, which were woven by her friend Evelyn Wyld's workshop, alongside modern art by her elite circle of artists.

It's no surprise that, shortly after she opened the gallery, Gray turned to her next challenge—teaching herself architecture. She bought books, took drafting classes, toured building sites, and tagged along with her lover Badovici, who was fifteen years her junior. In 1926, when Gray was forty-eight years old, she began to design a holiday

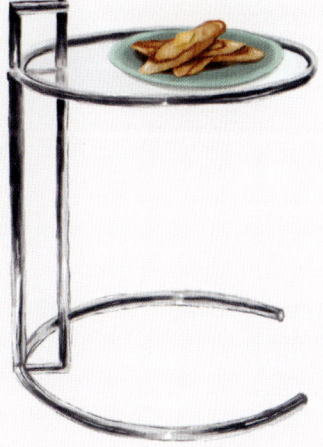

home for the couple to share. The retreat's name was coded in romance. *E* was for Eileen, 10 for *J* for Jean, 2 for *B* for Badovici, and 7 for *G* for Gray. The plot she chose for E-1027 was on a rocky outcropping in Roquerbrune, near Monaco, with no roads leading to it. It was impossible to get a truck to the site to clear the land or to bring in building materials. But Gray was never one to be afraid to get her hands dirty. She had worked continually with lacquer, even though it caused a painful rash all over her skin, so naturally she was fine with hauling supplies to the site and removing debris from it by hand with a wheelbarrow. Her reward each evening was a swim in the sparkling Mediterranean in front of her future home. For three years, she hauled supplies back and forth, working closely with the contractors and making improvements to the design on the fly.

Gray designed a sumptuously minimalist interior that was meant to intuitively fulfill the couple's needs. It was a marvel of multipurpose built-ins and features, including headboards with reading lamps, panels that folded or opened to create tables or privacy screens, dressers with drawers that fanned out so one could easily locate an item, and a cork tea tray to quiet rattling cups. There was not one thing in the house she did not

design, and her rugs, wall hangings, and other furniture made E-1027 a continuous, harmonious, intuitive work of art. Badovici checked in every so often and gave his opinions. So did Le Corbusier. He was furiously impressed, his ego completely disrupted by the realization that a self-taught architect, who was also a woman, could make such a beautiful project. When the couple moved into E-1027 in 1929, Badovici dedicated an issue of his magazine, *L'Architecture Vivante*, to the project and named himself joint architect therein. The article was a hit, and soon other publications were writing about the modernist masterpiece he'd allegedly codesigned. It wasn't long before subsequent articles listed only Badovici, with their writers encouraged by an increasingly obsessed and blindingly jealous Le Corbusier determined to erase Gray from press, museum exhibitions, and galleries. Gray left Badovici and E-1027 in 1931. She built herself a two-bedroom house with a large terrace, which she called Tempe à Pailla, not far from E-1027. Gray had moved on, or so she thought.

One day in 1938, while visiting Badovici and his new girlfriend at E-1027, Le Corbusier crossed the line of respect and violated the architects' code. Unable to move past his jealousy, Le Corbusier took destructive action, pulling out his paints and covering eight of Gray's pristine white walls with garish, lewd murals, one of which portrayed Gray and a female lover in the nude. Worse, *he* was in the nude while painting it. And even worse still, the ever popular Le Corbusier purposely solicited press for the murals, making sure Gray's name was not mentioned in the articles. The shy and reserved Gray was no match for Le Corbusier, his brash personality, and his loose lips.

When World War II came, Badovici and Gray were each forced from their respective homes. Both structures were badly looted, and E-1027 was used for target practice by the Nazis. After the war, Gray moved back to Paris, where she lived quietly for the rest of her life, continuing to design all the while.*

Gray eventually received the acclaim she deserved, though only after the boys' club had died off. In fact, she would have to wait until her nineties to get the recognition she had earned. In 1968, architectural historian Joseph Rykwert wrote an article in *Domus Magazine* paying tribute to Gray. Suddenly, the design world was obsessed with the "newly discovered" woman of the mod-

ern movement. Even then, the furniture she had designed in the 1920s and '30s still felt fresh and edgy, so she partnered with Zeev Aram of Aram Designs, who would bring her pieces to the modern market. The company continues to sell her designs today. In the early 1970s, her originals began to appear at auction. Yves Saint Laurent bought her 1919 Dragons Chair for $2,700 in 1973, a sum that Gray found absurdly high. YSL's stamp of approval enlarged the market for and awareness of Gray's work. In 2009, that same chair would be sold as part of the YSL and Pierre Bergé collection at Christie's auction house. The final price was a whopping $28.3 million, the most ever paid for a piece of contemporary furniture.

When Gray died in Paris in 1976 at the age of ninety-eight, E-1027 was in a state of disrepair. In 2015, director Mary McGuckian paid tribute to Gray and her villa in the biopic *The Price of Desire*, which is filmed entirely at E-1027. The production, along with grants, funded the complete restoration of the villa inside and out, returning it to a condition as close to Gray's vision as possible. E-1027 is now a museum dedicated to Eileen Gray.

---

* Though she would never return to E-1027 for fear of seeing her vision disrupted, the building did give her one final gift—poetic justice for Le Corbusier. He never quite got over his obsession with E-1027, and after he failed to buy the estate, he built a small cabin almost directly behind it. On the morning of August 27, 1965, Le Corbusier had a fatal heart attack while swimming in the waters in front of E-1027.

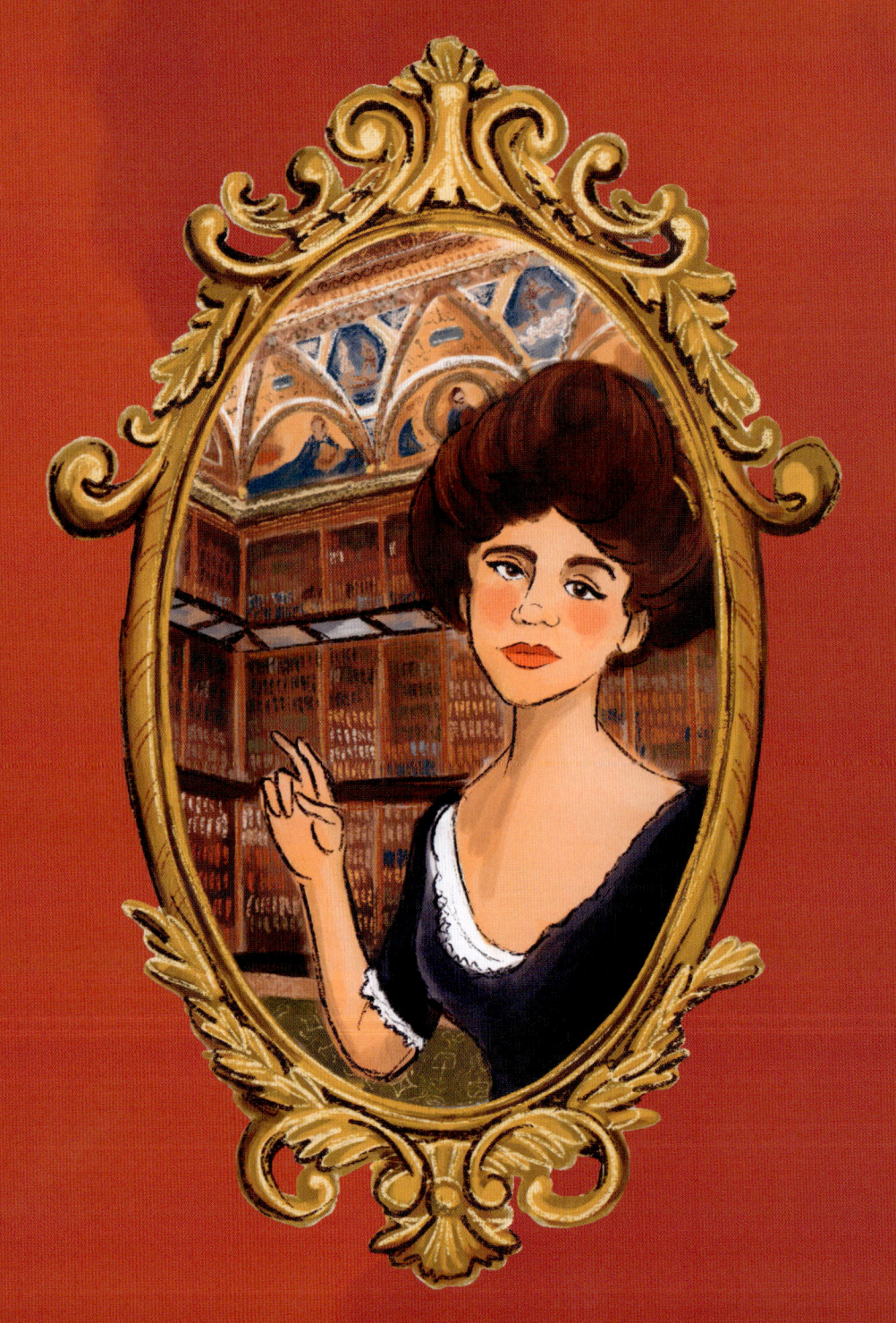

BELLE DA COSTA GREENE

VISIONARY OF THE MORGAN LIBRARY

NOVEMBER 29, 1879–MAY 10, 1950

The Morgan Library & Museum in New York City is a living monument to Gilded Age opulence: a sumptuous collection of rare books and artistic treasures collected by legendary American financier John Pierpont Morgan and forever displayed in a brownstone complex on Manhattan's Madison Avenue. Each year, nearly a quarter million visitors gawk in wonder at the early edition books, Renaissance paintings, historical manuscripts, Old Master drawings, and Chinese porcelains, all fantastically arranged in the luxurious interiors that were once Morgan's private home. With a mission of "bring[ing] to America as many of the finest objects of European civilization," Morgan helped establish one of the most important library collections in history. However, the real credit for this exquisite collection goes to one woman: Morgan's personal librarian, the incredible visionary Belle da Costa Greene. Greene not only shaped this incredible collection through her dedication and determination, she also created the first library with a sharing system, making the content accessible to scholars, students, and universities which otherwise could not afford to acquire these expensive works. She was thrust into a world of high society through her work with Morgan and with that position wielded an incredible amount of power for a woman in the first half of the twentieth century.

J.P. Morgan first hired Greene—an exceptionally smart woman with a complicated secret that could have discredited her important work—in 1905. She had begun life as Belle Marion Greener, the daughter of Genevieve Ida Fleet and Richard T. Greener, who were both from prominent African American families. Her father Richard was the first African American to graduate from Harvard in 1870. He spent his life as an activist, attorney, professor, diplomat, and dean of Howard University. For the first sixteen years of her life, Belle and her five sisters were themselves part of a prominent Black family. They moved from Washington, DC, to New York in 1885, when Richard took a position as secretary for the Grant Monument Association, where he led the fundraising initiative to construct the official mausoleum of President Ulysses S. Grant. When Belle was eighteen, though, her life changed forever. Her father was offered a job as a U.S. commercial agent in Vladivostok, Russia; her mother was not interested in relocating their family so far away. Richard took the position anyway and left his family behind.

Distraught and angry, Genevieve decided to cut all ties to her husband and start anew with her daughters. Alone in New York, she also made a decision to reinvent the family—as white. The Greeners were light-skinned and had been mistaken as white on occasion. So she adjusted their surname, changing it to what she considered the more "American" sounding Greene. Genevieve changed her maiden name to the Dutch-sounding Van Vliet, and Belle swapped her middle name of Marion for the more European sounding da Costa. They recast their heritage as well, claiming their ancestors were Portuguese to explain their darker complexion.

After being brought up as an affluent African American and the daughter of an activist, this shift in identity must have been confusing for Greene. But Blacks presenting as white if they could was not an uncommon occurrence in Jim Crow America. Many African Americans or people of mixed race sought any path available to escape the extremes of racial discrimination and make better opportunities for their families.

For Greene's entire professional life, then, she was perceived as white. This began as soon as she turned eighteen, as her father Richard refused to support any of his children after that age. Instead of extensive schooling, Greene got a job right away as a cataloger at the Princeton University Library. Because of this job, she developed a love of rare books and the work of reference librarians. While at Princeton, she met Junius Spencer Morgan II, a fellow bibliophile and Princeton alumnus who regularly donated rare volumes to the university's library. Junius recommended Greene to his uncle J.P. Morgan, whose private library was being built in Manhattan. Impressed by Greene's taste and skill, Morgan poached her from Princeton in 1905 to work as an assistant librarian at his own venture. Soon, the twenty-six-year-old was making a whopping $75 (over $2,500 in today's dollars) a week as his employee.

Her first task at the library was to unpack boxes and boxes of Morgan's existing collection which had been sent from storage over to the nearly complete building that would serve as the main part of the library. The edifice had been designed by Charles McKim of famed architecture firm McKim, Mead & White, and Morgan spared no cost on its construction, which was finally completed in 1906. By that point, Morgan had already become known as a great American financier, with investments and industrial organizations worth more than $25 billion in today's dollars. He changed the face of corporate finance during the Gilded Age, as his expertise and corporate holdings accrued him great influence in U.S.

markets and made him one of the richest men in history.

Once the classic marble library was finished and Morgan moved his office in, Greene's job quickly changed. Morgan grew fond of her, and soon she was managing his entire collection, communicating daily with rare book dealers, auction houses, museums, and other scholarly libraries to acquire the perfect pieces. The trust between Greene and Morgan strengthened, as did their friendship. She lovingly nicknamed him "Big Chief" and began advising him on the collection's direction. With his vast wealth, she knew he had the means to build an important library that could change the face of what it meant to collect books. She believed Morgan's library should be preeminent, serving as a benchmark for other collections to measure themselves against, so she began to push the boundaries of what he acquired beyond books. Greene encouraged the purchase of pieces that met the same criteria she had for books—those that were rare, important, and a teaching moment from history. Under her direction, the collection grew to include masterpieces like the medieval reliquary the *Stavelot Triptych*. She also oversaw the acquisition of the first pieces of Islamic art in the collection—she knew that Persian art wasn't a passion of Morgan's, but both felt it was important to have it represented in his holdings.

Having the complete trust of someone like J.P. Morgan thrust Greene into the high-society spotlight. As the face of the collection, she was sent to public auctions and sales on Morgan's behalf and became known there for her shrewd negotiating. She once bragged about acquiring a rare book for $48,000, talking the dealer down when she knew that Morgan had approved her to spend $100,000. These prudent purchasing habits landed her in newspapers and society pages, which touted her as an intelligent sensation who pushed boundaries in the male-dominated worlds of art and literature. Her glamorous and flamboyant style was praised (luckily!), and pictures and drawings of her began to appear alongside articles. The press and public simply could not believe that a librar-

ian could be so young, fashionable, and wildly intelligent, nor could they believe that Morgan would entrust *a woman* to handle his business. Greene used this newfound publicity to push for higher wages for other librarians, since she knew these were predominantly women whose families depended on their paychecks.

Being linked to Morgan also gave Greene access and influence in a world of men. Women were not usually the ones negotiating at auctions and with dealers or conducting business with men. But with Morgan's approval, Greene operated on equal footing with the businessmen she routinely dealt with, and even bested them when she held Morgan's purse. Her connection to Morgan and clear taste level also opened an endless rotation of invitations to society balls, teas, events, and private clubs, which she enjoyed just as much as dressing stylishly for the occasions. She also had her portrait taken by professional studio photographers and rendered by artists, in a tradition normally reserved for society women.

Morgan died in 1913, leaving Greene to wonder what would become of the library—and her position. In his will, he left $50,000 to Greene (about $1.3 million today), along with instructions to his son Jack that Greene stay on as librarian with her

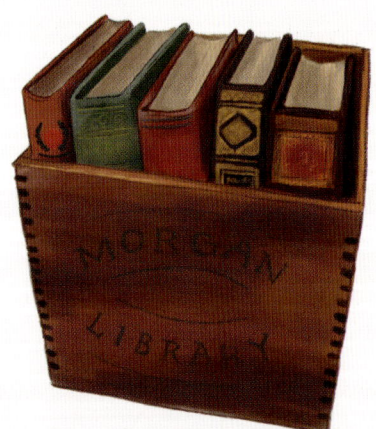

salary, which was by this point $10,000 a year (nearly $300,000 today). For a year, she reassessed the 7,000 pieces in the collection, selling off or donating some of the fine art to museums like the Metropolitan Museum of Art to raise money to buy more literary and illuminated manuscripts.

After World War I, Greene and Jack began to discuss changing the scope of the library. She envisioned the collection as an incredible teaching resource and wanted to give the public unprecedented access to the rare volumes. With the younger Morgan, she transformed a book lover's paradise into a lending museum with excellent research facilities. In 1924, he officially incorporated the Pierpont Morgan Library as a public educational institution, with a $1.5 million endowment to boot. Greene was named as the museum's first director.

She added 5,000 additional volumes to the collection, annotating them, adding commentary by visiting scholars, and creating a cataloging system. She also spearheaded initiatives that were, at the time, unknown to other research libraries, including an active loaning program to other institutions and a calendar of special exhibitions that showed off rarely displayed works from the Morgan Library and elsewhere. Greene broadened the library's educational outreach by hosting special lectures and seminars, which were open to the public, as well. The library museum grew, and an annex was opened in 1928, in which she curated forty-six special exhibitions. An added reading room gave visitors access to 17,000 volumes, though her innovations in allowing the public to interact with the collection extended even beyond the museum's walls. She established the first example of "remote" access to a library, creating copies of important works to disperse to other libraries—quite a feat of knowledge sharing in a pre-internet world. Similarly, she created a photography department, which was responsible for reproducing works and photographing works with infrared film for study. She formed deep bonds with other libraries and institutions, setting up a network of scholars who could have access to all of their collections.

Greene died of cancer in New York City in 1950. She was notoriously private and, in the weeks before her death, burned all of her personal papers and correspondence. We are lucky enough to know a snippet of her personality thanks to the preservation of the letters she sent to her lover Bernard Berenson, an Italian Renaissance expert she consulted with regularly for the library.

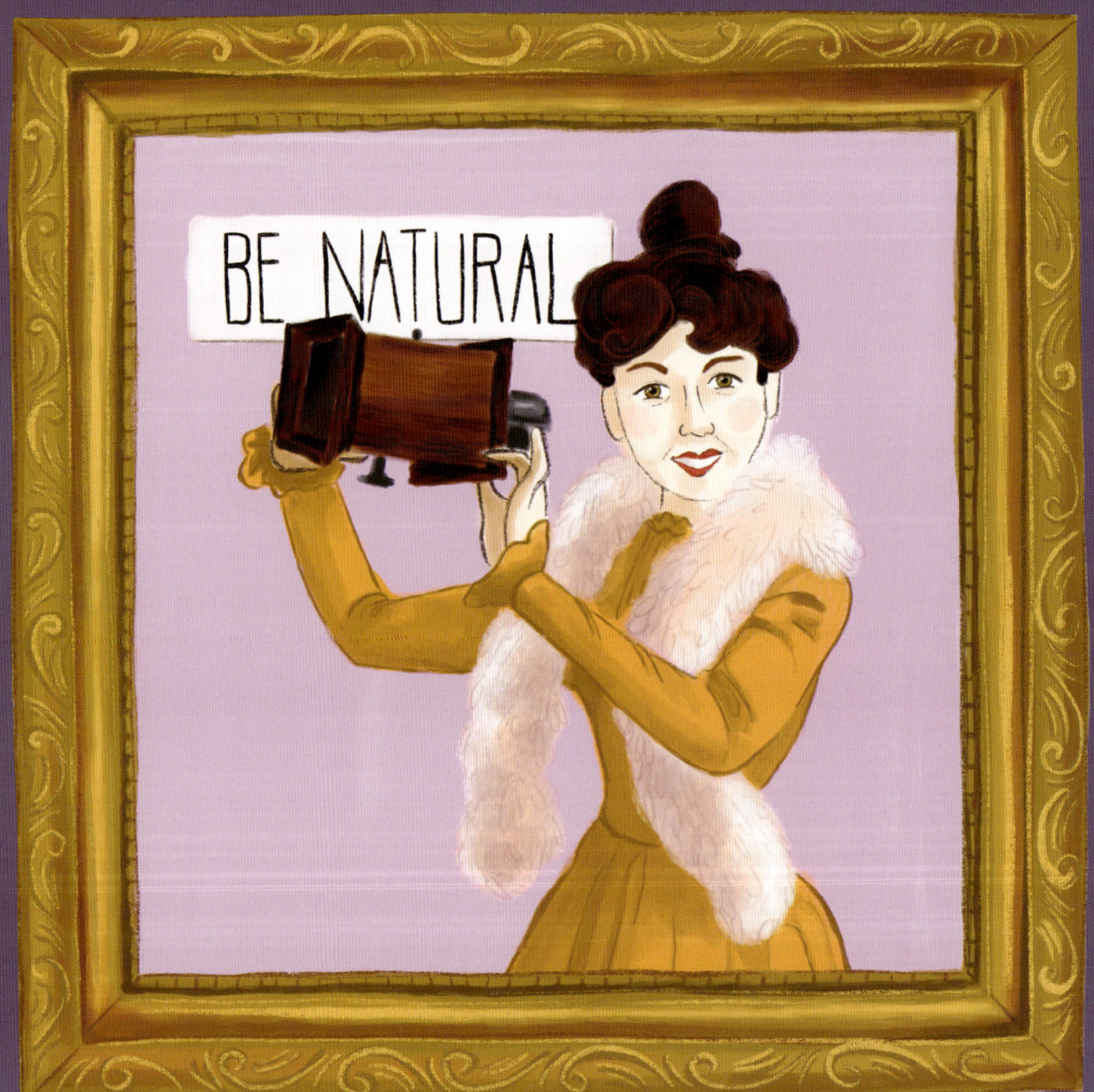

ALICE GUY-BLACHÉ

THE MOTHER OF THE MOVIES

JULY 1, 1873–MARCH 24, 1968

Can you imagine a life without movies? Movies have had an undeniable impact on our culture and our lives. For more than a century, narrative films have made us roar with laughter and clench our teeth in fear. They've made us bawl uncontrollably from the safety of our couches or under the cover of darkness in a movie theater. We go to the movies to experience love, loss, action, adventure, and joy alongside friends and loved ones, as we enjoy a side of salty popcorn and an oversize soda. Movies are the great escape. They inspire, teach, and influence us by connecting with our emotions as we gaze at the big screen. With a magical mix of storytelling, visuals, technological effects, and artistic expression, good movies have the power to change not only the individual, but society, which is incredible for an art form that's not even 150 years old. This absolute power—to both entertain and impact—was the vision of one person: a secretary-turned-director named Alice Guy-Blaché.

How did Guy-Blaché take on such an outsize role in the world of cinema? It began on the afternoon of March 22, 1895, when Auguste and Louis Lumière famously debuted the first projected motion picture, by invitation only, to an audience of 200 lucky guests in a room at the Society for the Development of the National Industry in Paris. The film—*Workers Leaving the Lumière*

Factory—went exactly as its title foretold. It was comprised of forty-six continuous seconds of workers, mostly women, walking out of the Lumière factory in Lyon. Without any real storyline, it was more of a demonstration, much like others of its kind at the time. The real star of the display was the Lumière brothers' new Cinématographe, a revolutionary three-in-one movie camera that could record, develop, and project film for the first time.

After all, most films of the day were kind of dull. They wowed audiences with their feat of engineering, as seeing moving pictures for the first time was surely a transcendent experience at the turn of the twentieth century. But these first films lacked any sort of narrative. Called "spectacles" and "demonstration films" by their makers, they were intended to show off camera equipment rather than content. Generally, they offered short scenes of a few seconds from life, captured from one vantage point. A family on

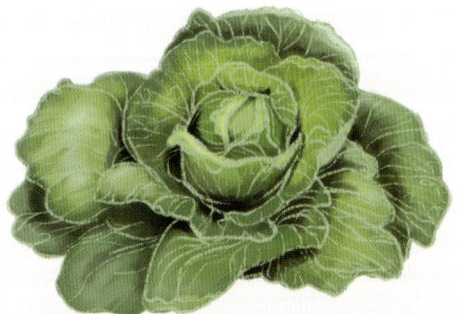

a farm, a street corner in New York, a group of blacksmiths hammering an anvil—these simple vignettes were the extent of early film. While it is amazing for today's audiences to see these snippets of life from long ago, cinematically they are more novelty than art.

Twenty-two-year-old secretary Alice Guy-Blaché was in the audience on that fateful day in March, along with her boss Léon Gaumont of the Gaumont Film Company. Although the Cinématographe presentation was exciting, Guy-Blaché was unimpressed with the film. The leading film companies at the time, such as the Lumières, the Pathé Frères, and Gaumont's own outfit, as well as Thomas Edison and his Black Maria in America, were focused on outdoing each other techni cally. Each was clamoring to make the very best and most modern camera equipment. In one demonstration, the Lumières had clearly proven they were leading the race. Their camera was the first to project a moving image so large an audience could experience the film together and stood in contrast to the machines that viewers were required to look down into, which created an individual experience. Despite this advancement, Guy-Blaché was bored by the content. That very boredom sparked something within her, and she left the makeshift theater with a head full of ideas. Uninterested in the race to achieve movie camera perfection, she was focused on the film itself. She saw a potential that the others did not: What if film could be a medium for telling a story, rather than documentation? This deceptively simple idea would revolutionize the industry forever.

That afternoon, back at the office, Guy-Blaché asked Gaumont if she could borrow a camera to experiment with a film of her own. She had always created little stories and tales to entertain her family and friends. What if she brought one to life and used Gaumont's equipment to film it? She quickly got to work, enlisting some coworkers to help her build a set and act in a narrative she wrote.

By the early months of 1896, her first film was ready. It was a fictional fantasy called *The Cabbage Fairy*,* in which a newlywed couple wanders through a field of cardboard cabbages and are overjoyed when they find a baby behind one of the leaves. The moving picture was choppy, with the effect of Guy-Blaché cranking the film seen every few seconds, but it was revolutionary. Never

before had a studio considered storylines, scripts, actors, sets, or costumes. The first narrative fiction film was born, and its concept spread like wildfire. Within weeks, movie production houses around the globe had switched their focus from showing off their equipment to producing narrative films of their own. Guy-Blaché was promoted to full-time director, becoming the first woman to achieve that distinction.

Guy-Blaché fell into the film industry by accident. At only eighteen, she unexpectedly lost her father and was thrust into the workforce to help support her mother. Being both educated and ambitious, she trained as a typist and stenographer—a new field that enabled women to make a decent wage. After a stint as a secretary for a varnish factory, Guy-Blaché was hired by a photography equipment and supply company that would later become the Gaumont Film Company.

After the success of *The Cabbage Fairy*, she immersed herself in the art of filmmaking. From 1896 to 1906, Guy-Blaché thrived as Gaumont's head of production and as the world's first female director. She wrote, produced, and directed

---

* That original version of *The Cabbage Fairy* has sadly been lost to the ages, but Guy-Blaché, always seeking to improve upon her own work, would remake this story two more times—in 1900 and 1902. In these versions, which anyone can watch on YouTube, Guy-Blaché has recast the newlyweds as a glamorous fairy, who dances among the cabbages finding babies.

narrative films on many topics for Gaumont, demonstrating her range through emotionally engaging, humorous, witty, and complex characters and sets. Guy-Blaché wasn't afraid to address gender roles or sexuality in her work, and was the first to feature pregnancy on film, as well as the first to showcase an all Black cast in a film. She was also known for writing quality roles for children. Her ability to connect with audiences gained her an award at the 1900 Universal Exposition in Paris. Soon, she was even hiring assistant directors, including Louis Feuillade, whom she taught everything she knew.

Guy-Blaché's exquisite knack for storytelling was only enhanced by her growing cinematographic skills. Through her experiments, she was the first to develop special effects like double exposure, split screen, close-ups, and running film backward. She colorized films with hand tinting and was one of the first to use synchronized sound, utilizing Gaumont's "Chronophone," in which sound was recorded and played on a disc in tandem with a film. In 1906, she reached even further—and made headlines—with her film *The Life of Christ*, based on the Tissot Bible. It was her largest production to date, with 300 background actors and twenty-five discrete episodes. Even at the time, Guy-Blaché was given proper credit for her role in the film's production by newspapers and film industry periodicals. She was the boss and happy in her role.

That would all change in 1907, when she married Herbert Blaché, a coworker who would soon be appointed production manager for Gaumont's U.S. branch. Blinded by love, Guy-Blaché quit directing—much to the chagrin of Gaumont—and moved to New York. Soon, Guy-Blaché and her husband started the Solax Company with partner George Magie, making Guy-Blaché the first woman to run her own studio. Solax would become so successful that it outgrew the Flushing, Queens, facility where it began. Its founders moved production to Fort Lee, New Jersey (which was becoming the precursor to Hollywood), where they built a $100,000 state-of-the-art film production facility. In this new facility, Guy-Blaché produced three films a week, using a stable of actors—another prototype that Hollywood studios would adopt.

Guy-Blaché continued to work tirelessly—throughout her two pregnancies, after the birth of their children, and even while deathly ill with the Spanish flu. Jealous of her success, Herbert started the competing Blaché Films and in 1919 ran off to Hollywood with an actress, leaving Guy-Blaché and her children destitute. Worse, he took credit for *all* of her films made at Solax, and adding salt to the wound, everyone believed him.

By the 1920s, the film industry had changed in ways that would not favor talents like Guy-Blaché. Studios turned to the deep pockets of Wall Street investors, who pushed many women out of the industry in their quest to establish their influence. As part of this tragic trend, Guy-Blaché directed her last film in 1919. Unable to find a job, she filed for bankruptcy in 1921 and divorced Blaché the following year. (Good riddance.) She moved back to France with her children and sold her jewelry, then her furniture, to make ends meet.

This low point in Guy-Blaché's life was compounded by her former boss, Léon Gaumont, when he published a book on the history of Gaumont Film Company that made no mention of her whatsoever. Her films were attributed to other directors, including her underling Feuillade, who had since become famous. Back in Paris, she found that other women were given credit as the first female directors, with her own name absent from articles and unknown to film historians. Refusing to be erased, Guy-Blaché began to fight for her rightful place in film history. Gaumont agreed to revise the book and reveal her true contributions, but he died in 1946 before the new edition could be published.

Knowing that she must be her own advocate, Guy-Blaché spent the last years of her life furiously trying to locate the nearly 1,000 films she had a hand in from 1896 to 1920. Around 150 works survive, largely shorts along with twenty-two feature-length films. She cataloged their titles and reached out to countless reporters, film historians, and colleagues, as she set the record straight and introduced her work to those who had not encountered her in their schooling or teaching. She refused to be erased by the writers of history.

In 1964, Alice Guy-Blaché and her daughter Simone moved to Wayne, New Jersey. She later died in a nursing home there, on March 24, 1968. She left behind a roster of 1,000 films and an equally impressive list of cinematic innovations. More important, Guy-Blaché was the first person who thought that movies should make us feel. She created the language of film that would bring magic to the silver screen for generations to come.

In 2012, a hundred years after her high point, the Fort Lee Film Commission updated Guy-Blaché's headstone. Her gravestone in Maryrest Cemetery, Mahwah, New Jersey, now reads, "Alice Guy-Blaché, first woman motion picture director, first woman studio head, and the president of the Solax Company, Fort Lee, N.J."

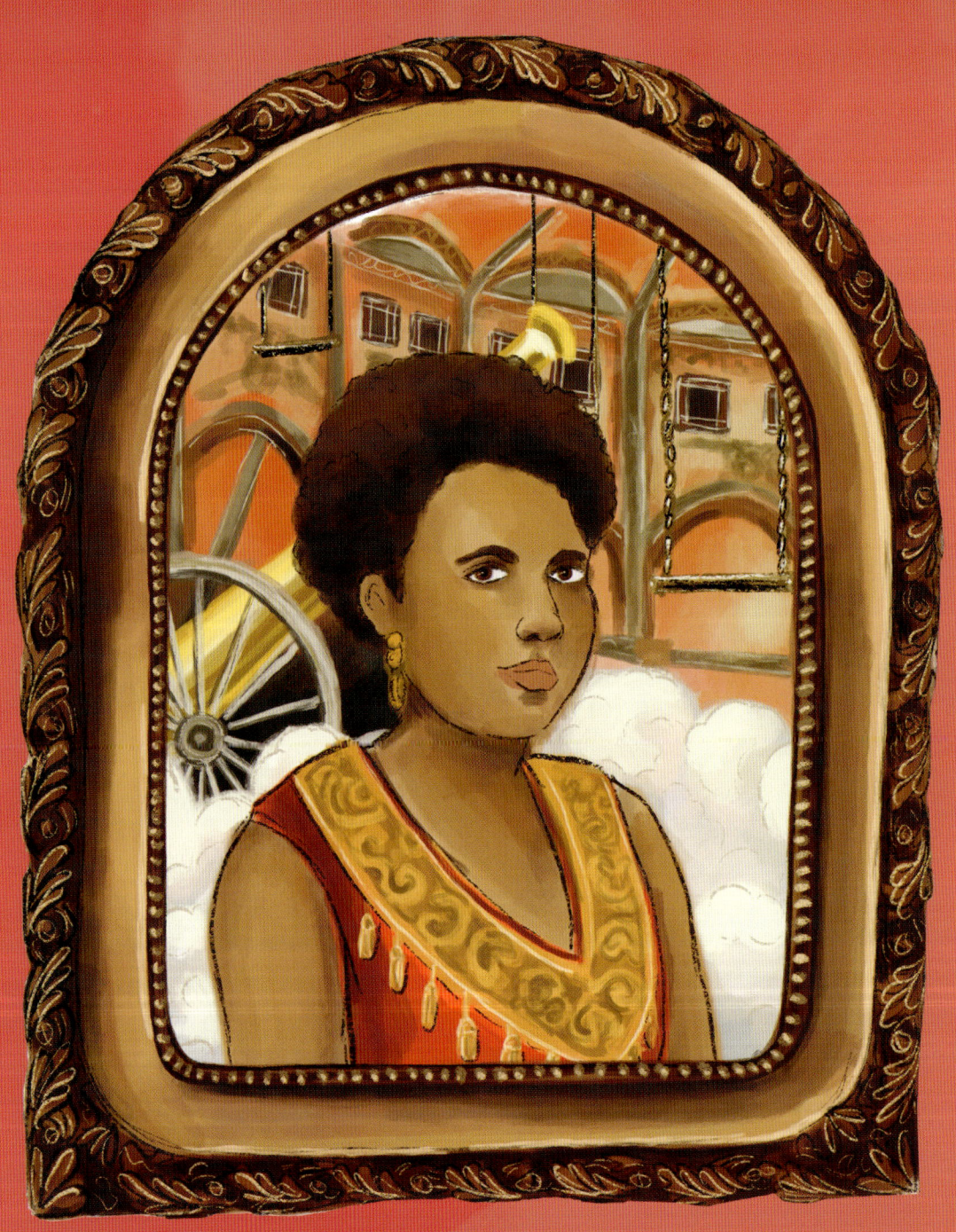

MISS LA LA

THE CANNON WOMAN WHO WAS AN IMPRESSIONIST STAR

APRIL 21, 1858–AFTER 1919

More than a decade after he had focused on painting young dancers in the ballet schools of Paris, Edgar Degas visited the circus. It was the late 1870s, and the headlining act of the popular Cirque Fernando near Place Pigalle caught the artist's eye. In the center of the ring, a young Black woman called Miss La La clenched her jaw tightly around a rope, her body suspended, with limbs dangling freely in the air. Degas watched in astonishment as the rope was hoisted higher and higher, until the young performer was just under the peak of the circus hall, nearly 100 feet above him. Using only her teeth to hang on to a specially made mouthpiece, Miss La La seemed to spin effortlessly way above the audience, twirling into a graceful tornado before being lowered to take her bow to the roaring delight of the crowd.

Miss La La, who was twenty-one years old at the time, probably never imagined that this particular performance would be the event that would place her in history books. By the time the circus had become a favored source of inspiration for the bohemian artists of Montmartre, she was already a seasoned professional, having begun at age nine and performed thousands of times with the great circuses of Europe. This night at Cirque Fernando was like any other in a string of sold-out shows, but Degas's presence is why we know her today.

Anna Olga Albertina Brown was born on April 21, 1858, to Marie-Christine Borchardt, a white German-Prussian, and Wilhelm Brown, a Black German. Borchardt and Brown were working in local circuses in Szczecin, now part of Poland, when they fell in love. They raised their daughter behind the scenes of the fairground, and when she showed promise, they enrolled her to perform as an acrobat and aerialist. Aerialists, trapeze artists, and daring performers were the biggest circus acts of the time, so Miss La La's success grew as she toured Europe.

Small and muscular, La La was as much an impressive athlete as she was a star performer. Her claim to fame was her incredible strength, which she demonstrated for audiences at daring heights. One of her most popular acts was called the Cannon Woman. For this routine, La La would hang upside down from a trapeze by her knees, with a chain attached to her special mouthpiece gripped in her teeth. Instead of one of her fellow performers hanging from the chain, as one would expect, there was instead something truly remarkable. A small cannon—weighing in at 150 pounds and rumored to be salvaged from the U.S. Civil War—swung above the crowd, suspended between La La's teeth. In this stunning act, her clenched jaw was the only thing keeping the monumental weapon from tumbling to the ground. She would be hoisted even higher, and then the unthinkable would happen—the cannon would be fired midair! Her strong body would absorb the pushback, sending her into a gracefully chaotic twirl before her muscle control would stop her just in time to take her bow, the cannon still on the chain between her teeth. La La used her jaw strength on other performers as well. Another popular stunt had her hook only one knee on a trapeze bar, then alternate lifting other performers from a bar that hung from her teeth. While this act never ceased to impress, it was the cannon performance that wowed every time.

Degas was just as mesmerized by La La's harrowing acts as the rest of the audience. For four nights, in January of 1879, he bought a single ticket to the Cirque Fernando to study La La. His eyes would widen with amazement, and he looked away only in small bursts to sketch furiously in his notebook. (Degas, a lifelong bachelor, was rumored to be obsessed with La La and even mentioned her in his diary.) From these shows, Degas made a flurry of drawings, four pastels, and one final oil painting, simply titled *Miss La La at the Cirque Fernando*, which was exhibited at the Fourth Impressionist Exhibition in Paris in 1879.

Instead of showing the gimmick of the cannon act, Degas chose to depict La La suspended alone without the fanfare, floating ethereally against the ornate ceiling above the crowd as if the painting's viewer is among the audience.

The artist's sketches reveal that over his nights spent at the circus, Degas sat in different seats, drawing different angles of La La as she soared above the crowd. The earliest drawing shows La La from a full-frontal perspective. The sketches and pastels also show that the artist experimented with La La's skin color and tone, using varying shades of brown as well as oranges and greens. In the final oil painting, which can be seen at the National Gallery in London, Degas chose to show La La from a profile position, her face curiously obscured. Her skin tone was also lightened, blurring her mixed racial background. The brown of her legs appear to be thick stockings, with folds visible just behind her knees. Historians have since argued about whether the artist's intention was to hide the performer's identity and throw her race into question. Regardless of his motivation, the painting is unique among Degas's work. It remains the only circus painting he ever made and features the only identifiable person of color in all of his works.

Whether Degas meant to obscure La La's race remains a mystery, but others certainly used her skin color to drive ticket sales. Although La La was a headliner in her field, she was not immune to her bosses profiteering off of her racial identity. Venues regularly used La La's Black heritage as inspiration for racially motivated stage nicknames, meant to lure white audiences. Among those that were emblazoned across posters and ads were the Black Venus, Venus of the Tropics, Olga the Negress, the Black Pearl, African Princess Olga, and Olga the Mulatto. These names were meant to cast an air of mystique around La La, enticing the audience with "exoticism," which was highly fetishized in the late nineteenth century. One venue in England went so far as to concoct a complicated tale around La La to sell tickets. They told prospective audiences that she was an African princess from a fallen kingdom, left without a throne. The story took a grim turn, as it went on to say that La La was sold into slavery and forced to perform in a circus in the South of France, before deciding to pledge her devotion and allegiance to Queen Victoria in England. This was all obviously completely preposterous and a ruse to sell tickets, as if a tiny woman hanging from the rafters by her teeth needed more allure.

Despite these offensive names and fabricated tales, La La enjoyed a freedom that other women in her social position did not. The circuses of Europe were a more accepting environment than society in general, offering a reprieve in the sexist and racist nineteenth century. The circus, marked by comradery and a unique set of ideals, held women in higher regard, recognizing them as talented performers and granting them freedoms that other women did not enjoy during the Victorian era. Their death-defying acts as trick equestrian riders, aerialists, and trapeze artists earned them higher wages than their male counterparts, due to the risks taken each night—and the audience's bloodlust at the possibility of seeing them fall. Because of this, many women were the top earners of their troupes, which enabled them to be financially independent at a time when the vast majority of women were expected to be homemakers and mothers. (It was also socially acceptable to wear pants in the circus, which women confined to the general population were not permitted to do.) With its crews of outcasts and the marginalized, the circus was also a place where performers of

color could find fame, success, and acceptance, though racial exploitation was still rampant—especially in sideshows and freak shows, which Miss La La was not a part of.

Miss La La had a long and lucrative career. She performed alone, as well as in troupes. Her first was Troupe Kaira, which was a foursome comprised of La La and three white performers: Kaira la Blanche, petite Kaira (a child), and a man named Popischill. La La and Kaira la Blanche later broke off and formed their own troupe, calling themselves Les Deux Papillons, or The Two Butterflies. The pair would toss each other through the air in a complicated trapeze act. Kaira was a dear friend of La La's, and together they performed in some of Europe's most famous halls, including the London Hippodrome and the touted "most famous cabaret in the world," Paris's Folies Bergère. They worked together until 1888, when Kaira tragically fell to her death while performing, when she was just twenty-four years old.

La La and Kaira were also the subjects of commercial artworks, appearing in beautiful renderings on Art Nouveau posters that advertised their acts. "Les Papillons: NOIR et BLANC" (Butterflies: Black and White) made for appealing advertising. Belle Époque poster artist Jules Chéret focused on just La La and her cannon act on a poster for a performance at the Folies Bergère in 1880. Chéret's lithographs have become a beloved record of the legendary acts in this venue and are also known for the free-spirited, strong style in which he painted women. Some even call him the "father of women's liberation," which seems a bit of a stretch, although it leaves La La in good company.

The circus posters provide a gorgeous record of La La's accomplishments, but it is because of Degas's popularity and legacy in art history that contemporary scholars are talking about her today. The reexamination of master paintings by both contemporary feminist and BIPOC scholars has started a fascinating conversation about the women whom art history's biggest names chose to paint and why. In the process, they have freed these figures from their anonymity. Through their research, these scholars are not only giving names to faces (although Degas does name Miss La La), but also contextualizing their lives and how they were woven into those of the artists who painted them. It feels a bit like uncovering a mystery, learning that the woman in a painting was an actual person with a fascinating life and accomplishments all her own.

After Kaira's death, La La fell in love with a fellow circus performer. Emanuel Woodson was an African American contortionist from a family of performers in St. Louis. After the two were married in 1888, they formed their own troupe, called the Three Keziahs, and toured France and Germany. By the early 1900s, the couple had had three daughters and had settled in Brussels, where they were highly regarded. La La retired from performing, and Woodson became the manager of a luxurious venue called Palais d'Eté. After her husband died in 1915 of liver failure, records show that La La applied for a U.S. visa, likely spurred by the onset of World War I. Whether La La and her daughters made it to the United States remains a mystery, as there are no other records of her after her visa application.

Several studio photographs of Miss La La, alone and with members of Troupe Kaira, remain. One even includes the cannon she costarred with every night. They show a diminutive yet focused athlete, comfortable with and confident in herself during an era when women were expected to be home, the working class was expected to stay within their station, and slavery was just barely in the rearview mirror. La La was more than an art model or a figure in a famous painting. She was a career-minded powerhouse who should be remembered as a great athlete today.

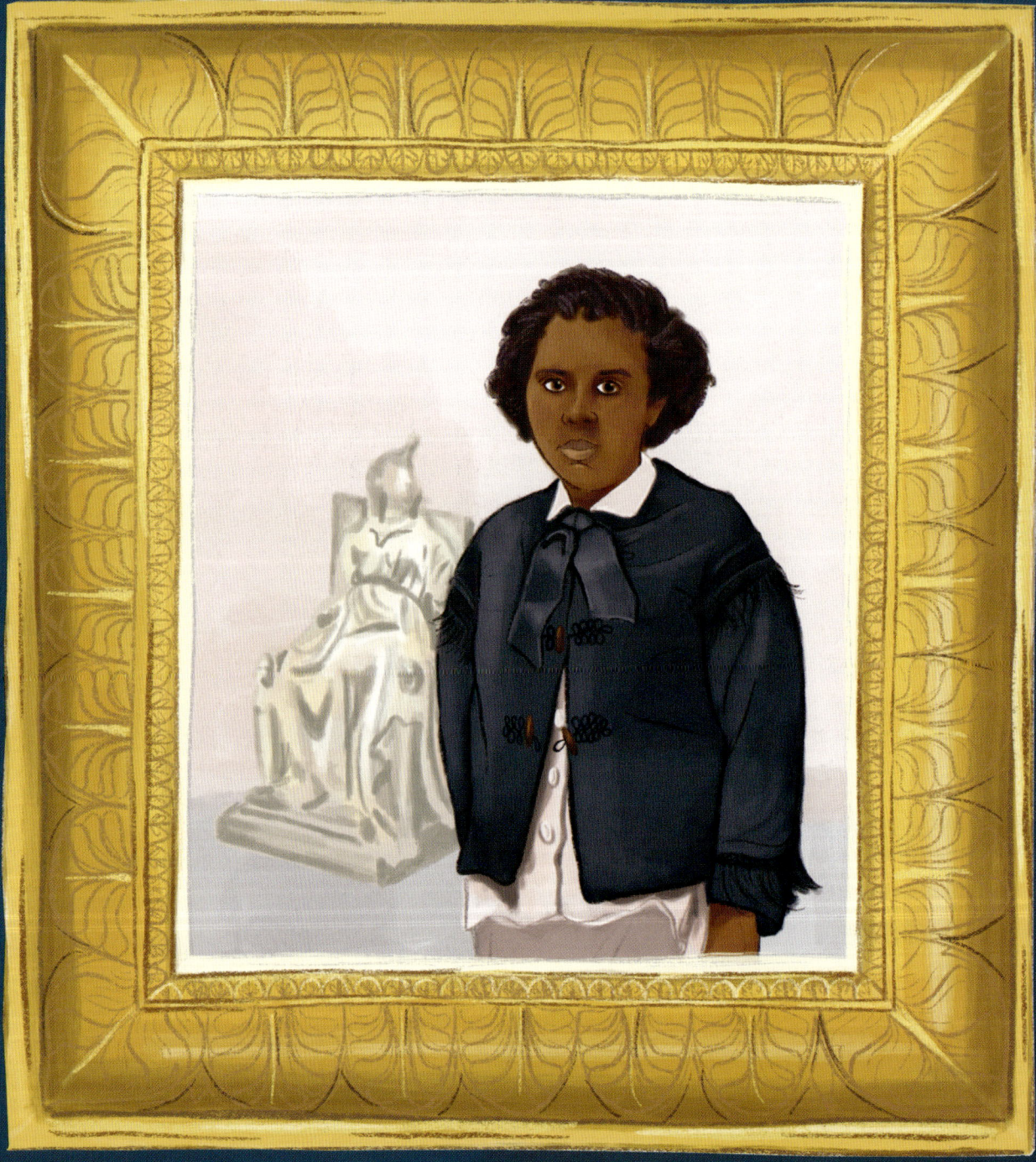

EDMONIA LEWIS

THE QUEEN AND CLEOPATRA

JULY 4, 1844–SEPTEMBER 17, 1907

In 1988, art historian Marilyn Richardson began a quest to find a missing sculpture. It took her to the most unlikely of places—a shopping mall outside of Chicago. The piece in question was a 3,000-pound marble sculpture called *The Death of Cleopatra*, carved in 1876 by Edmonia Lewis, a prominent, yet largely forgotten, nineteenth-century artist of African American and Native American descent. Lewis rose to prominence during her lifetime and was considered the first professional BIPOC sculptor, but somewhere along the line she faded into obscurity—not entirely unlike her sculpture of the Egyptian queen. But the sculpture, at least, was about to be unearthed once more. A scavenger hunt comprised of inquiries and phone calls had led Richardson to a back storage hallway of the Forest Park Mall. There, sandwiched between coils of holiday lights and tinsel-covered Christmas trees, sat Queen Cleopatra in repose. She had remained undisturbed—apart from the shuffling of seasonal decor—for years. Up to that point, both sculpture and sculptor shared the same fate, with both absent from history. But Richardson's find that day changed the trajectory for both. Cleopatra would be released from her suburban tomb and find a permanent home on display at the Smithsonian in Washington, DC. This, in turn, put her creator Edmonia Lewis back in the news and a step closer to the canons of art history where she belonged.

Nearly a century and a half before Queen Cleopatra was liberated from her hallway, Lewis was believed to have been born on the Fourth of July around 1844, near Albany. She was often cagey about her background, including her birth year and heritage, but we know she was a young woman when the Emancipation Proclamation was signed in 1863. Lewis's parents died when she was a child, after which she and her older half-brother Samuel moved to Niagara Falls, New York, where they lived with her mother's two sisters, who were Mississauga Ojibwe. They were happy with their aunts and their way of life. The children helped sell moccasins and Ojibwe baskets to tourists and spent their downtime connecting to the land—fishing, hiking, and playing in nature. Samuel moved to California in 1852 and made a fortune during the gold rush. (He was a barber, and it is unclear whether he panned for gold or just cut a whole lot of hair.) This wealth allowed him to pay for his sister's education and make sure she wanted for nothing.

School was rough for Lewis, both as a child and a young adult. She had become unaccustomed to the order of formal education while living with her aunts, although she was intelligent and had the grades—from her pre-college education at New York Central College—to prove it. When she was fifteen, Samuel paid for his sister's tuition at Ohio's Oberlin Academy Preparatory School, followed by Oberlin Collegiate Institute for post-secondary education. There, Lewis studied art and briefly called herself "Mary." Oberlin was founded as an idealistic institute by members of the Christian revival movement and was known to espouse abolitionist ideals. It was the first college in the country to admit African American (1835) and female students (1837), promoting a program of coeducation. Sadly, these progressive beliefs did not suffuse the town in which the school was situated. In spite of the lofty goals of Oberlin's administration, Lewis faced racial discrimination from townspeople and in the classroom. As one of only thirty BIPOC students in a school of 1,000, she found that most of the students and teachers completely ignored her in class, which layered a dehumanizing patina atop her education. She found refuge at home, though, boarding with the kind Reverend John Keep and his family. Reverend Keep was a white abolitionist and the member of Oberlin's board of trustees who had cast the deciding vote that allowed African Americans into the college. Keep and his wife were outspoken supporters of rights for both women and African Americans, and Keep was known to weave these messages into his sermons. The couple opened their home to female Oberlin students who did not have relatives in the region.

The Keeps treated Lewis like family during the four years she lived with them, but even they could not protect her from the horrible racial injustices of the day. The worst incident was when two of the Keeps' other female boarders falsely accused Lewis of poisoning them after drinking wine spiked with Spanish fly (an aphrodisiac). The two girls became violently ill, hanging on the edge of life for a few days before both made a complete recovery. When the story got out, the finger was pointed at Lewis, and a group of men grabbed her while she was walking home from class in the dead of winter as retaliation. The group beat her to within an inch of her life, leaving her for dead in torn clothes in an open field. Later, while Lewis was still abed recovering from her injuries, she was arrested and put on trial, where she was acquitted for lack of evidence. She stayed enrolled at Oberlin and continued to live with the Keeps, but the assault left her isolated and fearful. When she was accused of stealing art supplies a year later, she decided she was done with Ohio.

The Keeps, still fully supportive of Lewis, wrote to abolitionist friends in Boston, who helped facilitate an apprenticeship for her in the studio of sculptor Edward Augustus Brackett. By the end of 1864, just a year after arriving in Boston, she had opened a studio of her own. In her studio, she chose famous abolitionists and Civil War heroes for her subjects, sculpting medallion portraits and marble busts. Her Neoclassical style and thematic choices made her popular among the New England abolitionists, a position that was only reinforced by frequent articles and interviews with her printed in abolitionist publications. Lewis became the first African American and Native American sculptor to achieve national—and later international—success thanks to the support of her community in Boston, but this acclaim proved to be a double-edged sword. While Lewis enjoyed the positive reception and the regular commissions, her circle of support greatly limited her scope as an artist. She was the BIPOC woman who sculpted abolitionist-friendly art. She began to feel more like a novelty than an artist.

In 1866, Lewis used her abolitionist contacts to raise money for the next step in her artistic career. She sold an open edition of plaster casts of one of her most famous busts—fallen abolitionist hero Colonel Robert Gould Shaw, commander of the African American Civil War regiment. The casts sold for $15 each, and she made enough money from the sale to head off to Rome.

In Italy, Lewis blossomed. She was free. She did not feel the constant discrimination in Europe that had plagued her in the United States. Here, she wasn't an African American artist, a woman artist, an abolitionist artist. Rome judged the art, not the artist. Once established, she felt her race and gender were secondary. Lewis quickly fell in with a group of American expat female sculptors who gave her the support system she had never before known. She rented a studio that once belonged to one of her idols, eighteenth-century sculptor Antonio Canova, and soon she began making the best work of her life.

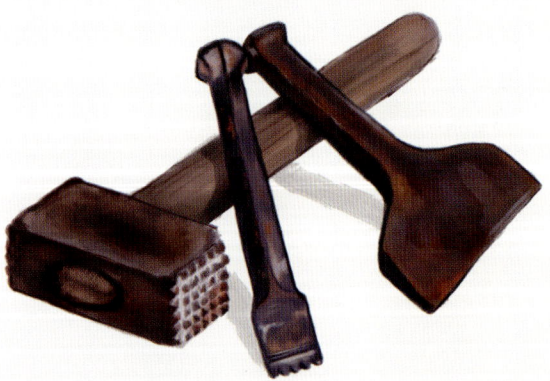

Free from the constraints at home, Lewis was at liberty to make the work she wanted—for the most part. She did feel a quiet undertone of racism, even in Italy. To account for that, Lewis made sure her female figures had European features, so the white audience would not read them as self-portraits. Still, her pieces from this period marry her African American and Native American heritage with the traditional Neoclassical style in which she was trained and feature BIPOC from her life, carved in gleaming white marble, fantastically mixing old and new.

In Italy, it was customary for artists to sculpt small models in clay, then have Italian artisans translate the model to a large marble. It was assumed and insinuated that all women followed this practice. Lewis, bucking tradition, carved her own marble—an arduous task that ensured everyone knew how good she was. She began to get extremely well-paying commissions, and in 1870 she had a major exhibition in Chicago, followed by another in Italy the following year.

Then came the Centennial Exposition in Philadelphia. For her showstopping contribution, Lewis chose to depict Cleopatra moments after death, the asp that ended her life nowhere in sight, with her body slouching lifelessly. Raw and emotional, the sculpture is a departure from the usual portrayal of Cleopatra as living temptress looking contemplatively at the asp. The piece caused quite a stir and was reported to be the most visited artwork at the exposition, as well as the most covered by journalists.

So how did this spectacular, two-ton sculpture become lost?

The reasons are as random and unclear as what we know about the remainder of Lewis's life. She went home to Europe after the exposition, but in 1877 returned to the United States to sculpt a portrait bust commissioned by Ulysses S. Grant, who was then president. That same year, Cleopatra was boxed up and sent to Chicago for the 1878 Interstate Exposition. But in the 1880s, Neoclassicism suddenly became extremely gauche, and Lewis's reputation went along with it. She pivoted to working for religious clients, making a living sculpting altars and statuary and turning her back on her personal work for good. Concurrently, Cleopatra was bought as decor for a Chicago saloon, then became a headstone at a track in Forest Park for a horse named after the Egyptian ruler. In 1896, Lewis moved to Paris, then to London in 1901, where she died from chronic kidney failure on September 17, 1907. The track in Forest Park was bought by the U.S. Postal Service, and Cleopatra was eventually moved to a storage room large enough to fit the massive sculpture—which happened to be at the mall. Once Richardson found her, Cleopatra was given a $30,000 restoration to take care of the extensive damage she had endured over the years, including paint, scratches, a broken nose, missing fingers, and surface pitting. She's been at the Smithsonian American Art Museum since 1994.

As for Lewis? In 2017, a man named Bobbie Reno raised enough money on the charity platform GoFundMe to restore Lewis's gravestone at St. Mary's Catholic Cemetery in London. In 2022, Oberlin took steps to right the horrible wrongs done to Lewis while she was a student by opening the Edmonia Lewis Center for Women and Transgender People and awarding her a ceremonial posthumous degree. That was the same year the U.S. Postal Service honored her with a stamp.

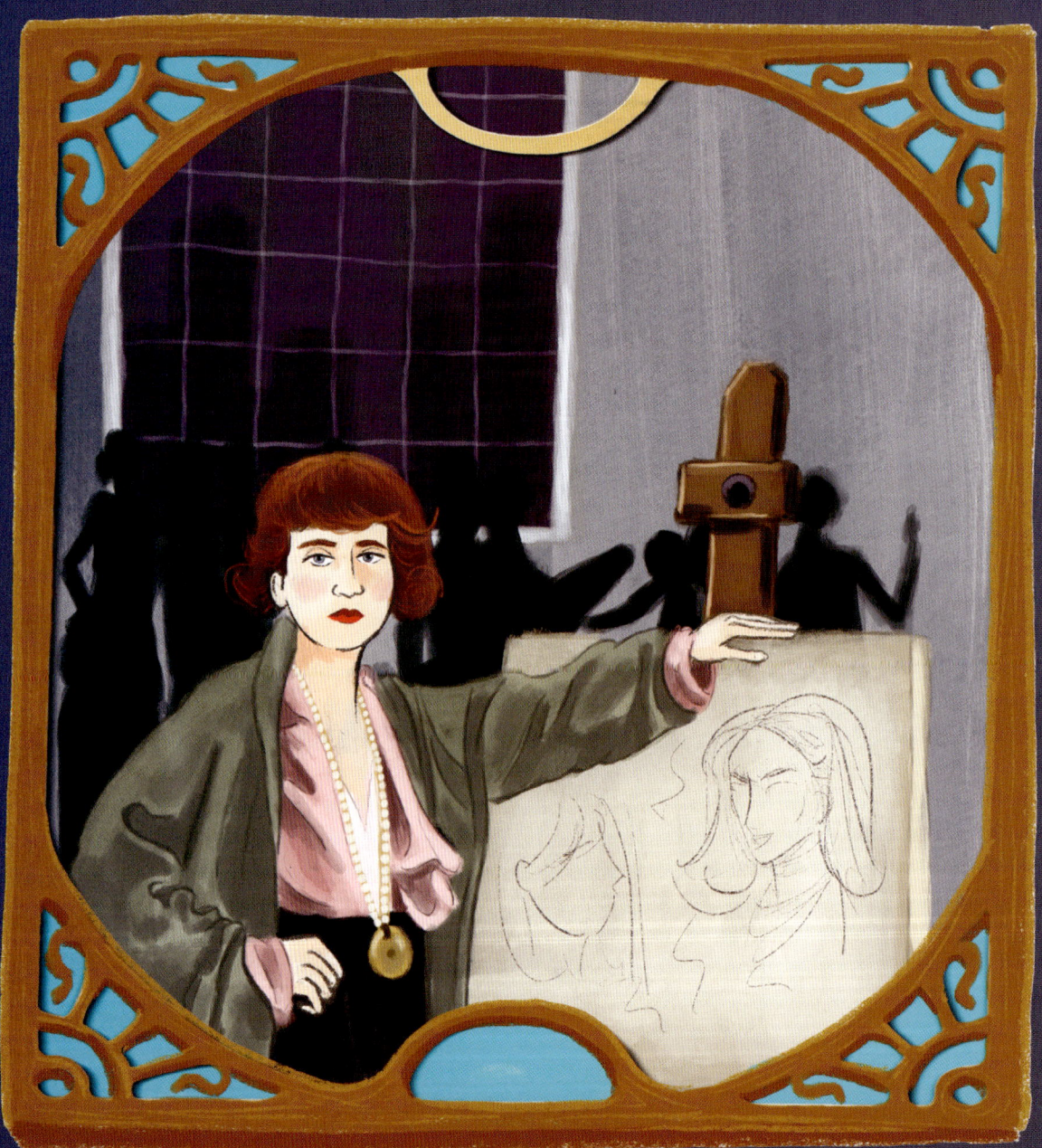

NEYSA McMEIN

ROUND TABLE REBEL

JANUARY 24, 1888–MAY 12, 1949

As the notion of modern, feminist womanhood evolved from the New Woman at the turn of the twentieth century to the even more daring flapper of the 1920s, portrayals of women in fashion magazines developed alongside it. Modern women no longer identified with the stoic, nurturing mother archetype or the pinch-waisted, stylized "good girls" that had previously appeared in popular magazines. Periodicals like *McCall's* and the *Saturday Evening Post* began to depict fashionable women who were glamorous, confident, and, above all, had an air of autonomy that pushed back against the Victorian domestic ideals that traced their roots to the previous century. Illustrator Neysa McMein drew women as she knew them: as independent individuals who had a flare for fashion and a self-assured twinkle in their eyes—as she did herself. One of the most sought-after and highly paid magazine illustrators for nearly twenty years, McMein had artistic success that was only outshone by her active and culturally significant personal life. Throughout the 1920s, she was a member of the highly publicized Algonquin Round Table set. McMein's art studio became an extension of the Algonquin Hotel and the gathering place for the most famous cultural salon of the Prohibition era.

For nearly ten years, the wisecracking, witticism-trading group of writers, critics, and creatives known as the Algonquin Round Table met each weekday for quite possibly the world's longest, most famous lunch date. Headed by Dorothy Parker, Robert Benchley, and Robert E. Sherwood, the group was known as much for the antics of its members as their literary output. We might consider it the first clique to become famous for being famous. An invitation to join the table was exciting, as was gawking at the group from across the room. Envious actors, authors, and admirers alike crowded the Algonquin Hotel's restaurant throughout the 1920s with the hope of catching a glimpse of some of the famous faces who dined with these arbiters of New York theater and literature. Though lunch was an hours-long affair, the truly coveted invitation was after the Algonquin closed to prepare for dinner, when the Round Table members would trickle uptown to the 57th Street art studio of McMein. There, with other movers and shakers, they could continue the raucous gathering without an audience.

As writers, actors, directors, and celebrities filtered in—their lips and attitudes kept loose thanks to the large illegal gin still kept in the bathroom (it was Prohibition, after all)—McMein would hold court at her easel as the party raged on, usually working on a commission while dressed in a dusty artist's smock buttoned over one of her elegant evening gowns. She loved to work amid the chaos, with the buzz and excitement of the crowd serving as her best inspiration. Cole Porter and George Gershwin could often be found playing one of McMein's studio pianos (the latter debuted his sultry *Rhapsody in Blue* for McMein and her guests in 1924), and her celebrity guests like Charlie Chaplin and Tallulah Bankhead often sat for impromptu portraits, presaging McMein's portrait painting career later in life. Dorothy Parker and her first husband Eddie Parker lived upstairs, which added to the constant stream of literary and artistic personalities who wandered in and out of the studio. Most guests, though, would admit they were there to bask in the glow of the exuberant hostess who was the toast of New York.

Like her parties, McMein's personal life was daring and enigmatic. By her early twenties, she had traveled extensively. Aside from contributing to war efforts in France, she rode on horseback across the Algerian desert, traveled in Count Zeppelin's dirigible, and marched in countless suffrage parades in cities across the United States.

She was a known tastemaker, whose life and career were covered by tabloids and newspapers and whose opinion was sought after. She wrote magazine articles about beauty and fashion and sometimes worked in tandem with Parker, who would interview notables while McMein made their portraits.

Though she had built a career on the image of the modern, independent woman, McMein shocked her friends by marrying businessman Jack Baragwanath in 1923. But, in true McMein spirit, she kept her maiden name and left with several of her gentleman friends for a two-month European trip—without Baragwanath—just a few days after the ceremony. This was fine by her husband, as theirs was an open marriage in which McMein had public affairs with notables like Chaplin, Round Table member Benchley, and Broadway director George Abbott while Baragwanath was encouraged to keep up his reputation as a playboy. Despite the issues an open marriage can sometimes cause, theirs was a successful one, and the pair remained happily married and happily open even through parenthood. Their only child, Joan, was born in 1924.

While McMein's studio became *the* place to see and be seen throughout the 1920s, her illustrations were making her very rich. She was regularly employed by *National Geographic*, *Woman's Home Companion*, *McClure's*, *Collier's*, and *Photoplay*, and from 1923 to 1937, she was the exclusive cover illustrator for *McCall's* magazine. At her peak, McMein was the highest-paid illustrator in the country, earning up to $2,500 (almost $40,000 in today's dollars!) *per* illustration. She fought for the rights of herself and other artists when she was charged New York City sales tax on the illustrations she sold to magazines. Taking her case all the way to the Supreme Court, McMein argued that her drawings were merely licensed, not sold, since they were returned to her after reproduction. Her case, which she won, set a new precedent for commercial artists, which established that the IRS could not charge tax for artworks licensed for reproduction.

When the four-color printing machine replaced fashion illustrations on magazine covers with fashion photographs in the 1930s, McMein was unbothered. She continued to illustrate product ads. (She was the first to create the image of "Betty Crocker" in 1936, which was based on an amalgamation of workers she met at General Mills.) Her main practice, however, shifted to professional portraiture and painting actors, writers, and people of note, including presidents Warren G. Harding and Herbert Hoover, as well as Count Ferdinand von Zeppelin.

Though the star power of the Algonquin Round Table had faded by the time the group unofficially dissolved at the onset of the Great Depression, McMein continued to host boisterous parties. A new wave of artists, writers, and actors came to her apartment in New York or the house she and Baragwanath had bought on the North Shore of Long Island to be entertained. Rather than a meeting of the minds over bathtub gin, these gatherings were characterized by the crowd-pleasing party games that McMein became known for. She is thought to have invented and/or popularized a quick-fire version of charades, scavenger hunts, croquet, and a slew of clever word games that she and her celebrity friends perfected in the late 1930s and '40s. Her games were so popular that *Life* magazine did a feature on them in 1946.

McMein died of cancer in 1949, with her daughter Joan and husband Baragwanath at her bedside. Her will left a fund to the Whitney Museum of American Art for an annual purchase of artworks by American artists for the museum's permanent collection. Of the seventy-two pieces purchased, none were by McMein, whose illustrations of modern women from a female perspective were not considered by the museum to be "fine art."

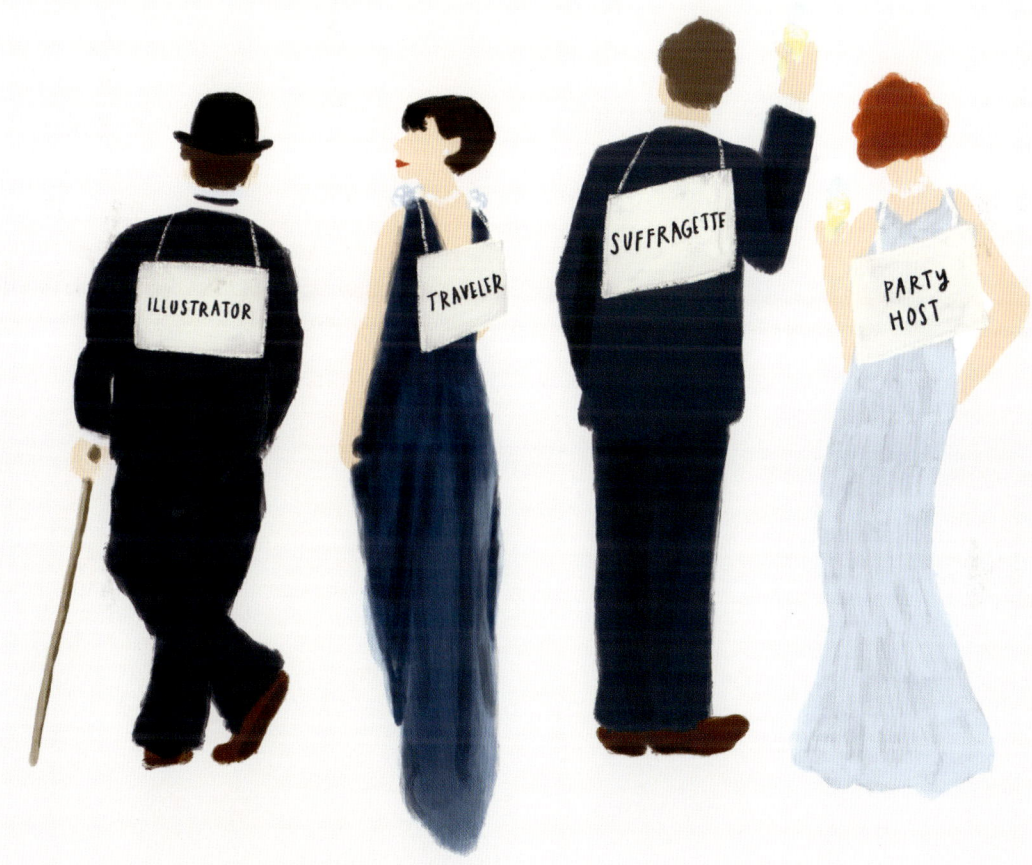

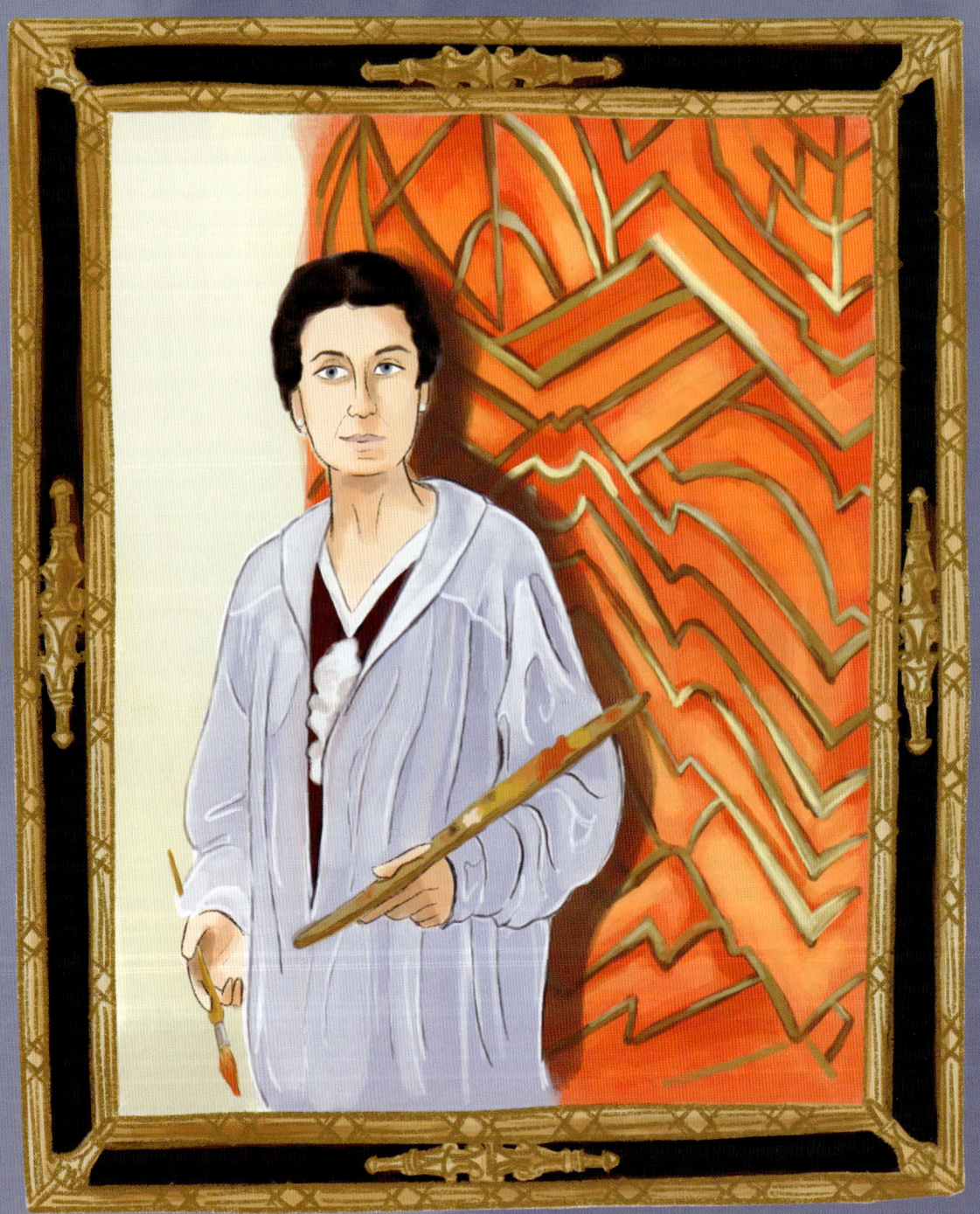

HILDRETH MEIÈRE

DOYENNE OF DECO

1892–1961

Since it opened in New York City in 1932, Radio City Music Hall has been regarded as an American icon, the "showplace of the nation." More than 300 million people have seen a show, movie, or event there in person, and countless others have tuned in to the theater's offers from home via television broadcasts—particularly of the Rockettes during the holiday season. Its recognizable silver marquee, soaring neon signs, and ornate facade are an Art Deco vision. The building's sleek and strong lines evoke modernism, though the style itself is a century old. The three oversize roundels that depict traditional Dance, Drama, and Song running along the 50th Street facade have become iconic themselves. At eighteen feet in diameter, the roundels feature bold enameled colors and dramatic Deco details that are easily enjoyed from the street. They were commissioned as part of the sculptures, friezes, murals, and ornamentation for the sprawling nineteen-building Rockefeller Center complex, which stretches from 48th to 51st Streets between Fifth and Sixth Avenues. As some of the first architectural decorations to be installed on the new complex, the roundels were instant emblems. They remain symbols of Radio City to this day, but they are also more than that. The roundels are the only examples, out of the hundred-or-so pieces that ornament the Rockefeller Complex, to be designed by a woman: the prolific unsung queen of Art Deco Hildreth Meière.

More than 100 years after it was first introduced, Art Deco has proven itself an enduring design movement, and it has yet to fully go out of style. With its geometric designs, bold jewel-tone colors, and exuberant use of metallic accents, Art Deco has retained an association with timeless elegance, luxury, and glamor. New York, with its numerous skyscrapers, is the quintessential Art Deco city. (Hello, Empire State Building, Chrysler Building, and Rockefeller Center, to name the most tourist-visited!) And so it shocked me to discover that Meière, a native New Yorker responsible for so many Art Deco works across the city, is not touted as one of the immortal legends of the movement. (The lack of attention given to her work is one of the things that inspired this very book.)

Meière was born in Manhattan in 1892. At eighteen, she spent a year studying painting in Florence, where she fell in love with Renaissance frescoes and vowed to become a muralist. Her formal education carried her to several art schools across the United States before she landed at the New York School of Applied Design for Women, at a time when Manhattan's Beaux-Arts Institute of Design would only admit male students. The school specialized in creative training "suitable" for women, including pottery, textiles, and costume design. Meière worked for a short time as a costume designer, before turning to her true passion of mural making. Her style, which combined Beaux-Arts with Byzantine mosaics, Egyptian wall painting, classical Greek vase painting, and Native American beadwork, caught the attention of famed architect Bertram Goodhue in 1921. Before his death in 1924, Goodhue signed Meière for several projects, including the Nebraska State Capitol in Lincoln and the National Academy of Sciences in Washington, DC. The talent and professionalism she exhibited in these projects soon made Meière one of the most in-demand muralists of her day.

During her prolific forty-year career, Meière realized some 100 commissions—most of which were impressively grandiose—across the Midwest and East Coast of the United States. However, the full breadth of her work can be experienced in New York, where she kept her studio and the residence she shared with her daughter. Her touch can be felt all over New York City, as if she had traced her finger along the spine of Manhattan, starting at the Temple Emanu-El (65th and Fifth Avenue) and moving down to St. Bartholomew's Church (53rd and Park), then a flick of the finger over to Radio City Music Hall (50th and Sixth Avenue), and following down to the AT&T Long Distance Building (32 Avenue of the Americas, Tribeca), before settling on the tailbone of Manhattan in the Art Deco gem One Wall Street (Wall and Broadway). (She also had a relief sculpture on the facade of Rockefeller Center's RKO Center Theatre on 49th Street, which was torn down with the building in 1954.) The projects range from religious (her decorative arch at Temple Emanu-El and half-dome of the apse at St. Bart's prove her vision can be easily translated for any creed) to secular, and all but the aforementioned roundels are massive and magical mosaics. Meière was a favorite collaborator of architects, partly because of her belief in the harmony between art and architecture (she did not think her work should upstage that of the architect, but should instead become inseparable from the project's overall vision), as well as for her keen interest in working with materials that challenged her. She executed her efforts in paint, ceramic tile, terra-cotta, wood, metal, and stained glass, but it is her mosaics that strike true awe in those who behold them. It's one of those mosaics that became the stuff of legend—and an elusive obsession of mine for years.

After grad school in the mid-2000s, I was writing for a design and architecture website, while also writing a blog about New York's hidden art treasures (Art Nerd New York). While researching an article about Art Deco in Manhattan, I heard rumors about a glittering, mosaicked room that supposedly lay dormant in a disused Art Deco building in the Financial District. One Wall Street, designed by Ralph Thomas Walker in 1931 for the Irving Trust headquarters, is a Deco gem that had stood largely disused since the nearby Twin Towers fell on September 11, 2001. The last remaining tenant, also a bank, had slowly moved operations uptown after that fateful day, but still owned the property. The rumor was that the fabled Red Room, a former banking hall with a wall-to-ceiling mosaic mural by Meière, was still intact. Although I had seen historic black-and-white photos from the 1930s, I read that the room was a heavenly amalgamation of gold, red, and orange tesserae, which made it appear to be engulfed in glorious flames. (Rather as if hell were a glamorous Art Deco masterpiece.) I tried to use my paltry credentials as a freelance writer to muscle my way into the building, writing to random names off the management company's website, but none replied. I even asked some of my urban explorer friends if they could get me in to no avail. With my contacts exhausted, I accepted defeat, but I never stopped mentioning the Red Room when I'd meet new associates in architecture or preservation, just in case they had an in.

Sometime in 2014, One Wall Street was quietly sold to developer Harry B. Macklowe, who planned to renovate the interior, including the Red Room, to create luxury apartments. For three years, I watched as photographs of the restoration, which was painstaking but successful, were released. The mosaic was largely intact, and a box of thousands of original tiles, fortuitously left by the Ravenna Company—which fabricated many of Meière's projects—ensured the restoration's accuracy. Finally, in 2022, I received an invitation by Macklowe's team to see the very room I had obsessed over fifteen years before. Experiencing something you've only seen in pictures can be a transcendent experience. I felt like I was entering a temple to Meière, and the soaring, glittering mosaics were every bit as beautiful as I'd read. Even better, the Red Room was slated to become

a retail space, meaning the public would be able to experience Meière's genius, rather than just the obscenely wealthy future tenants. I was thrilled to learn it would be the first American outpost of French department store Printemps, whose flagship location in Paris is capped with a stained glass Art Deco dome from 1923.

In her lifetime, Meière received many awards and was a leader in her field. She was the first woman to sit on the New York City Art Commission, served as president of the National Society of Mural Painters and vice president of the Architectural League of New York, and was the director of the Department of Mural Painting at the Beaux-Arts Institute of Design. She also served on the board of the Art Students League, the Municipal Arts Society, and the Advisory Committee of the Cooper Union Art School. In other words, she understood the value of leading by example and of giving back. Happily, the Red Room restoration has introduced Meière to a new generation of art and architecture enthusiasts.

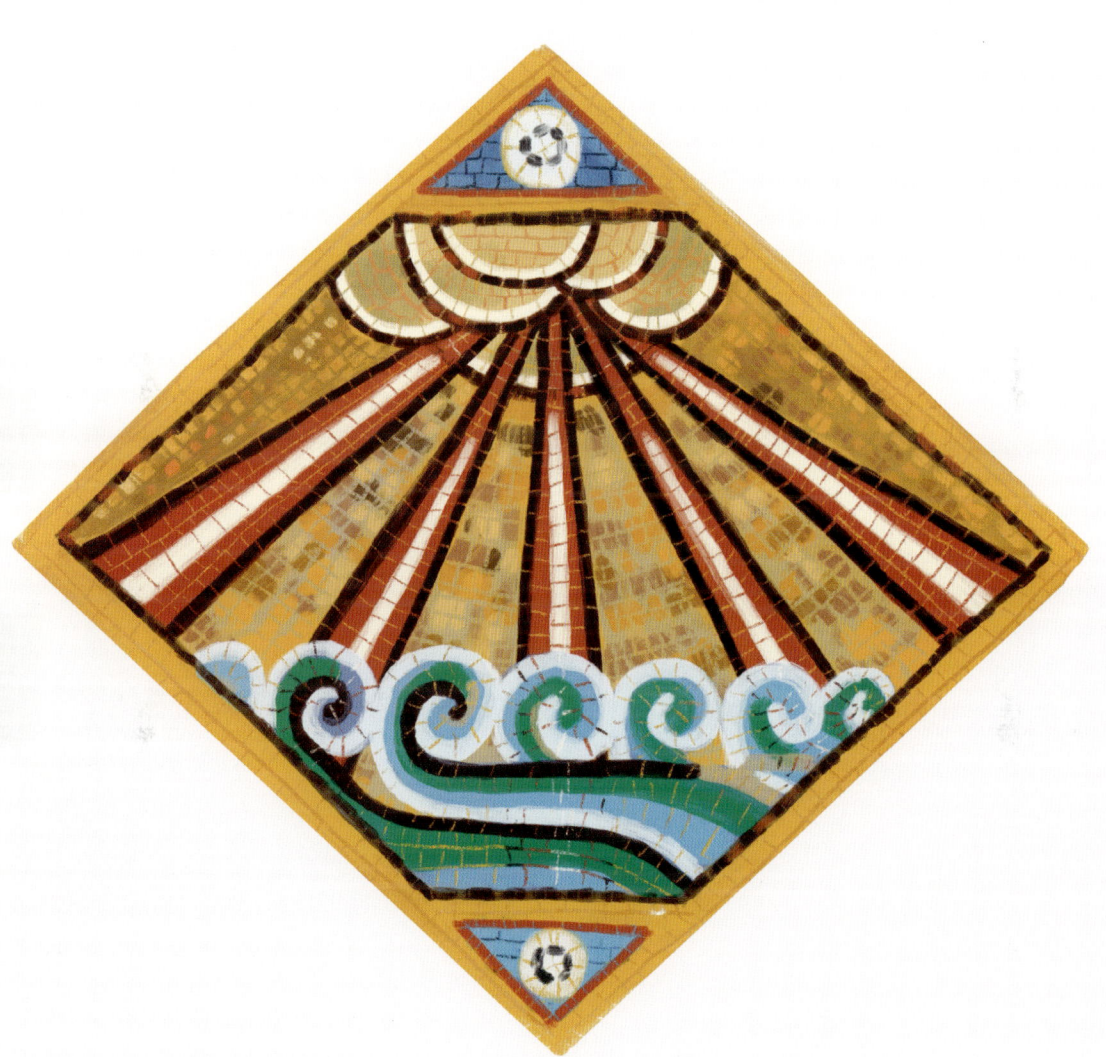

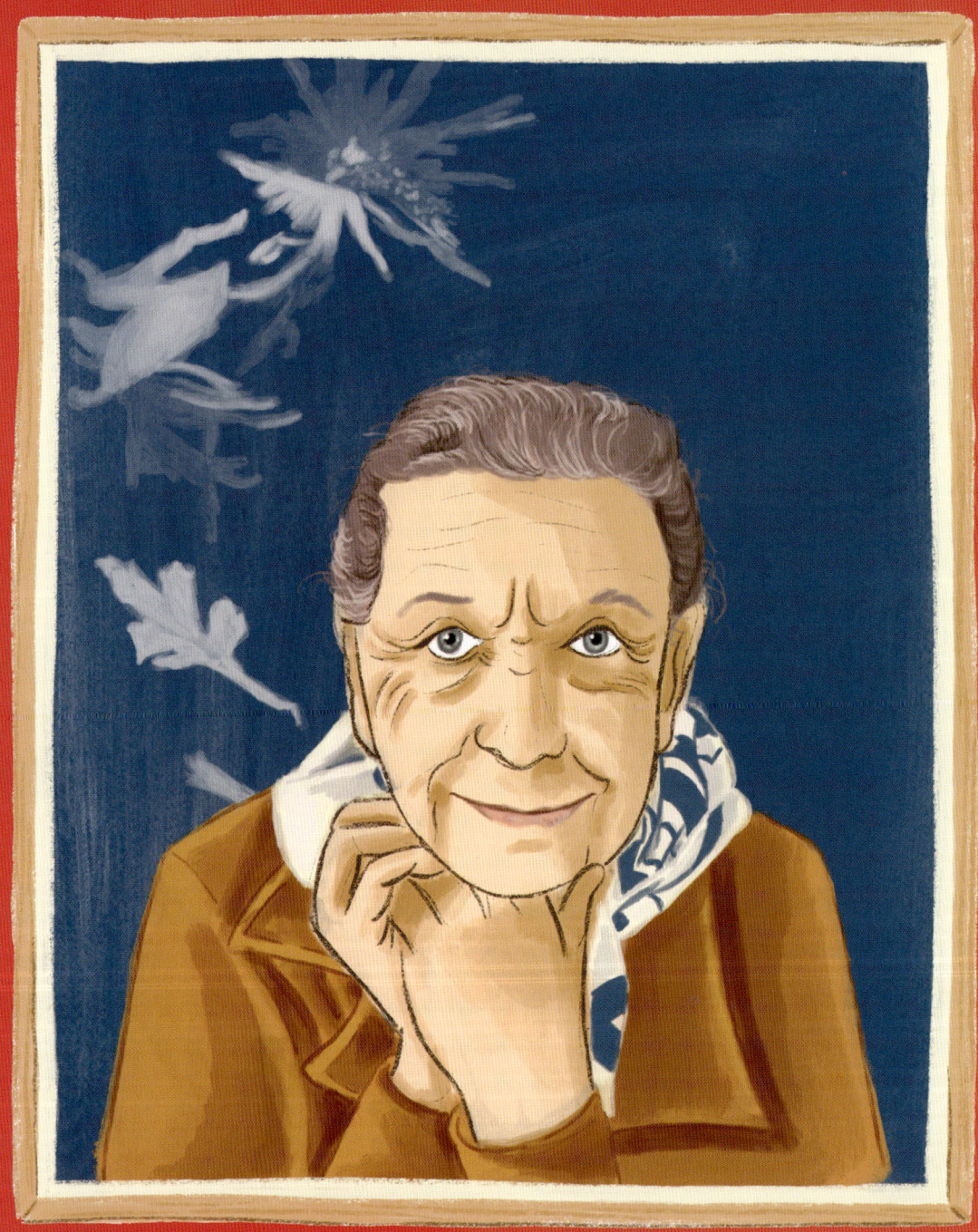

LUCIA MOHOLY

THE WOMAN WHO
SAVED THE BAUHAUS

JANUARY 18, 1894–MAY 17, 1989

In the grand timeline of design history, the Bauhaus School represents a tiny blip, lasting just fourteen years in all. Yet its impact was so great, it can still be felt a century later. Unifying all artistic mediums, the Bauhaus traded classical ornamentation for egalitarian simplicity. Under founder Walter Gropius, the movement exalted angular, clean lines and geometric abstraction. The Bauhaus was a grandiose leap into modernism, emphasizing new concepts like abstract and minimalist art, functional and industrial design, and an admiration for mass production.

But if not for one person, the Bauhaus may not have gone on to influence the entire design sphere as we know it. That person was Lucia Moholy.

In 1923, Moholy found herself packing up her Berlin apartment to head to Weimar, where her husband László Moholy-Nagy had been offered a teaching job at the exciting new Bauhaus School. In Berlin, Moholy supported the family financially, as her husband was still a young, and mostly unsuccessful, Constructivist artist. He had been largely reliant on Moholy both financially and creatively since their marriage two years earlier. She was busy in her own established career, working as a photographer, editor, and writer—reporting for local newspapers and, more interestingly, publishing Expressionist prose under the pen name Mr. Ulrich Steffen—to pay their bills. Still, she made time to work with her husband,

and her partnership in László's darkroom had helped him develop his artistic voice. The pair began collaborating on photography experiments early in their marriage, with their friends saying they were of "one mind" when creating art—yet it was always attributed solely to László. This Bauhaus opportunity, which was presented personally by Gropius himself, meant that László could leave the uncertain life of a fine artist to become the youngest instructor at the school. In time, he would grow into a leader of the Bauhaus movement. Ever the supportive wife, Moholy gave up her connections in Berlin and the couple relocated to Weimar.

Just four years earlier Gropius, a German architect, had founded the Bauhaus School with the belief that the end of World War 1 should usher in a new era of art and design. The Bauhaus ideal was the equality of all of art and design, positing that elements like architecture, fine art, crafts, interior design, and typography should all adhere to one unified vision. The objects and architecture that resulted were sleek, elegant, and highly functional—and easily mass-produced from minimal materials. Above all, the movement saw artists and artisans as equals, with one as important as the other.

The Bauhaus School also touted the equality of the sexes, admitting women when most art academies refused to enroll them. Still, while women were offered opportunities to take classes as well as to teach, they were largely funneled into courses deemed "appropriate" by Gropius, who was rumored to believe that women could not "see in three dimensions." (Yes, really.) Gropius believed women should focus on courses related to the domestic realm, like weaving and ceramics, which he saw as "feminine crafts" or "low arts." Ironically—and obviously—such objects are three-dimensional. (Incidentally, the ceramics, design objects, textiles, and furniture created by the women in these classes are truly exceptional and revolutionary. Artists like Anni Albers, Marianne Brandt, Otti Berger, Margarete Heymann, and many more are well worth reading about.) Because of this, when Moholy arrived in Weimar, she was expected, like the other instructors' wives, to make herself useful. Since she had training in photography, Gropius made her the official photographer of the Bauhaus School. This position was unpaid.

Moholy had already learned to push the limits of photography in and out of the darkroom. She had developed a distinct style that used multiple exposures, shadow play, and geometric arrangement to manipulate her subjects. She then taught these same techniques to László. Together, they experimented with photograms: camera-less images made by arranging objects like leaves or coins directly onto light-sensitive paper. The objects would leave ghostly black-and-white silhouettes after being exposed to light. Again, most of their photograms were attributed solely to László.

At the Bauhaus, Moholy applied her existing visual language to the strange new place. She was tasked with photographing all aspects of the school, first in Weimar, then in Dessau in 1925. She followed the practices of the Bauhaus, but no matter the subject, Moholy's distinct style shone through. It was clear that she had a sophisticated understanding of design. She shot from the practical, deadpan approach favored by the New Objectivists, which made her photographs of buildings comparable to her portraits of people. She loved to juxtapose starkly contrasting light and dark elements to draw awareness to the shapes made by negative space, which allowed the lamps and teapots she was photographing to pop off the page. She used the hard shadows cast by Bauhaus architecture to shift perspective and soft shadows to frame faces or create drama in her portraiture.

Moholy had grown up in Prague, as part of a nonobservant Jewish family in which her education and work ethic were encouraged early on. She began her career in her father's law offices before studying philosophy, philology, and art history at the University of Prague and photography at Leipzig Academy for Graphic and Book Arts. When she met László for the first time in Berlin in April 1920, her career had already taken her across Germany.

At the Bauhaus, it was László's turn to excel. Moholy helped him in the darkroom, with his correspondence and publications (acting as his translator, for which she did not receive credit), and with his courses. As he rose to prominence at the Bauhaus, Moholy wrote extensively in her diary about the loneliness that plagued her. She and László divorced in 1929, a year after they left Dessau, but remained close friends.

Four years later, Moholy would turn to her ex-husband when her boyfriend, communist Theodor Neubauer, was arrested by Nazis in her apartment. Fearing they would return for her as a Jew, she left most of her things behind except for her work. Her photographic negatives of the Bauhaus were the only ones in existence, so she wanted to keep them safe at all costs. She delayed her departure from Berlin to bring boxes containing nearly 560 glass negatives to László and his wife, who promised to care for them until it was safe for her to return.

Moholy spent the next few years outrunning the war, traveling from Czechoslovakia to Switzerland to Austria, before settling in London, where she would remain until 1959. She spent the last thirty years of her life in Zollikon, Switzerland.

In London, Moholy established herself as a teacher, commercial photographer, and author, writing the hit book *A Hundred Years of Photography, 1839–1939*, which is still used in art history classes today. She also ran a microfilm service at

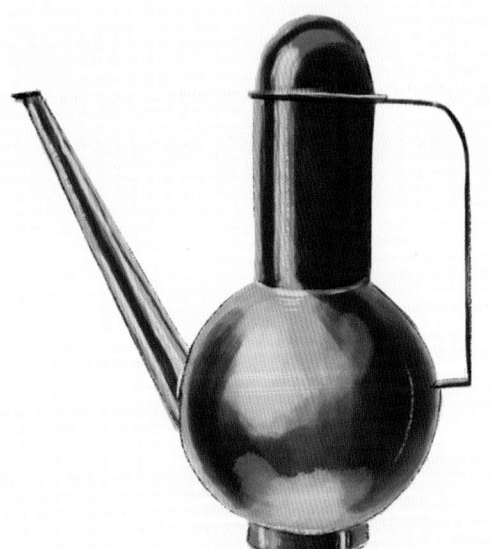

the London Science Museum, and later, in 1946, shot documentary films in the Middle East with UNESCO. Just before her first UNESCO trip, Moholy came across a catalog from a Bauhaus exhibition at the Museum of Modern Art in New York, which had been held eight years earlier in 1938. Between the book's covers were dozens of her photographs, both on their own and framed in the museum's galleries. Because of the war, the museum had been unable to transport examples of Bauhaus furniture and design objects, so Moholy's photographs were the main focus of the exhibition. She felt everything all at once: surprised, shocked, livid, relieved. She had assumed her negatives had been destroyed during the war, but here was proof that they survived! She was happy, until she read the signature in the corner of the photographs—Walter Gropius.

Many consider Gropius to be a god of design, and he agreed. Moholy soon discovered that, when László had had to flee Germany himself, he had asked Gropius to take her negatives back to the United States. In 1937, Gropius had been allowed to pack his home at his leisure, due to his friendship with several high-ranking Nazi officials. Once in the United States, Gropius had settled at Harvard University and quickly began to use Moholy's photographs as his own in pamphlets, articles, exhibitions, and books about the Bauhaus, which created a renewed interest in the movement around the globe.

Upon realizing her catalog of negatives had survived, Moholy wrote to Gropius. At first, she asked nicely for the work she had left with her ex-husband to be returned to her. But Gropius's reply would foreshadow a yearslong battle to come. Gropius began by saying she had *given* her negatives to him. He then offered to send her contact prints if she "wanted to make use of them herself." By this point, all three cities where the Bauhaus had established itself were occupied by the Soviets, who had drastically altered Gropius's surviving buildings. The Soviets had also enacted a photography ban that would last until 1980. Moholy's negatives were Gropius's only proof of his genius, and he guarded them fiercely. Without Moholy's negatives, he could have fallen into obscurity.

Moholy and Gropius went back and forth like this for years. He continued to claim ownership of the negatives, and she grew more and more impatient. Meanwhile, her photographs continued to be distributed under Gropius's name. Tired of being polite, Moholy finally hired a lawyer, and in 1957, Gropius was required to return more than half of her 560 negatives. He sent them COD in inappropriate packaging, causing several to become damaged.

In 1972, Moholy published the book *Moholy-Nagy: Marginal Notes*, in which she detailed her shared collaborations with her ex-husband, attempting to reclaim the artistic credit to which she was due. She died at her home in Zürich, Switzerland, in 1989 at age ninety-five.

Moholy's negatives are more than the Bauhaus's proof of life. They also demonstrate her role as an important artist in the movement who helped influence the growth of modern design across the world. Gropius donated fifty of Moholy's negatives to Harvard's Busch-Reisinger Museum, where they were originally housed as part of *his* archives. In recent years, though, the university museum has reattributed the negatives to their rightful creator: Lucia Moholy.

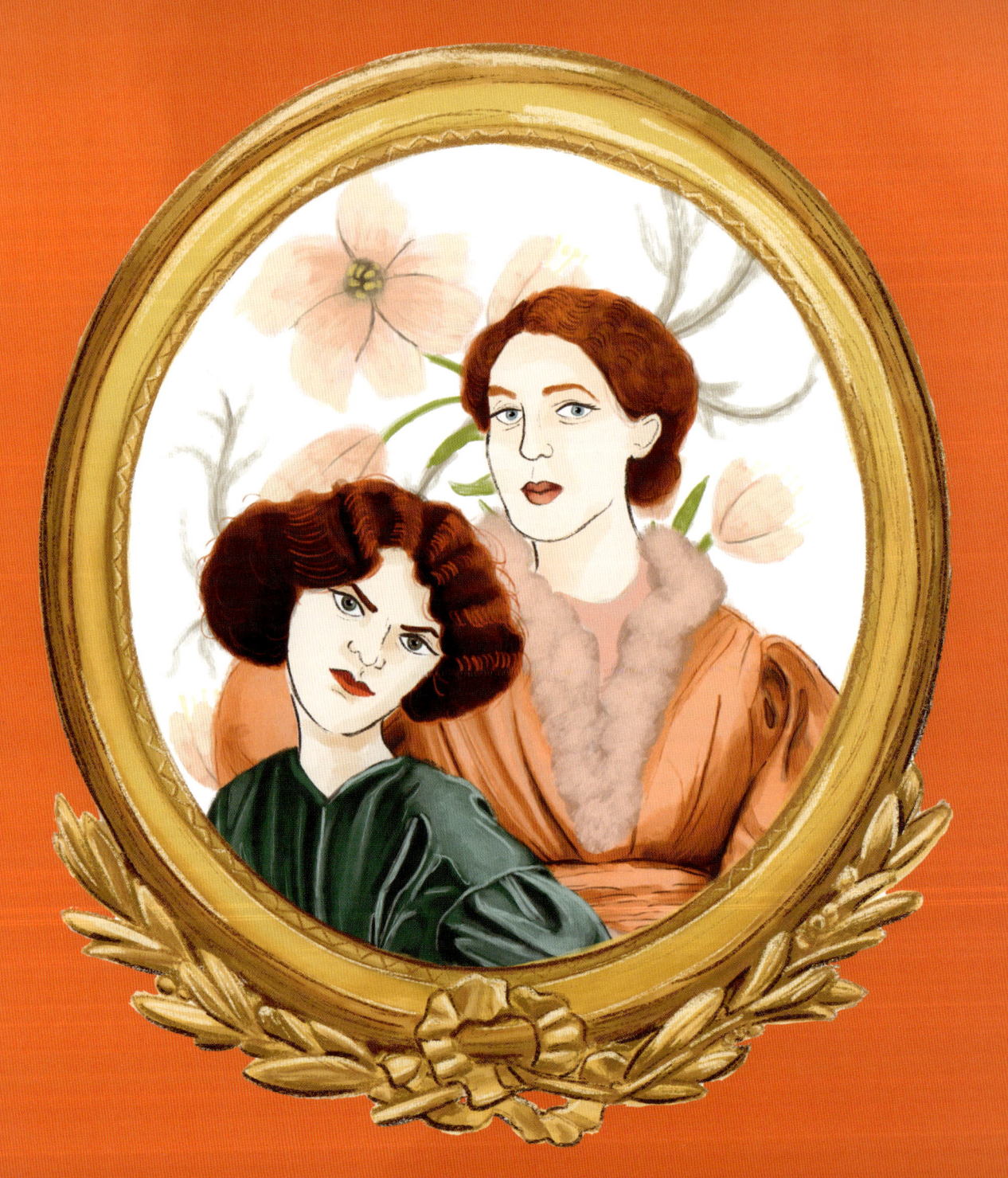

MAY & JANE MORRIS

ICONS OF ARTS AND CRAFTS

MAY MORRIS | MARCH 25, 1862–OCTOBER 17, 1938
JANE MORRIS | OCTOBER 19, 1839–JANUARY 26, 1914

More than 160 years ago, Morris & Co, a London design firm founded by William Morris, began to produce the gorgeously intricate, nature-inspired patterns that have since become a comfortably familiar design mainstay. The patterns, marked by organizational perfection, impeccable colors, and eye-pleasing subject matter—delicate flowers, the prettiest colorful birds, beautiful leaves—have somehow never gone out of style. William Morris, a historical heavyweight, Pre-Raphaelite artist, writer, socialist activist, and founder of the Arts and Crafts movement, has unsurprisingly been given the lion's share of credit for the almost mythical feat of creating timeless design. But it may have been the efforts of "& Co" that kept the Morris designs and name relevant across the centuries. The contributions of William Morris's wife Jane, a master embroiderer and driving force of the Pre-Raphaelites, and daughter May, a multitalented designer who undertook the arduous task of preserving her father's legacy, have been callously lumped into that "& Co" over the years. However, these two powerful and talented women are the key to our perpetual fascination with the Morris & Co aesthetic.

There is no doubt in my mind that most readers of this book would recognize Morris designs, whether they're familiar with the company name or not. The typical Morris & Co pattern is delicate, detailed, richly colorful, and mesmerizing. It feels familiar and traditional, but also sophisticated, elevated, and, above all, undeniably beautiful. There is a comfort in following the swirling lines of these designs from stem to bloom and around again. The botanical goodies of leaves, flowers, and fruits are arranged so tightly, so harmoniously, that the overall patterns are suited for almost any kind of material or surface—a design manufacturer's dream. It is no surprise that the Morris patterns remain tremendously popular, whether on blank notebooks at fancy stationery stores, on tiny trays and $35 tote bags at art museum gift shops, in capsule collections from clothing companies large and small, or on the signature fabrics of the famed department store Liberty of London, where William Morris was once employed as a designer. More than 600 original patterns are in the company's archive and licensed to appear on design products around the world. They are largely kept as they were originally designed, with the colorways the only aspect adapted over time to follow trends. No matter how many years have passed, the layered patterns with budding blossoms and furls have remained in fashion—thanks to the foresight of May Morris.

After the explosive changes of the Industrial Revolution, British designers were struck by a deep nostalgia for the days before the mass production of the machine age. A backlash against the poor quality of many factory-made goods launched a renewed appreciation for handmade traditions. The Arts and Crafts movement emerged from this yearning for the past, which favored not just a return to traditional artisanship, but also to medieval, romantic, and folk styles. William Morris's designs, which were initially hand-embroidered or block printed, were a beautiful example of these ideals.

May was born into the family business, which her mother Jane Burden Morris was also very much a part of. Jane, the daughter of a stableman and laundress, was born in a shoddy part of Oxford in 1839, but rose to prominence in the Pre-Raphaelite art scene despite her humble background. Her uniquely severe beauty—with a face of ancient Roman angles and an intense expression—captivated the Pre-Raphaelites so profoundly that painter Dante Gabriel Rossetti shifted his painting style to better reflect her features. The Pre-Raphaelites were a group of English painters, poets, and critics who believed paintings should be as realistic as possible, with the era before the Renaissance as their model. To look at a photograph of Jane is to immediately understand the power and inspiration she held over these artists. She modeled endlessly for paintings by the group and has been called "the face of the Pre-Raphaelites." She shared in their aesthetic and philosophical beliefs, and her wide-ranging knowledge and voracious love of reading soon made her a true member of the group, not just its muse.

Jane married William Morris in 1859, but continued a torrid, emotional love affair with Rossetti that lasted in various iterations for nearly twenty years—this despite her having a husband and Rossetti a serious addiction to a Victorian sedative called chloral, which contributed significantly to his untimely death in 1882. It's rumored that Morris said she was never in love with William, who was known to be emotionally unavailable, but she did care for him in her own way. As his wife, the "lowborn" Jane Morris was given the Eliza Doolittle treatment. William arranged for an education in etiquette and art, which Morris ended up adoring rather than resenting. She combined her newfound art education with her

experience with a needle and thread, becoming a masterful embroiderer for Morris & Co. Morris shared this gift with her daughters and her sister Elizabeth Burden, who was also a notable embroiderer and teacher.

Morris's children, Jane "Jenny" Alice (born in 1861) and Mary "May" (born in 1862), arrived as their father William became the face of the Arts and Crafts movement and just as he founded the firm that would become Morris & Co. Both children took to the family business, but Jenny was diagnosed with epilepsy at a young age and needed constant care. Like her mother and sister, Jenny excelled at embroidery, but her projects were limited to personal pieces that are now in the collection of the William Morris Gallery in London.

Though Jane was informally educated under her husband, she taught herself much of her skilled needlework. Her daughters did not face the impoverished upbringing she had, and so were highly educated in more traditional settings. At sixteen, and already a master embroiderer, May was among the first wave of students to study textile arts at the National Art Training School in South Kensington, London, which would later become the Royal College of Art. She saw thread in the same way painters do pigments and specialized in a free-form style of embroidery that built up varying colors of silk thread to mimic shading, which resulted in more realistic, dimensional designs. She was also a master of Opus Anglicanum, a medieval embroidery technique that used gold and silver threads on rich velvets.

May Morris's prodigal expertise in embroidery was rewarded when she took over as manager of the embroidery department of Morris & Co at just twenty-three. In this role, Morris oversaw a team who created all manner of embroidery for textiles, linens, and many ecclesiastic clients. She also contributed greatly to the Morris stock of botanical patterns for textiles and wallpapers. Many of the patterns in the Morris Archive originally attributed to William were done by May, including the perennially popular Honeysuckle (1883) and Horn Poppy (1885). She led the charge in the Morris & Co embroidery department for eleven years.

When her father died in 1896, the company would have been left to her . . . if she had been a son. But that was of little consequence, as May Morris had loftier plans for herself and took William's passing as an opportunity to move on. In the years that followed, she became a well-respected leader of the evolving Arts and Crafts movement,

a noted scholar of historical textiles, and, like her father, active in political Socialist circles.

The younger Morris stayed on as an embroidery adviser at Morris & Co, but turned her primary attention to educating the next generation of embroiderers and promoting the work of other women artisans. She toured the UK and North America lecturing on the past and present of embroidery, taught at various schools and created curricula, and was head of the embroidery department at LCC Central School of Art from 1899 to 1905. In 1907, she became a founding member of the Women's Guild of Arts, which was created to protect workers' rights as well as to establish a community for female artisans, since the existing Art Workers' Guild would not admit them. All the while, she regularly exhibited her work at major Arts and Crafts exhibitions and designed gorgeous jewelry, which is still replicated today. (Some originals can be seen at the Victoria & Albert Museum in London.)

Morris enjoyed her status as an impactful artist and figure in the Arts and Crafts movement. In her forties, she turned her attention back to her father, and undertook the arduous task of organizing, editing, and publishing his papers. Five years and twenty-four volumes later, *The Collected*

Works of William Morris were finally published (the last in 1910). Their existence has without question contributed significantly to William Morris's lasting popularity and impact.

The last twenty years of Morris's life were perhaps the most adventurous, and they were certainly dedicated to fun. In 1917, at fifty-five, she met Mary Lobb, a Land Army volunteer stationed in the town near the family's country retreat of Kelmscott Manor. Lobb was gardener of the grounds at Kelmscott. Morris had been unhappily married and divorced in the past—to the unremarkable Socialist Henry Halliday Sparling in 1890—after having had an unrequited, years-long flirtation with *the* George Bernard Shaw. She had given up on love until Lobb came along. The pair had a deep connection and a shared passion for outlandish travel. (For instance, they traveled across Iceland on horseback three times.) Together they explored the natural wonders of all corners of Great Britain, camping and wandering the lands and spending hours watching birds and other creatures, which Morris would then translate to embroidery. Lobb moved into Kelmscott Manor, where they found daily pleasures gardening, writing, taking bike rides, and reading travel tales together. They spent twenty-one happy years together, until Morris's death in 1938. Lobb would follow her the next year.

Jane and May Morris were an integral part of the Morris & Co legacy, and without them, the gorgeous designs may not have cemented their status as a coveted part of our contemporary consumer culture.

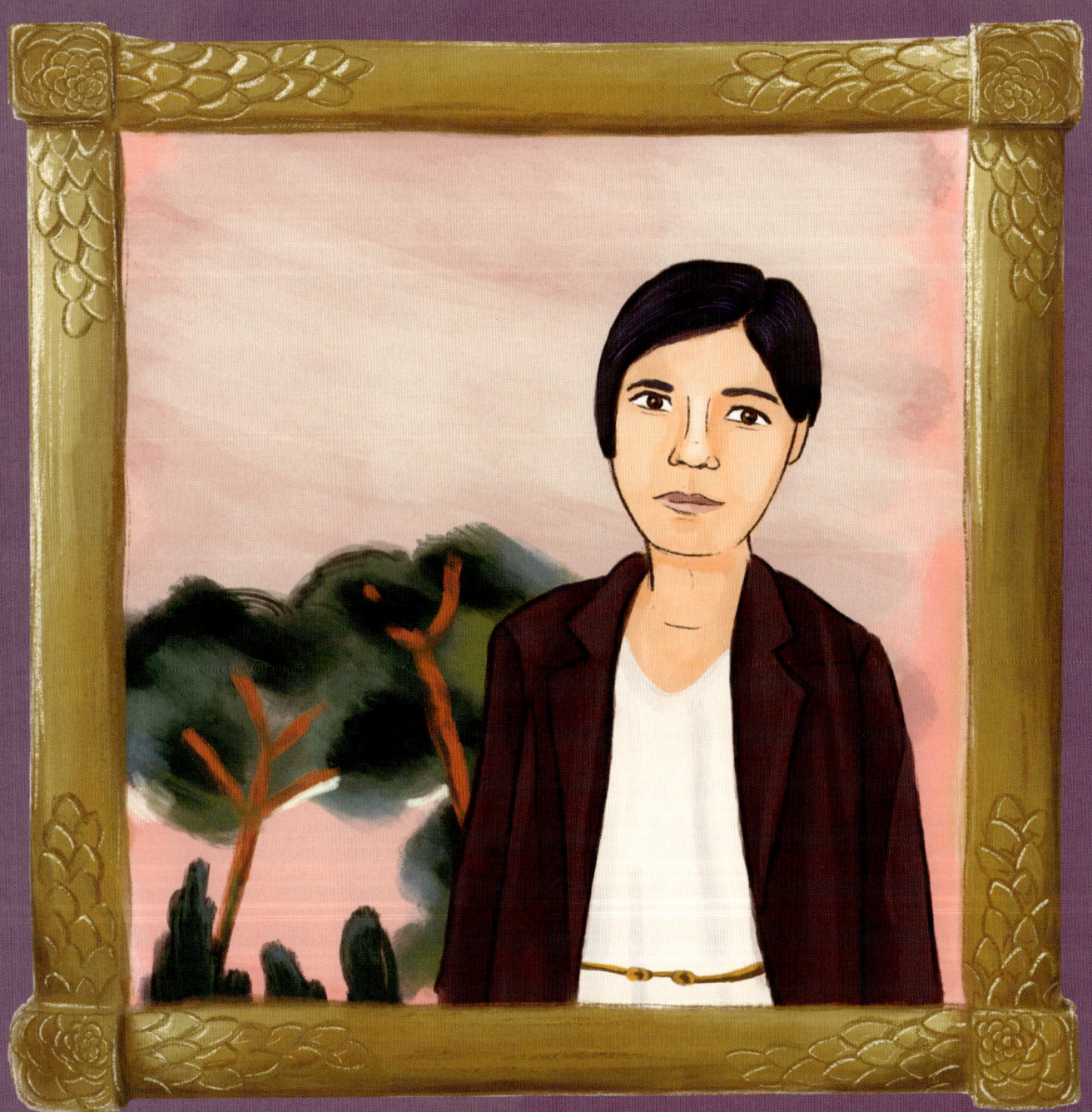

NA HYE-SŎK

GOOD FEMINIST, WISE POET

APRIL 28, 1896–DECEMBER 10, 1948

In 1930s Korea, little girls were raised to adhere to the cultural mandate of "Good Wife, Wise Mother." Good wives and wise mothers were said to be patriotic. Sacrificing their individuality for domestic harmony was considered their duty for their country. Those little girls who did not comply, the starry-eyed daughters who dreamt of growing up to be artists and writers, were threatened with the warning, "Do you want to become another Na Hye-Sŏk?" An outspoken feminist who used her pen and brush to speak out for female individualism during the volatile period of the Japanese occupation of Korea, Na was an important figure in Korean arts and literature, even if she was considered a dissident. During her lifetime, Na became a national celebrity as the first female professional painter in Korea. She was also widely known for her brutally honest takedowns of gender stereotypes. Her work was tolerated, and even celebrated, for much of her life—until it wasn't. Her blunt manner was both her strength and a weakness that sadly reduced her extraordinary story to a cautionary tale meant to crush dreams and put young women in their place.

From the get-go, Na was completely disinterested in the Good Wife, Wise Mother narrative. She grew up in Suwon, nineteen miles south of the capital city Seoul, in the early twentieth century and established herself as a formidable intellect while still only a child. Her parents were unusually supportive of her quest for an education and were unsurprised when Na decided to study an art form otherwise unknown in Korea: oil painting. At the time, Korea was a very traditional and insular country, still largely uninfluenced by Europe. When Na enrolled at Tokyo Arts College for Women in 1913 to major in Western oil painting, it is likely she or anyone else in Korea had only seen an oil painting once or twice in their lives—if at all. Tokyo set the perfect scene for the burgeoning feminist. Japan was in the midst of a liberal era, which was heavily influenced by Western culture. Na found her place among the students who marched in demonstrations, penned poetry, and read feminist magazines. (*Seitō*, which translates as Bluestocking, was the first, and included essays about sex, sexuality, and women's rights, written bluntly for the first time.)

This feminist awakening would set the tone for her life and work. Over the next few years, Na began to publish controversial essays, short stories, and poems on topics women were expected to keep their mouths shut about: sexual desire, sexuality, remarriage for widows, the double standard around expectations of chastity before marriage, gender roles (or the lack thereof) in child-rearing, the difficulty of childbirth, the negative effects of motherhood on professional women, and even a plea against the hanbok, the

traditional Korean dress that was quite uncomfortable and restrictive—much like the norms themselves. Her stories, considered the first feminist writing in Korea, were thinly veiled as fiction, though most readers understood they were largely autobiographical.

Na's literary prowess worked in tandem with her painting. In March of 1921, the first Korean feminist writer also became the first known Korean woman to hold an art exhibition. The exhibition was a wild success, and Korean art connoisseurs clamored to buy up the first oil paintings for their collections.

Na was on top of the world. Along with her creative and financial success, she had also found love, marrying the year before. Love marriages were still a rarity in Korea at this time, but without one, why would the immensely talented and financially secure Na have agreed to be tied down? Kim Woo-young fell in love with Na after she was arrested during the March 1st Movement against the Japanese occupation of Korea and he was appointed as her lawyer. (What an appropriate meet-cute.)

For a time, their marriage was bliss. Kim encouraged Na's career as an outspoken artist and writer, even after she gave birth to their first child in 1923. (They would have four in all.) In 1927, the couple got a once-in-a-lifetime opportunity to travel the world as part of Kim's job as a diplomat for the Japanese government. For three years, Na absorbed the cultures of the countries they visited together—Germany, Poland, Switzerland, Belgium, the Netherlands, Italy, Spain, and England, followed by a sixteen-month sojourn in Paris, a few months in New York, and a journey across the United States to San Francisco. In Europe, she became an even better painter, learning from the Impressionists and incorporating her feminist views into her works. She also engaged in a very public affair that became tabloid fodder.

With all that Na had accomplished—all the paintings, illustrations, forward-thinking articles, and poems that had gained her fame and admiration—it would be one action that ruined it all in the eyes of a judgmental public: divorce. After eleven years of marriage, her husband filed for divorce in 1931. The divorce was particularly unfair. In it, Kim had a judge declare Na an unfit mother, barring her from seeing her children again. Divorce was scandalous enough in Korea, but a woman having an extramarital affair was worthy of banishment. (Never mind that he had

had an affair all his own—because that was permissible in Korean society.) Her family refused to see her, as they were embarrassed by her well-publicized reputation as a "fallen woman." She was alone. And she had nothing left to lose. So she decided to spill it all spectacularly.

Confessions of a Divorce (also translated as *Divorce Testimony*) was published in 1934. It read like the juiciest, most scandalous tabloid—the kind you're a teensy bit embarrassed to be seen holding. *Confessions* spilled *everything*: details of her married life, her affair with Choe Rin, complications of her divorce, her love for her children whom she was forbidden from seeing, her alienation from Korean society as a fallen woman, double standards in marriage, and what it is like to lose everything. She called out Korean society for upholding the false narrative that an educated woman is an unhappy one, exposing the lie that education needlessly complicates a woman's life by distracting her from domesticity. She railed against other indignities as well, like the double standard that men need not remain chaste when it is demanded of women, the commonplace occurrence of sexual assault in marriages, and other hypocrisies and ironic truths—when I said everything, I meant *everything*. It was defamatory, salacious, and, for the most part, pretty close to the truth. But the truth hurts.

It wouldn't be long after the publication of *Confessions* that Na hit rock bottom. Na dreamed of returning to Paris: a place she had once said killed her, but also made her a real woman. When she had first traveled there, she discovered that in Paris she could be a person, while in Korea she had been a pawn. In her exiled state, she worked on her most ambitious exhibition to date, mounting 200 works. The show was impressive, but no one came to see it. As an artist, the only thing worse than a bad review is indifference. With hatred, the artist has at least accomplished their goal of stirring up emotion and eliciting a reaction. But Na's third and final exhibition was completely ignored.

Life as an outcast was difficult, but one without her children took a heavy toll on Na's mental health. She began to unravel. Unwelcome virtu-ally everywhere she had previously known, she began drifting. For nearly ten years, she became a wanderer without an anchor point, searching for place and purpose while still holding out hope that her children would find her and forgive her. She died in a charity hospital in Seoul on December 10, 1948.

Confessions of a Divorce is one of the most badass feminist historical artifacts. Reading her words from the distance of nearly a hundred years, you can still feel the burn of some of these injustices present today. And even in her pain, Na still managed to create works of tremendous power. A year after her life imploded, Na wrote a poignantly beautiful and wise poem called "No Need to Savor Youth" (1935) that came to me at a time when I am questioning my own worth in "middle age"—whatever that means. Her words filled me with gratitude and reminded me that aging is a privilege. In the end, she was our Wise Mother.

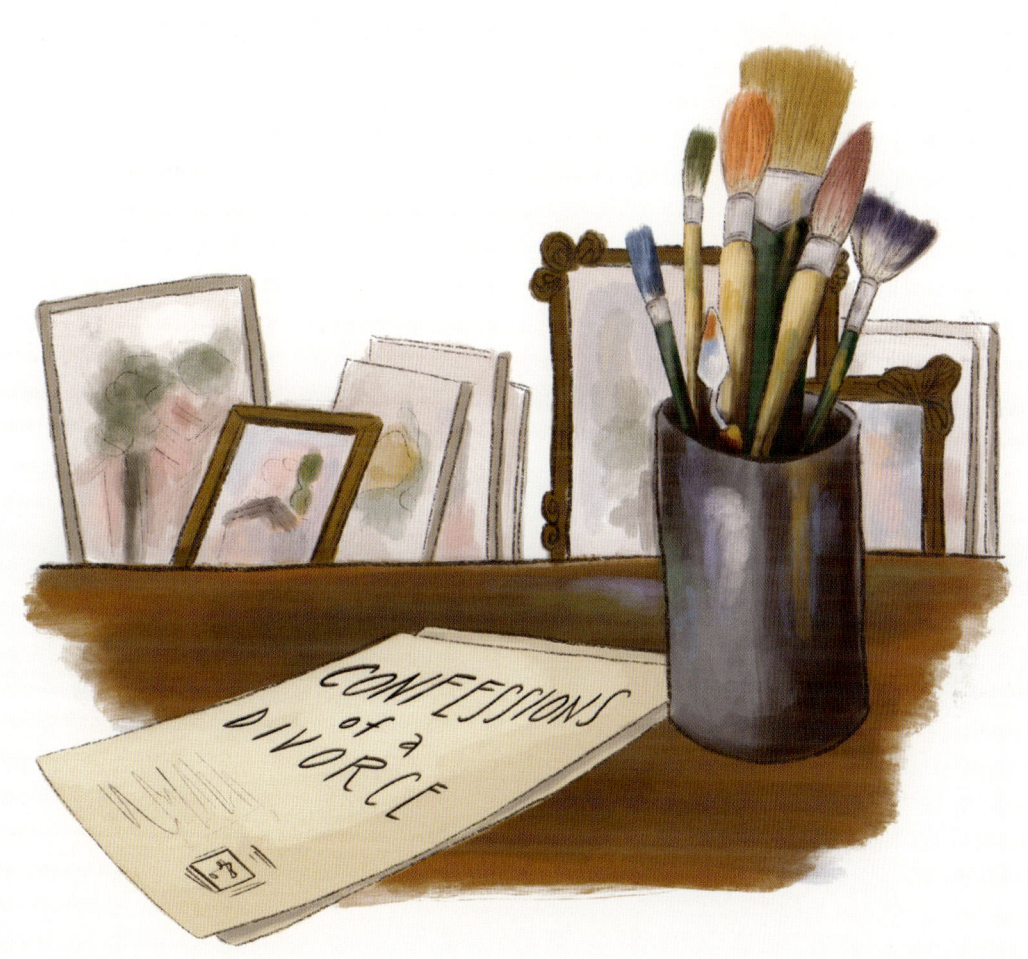

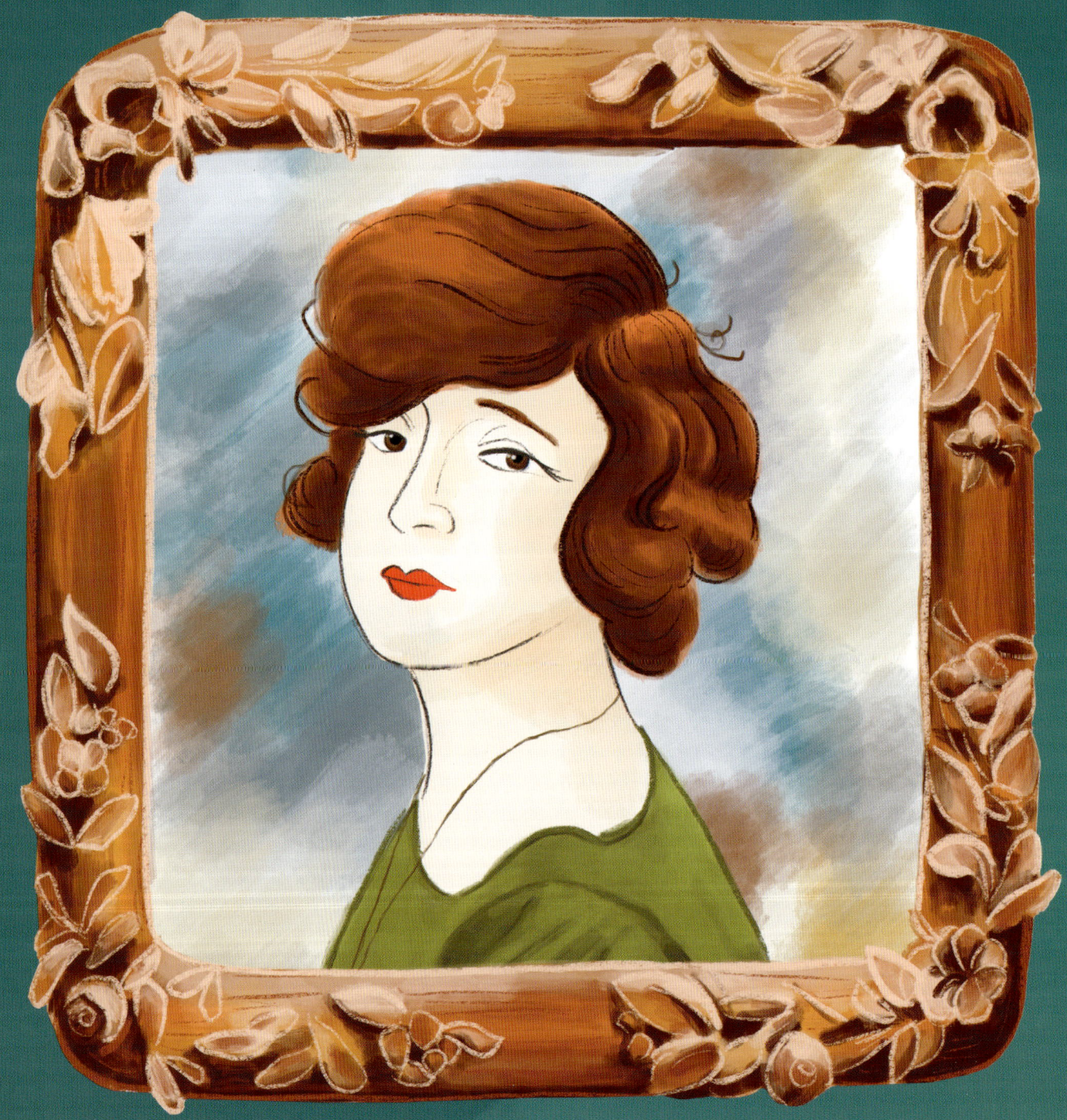

FERNANDE OLIVIER

MEMOIRIST OF THE BELLE ÉPOQUE

JUNE 6, 1881–JANUARY 29, 1966

More than 100 works of art bearing Fernande Olivier's likeness can be found in museums, galleries, and private collections around the world. She was sketched, painted, and sculpted by some of the greatest artists from turn-of-the-twentieth-century Paris. Olivier stands out, despite the varying hands and artistic styles used in these works. She is recognizable for her signature thicket of hair, piled high on her head, or her deep brown eyes that often look out to the viewer.

Olivier was a well-respected model, accomplished artist, and fantastic writer, but unfortunately, a single relationship in her early twenties eclipsed her own achievements—at least in public discourse—for the remainder of her life. When Olivier met the twenty-two-year-old Pablo Picasso on the street near his studio, he was just another starving artist who had moved to Paris to make it big. During their torrid, nearly seven-year relationship, Picasso created sixty works depicting Olivier, including the groundbreaking *Les Demoiselles d'Avignon*, which he painted when the couple shared a small room in Le Bateau Lavoir. Though they parted ways for good in 1911 when Picasso left her for Eva Gouel, he would continue to control Olivier by preventing her memoirs from being published during his lifetime—a move that left her nearly destitute. When her memoirs finally came out in 1988, the book was an immediate commercial success, though one that Olivier would never know. Her writing offers a vivid slice of life during the Belle Époque.

She tells of personal tragedy, of the intellectual satisfaction among now-famous artists, and of the rise of Picasso from an artist in poverty to one who enjoyed international success. Her books would surely have made her a star on her own. Instead, she was stifled by a man whom she dated in her twenties.

It is no secret that Picasso was a misogynist who siphoned energy from the women in his life. He famously said horrid things like, "There are only two types of women—goddesses and doormats," "Women are machines for suffering," and, my favorite, "Every time I change wives, I should burn the last one. That way I'd be rid of them. They wouldn't be around to complicate my existence." One may wonder why a woman would choose to begin a relationship with someone who came with such a glaring warning label. But when Olivier met Picasso, he had yet to achieve fame or earn the controlling reputation that is so often dismissed in art historical depictions of his so-called genius.

By 1904, when she first ran into Picasso, Olivier was already a fixture in the Parisian art world. At the time, she was earning a decent living as a popular artists' model, known as "La Belle Fernande." She was a favorite of painters Ricard Canals, Kees van Dongen, and sculptor Laurent Debienne, whose techniques she studied as they studied her. This nearly symbiotic arrangement allowed Olivier to regularly leave modeling sessions inspired to make paintings of her own when she got home. Her rough childhood had lured her to the Parisian artistic enclave of Montmartre, where she could hide in plain sight from the troubles of her past. That year, Picasso had permanently relocated to Paris and taken residence at the famous, although squalid, Bateau Lavoir. Olivier found him impoverished and with poor hygiene, but his paintings left an impression on her. Soon they were officially a couple, and Olivier moved into his stark room at Bateau Lavoir. Although Picasso knew Olivier for her hard work as an artists' model, he required that she quit her jobs and remain available to him at his studio as his personal model, hostess, lover, domestic servant, and all-round security blanket.

At first, she didn't mind. Modeling was hard work that required most of her waking hours. With Picasso, she was free to sleep as long as she liked. Olivier grew accustomed to spending evenings with him at the cafés, where Max Jacob and Guillaume Apollinaire made her feel like one of the family while giving her an education on literature and art theory. For a time, they were happy. Her presence ushered Picasso out of his depressive Blue Period and into his productive Rose Period.

Even when Picasso began to lock her in his studio when he went out, she did not leave him. Nor did she after finding nude drawings of the thirteen-year-old girl Olivier had brought from an orphanage to live with them. Their torrid relationship continued as Picasso's career gained traction, and during that time they spent periods in small towns in France and Spain. Eventually, the artist's success allowed them to move out of the Bateau Lavoir, and Picasso set up a real studio. Olivier stayed with him through his next phase, during which he appropriated the styles of African masks he found in Paris, and into the Cubist work that would become his signature achievement. But as time passed, his irrationality increased, and he evolved into an impossible tyrant—a reputation that followed him into the history books. Despite Picasso's controlling games and their endless fights, Olivier stayed in the relationship until he ultimately left her for his next mistress in a pattern that would continue his entire life.

Living with Picasso was difficult, but it had offered the greatest stability Olivier had ever

known. Her life up until that point had been a series of trials. She had been born Amélie Lang in a suburb east of Paris in 1881 to an unwed maid and a married man. She was then pawned off on her birth father's stepsister, whose resentment would lead to a childhood of abuse. In Olivier's diaries, which she began at age fifteen, she describes her life of unending unfairness and horrific situations with humor, wit, and sophistication beyond her years. Her words are descriptive and raw, providing a window into a nineteenth-century girlhood that was difficult and painful. Her aunt's cruelness scared any friends away, and when a friend of the family maid forced himself on Olivier when she was nineteen, her aunt made her marry her assailant. Olivier's marriage to Paul Percheron comprised a traumatic cycle of effusive displays of affection and vicious physical and sexual abuse. It lasted almost a year before Olivier found the strength to run away after a miscarriage left her unable to bear future children. In 1900, she escaped to Montmartre, where she changed her name to Fernande Olivier. But she never sought an official divorce from Percheron out of fear that he would find her and murder her.

After Picasso left, Olivier had little to support herself, having been out of the workforce for seven years. She got on her feet financially by selling some of the drawings Picasso had given to her, then made ends meet through various jobs as a tutor, secretary, cashier, and by performing poetry at the Lapin Agile. In 1929, she returned to writing and began to chronicle her time with Picasso, which had ended nearly twenty years before. Six chapters of her memoirs about their life together were serialized and published in *Le Soir*, a Belgian newspaper. The publication took place at the height of Picasso's stardom, and the public ate the revelations up. Olivier was thrust into the spotlight and her writing was praised by critics around the world, to the absolute detriment of her ex. Picasso hired a lawyer and threatened to sue *Le Soir* and anyone else who would publish Olivier's memoirs about him. He was successful in his efforts, and no one would agree to put out her books during his lifetime. Olivier made a modest living writing articles and essays about art, but it wasn't enough to truly sustain her.

Olivier's health began to decline. She developed severe arthritis, which put a stop to her writing career. Shortly after, she lost her hearing.

In 1956, she begged Picasso, who by then was extremely wealthy, for a stipend to compensate her for the money she had lost from the suppression of her book. He agreed to a modest sum despite his considerable reserves. (When Picasso died in 1973, his personal assets were valued at between $530 million and $1.3 billion in today's dollars. This vast fortune included 45,000 artworks, five homes, and a thick portfolio of stocks and bonds, as well as $32 million in *cash* and more than $9 million in gold.)

Olivier's memoirs, which were divided into two books, would eventually be published to critical and audience acclaim, though she did not live to enjoy the praise. *Picasso and His Friends*, which detailed the exciting time when the Bateau Lavoir was a hotbed of creativity, was published in 1965, just before her death at age eighty-four in January 1966. *Loving Picasso*, the intimate memoir Olivier wrote of her difficult childhood and her relationship with Picasso, would not be published until 1988. Both are widely regarded for their historical importance and prose.

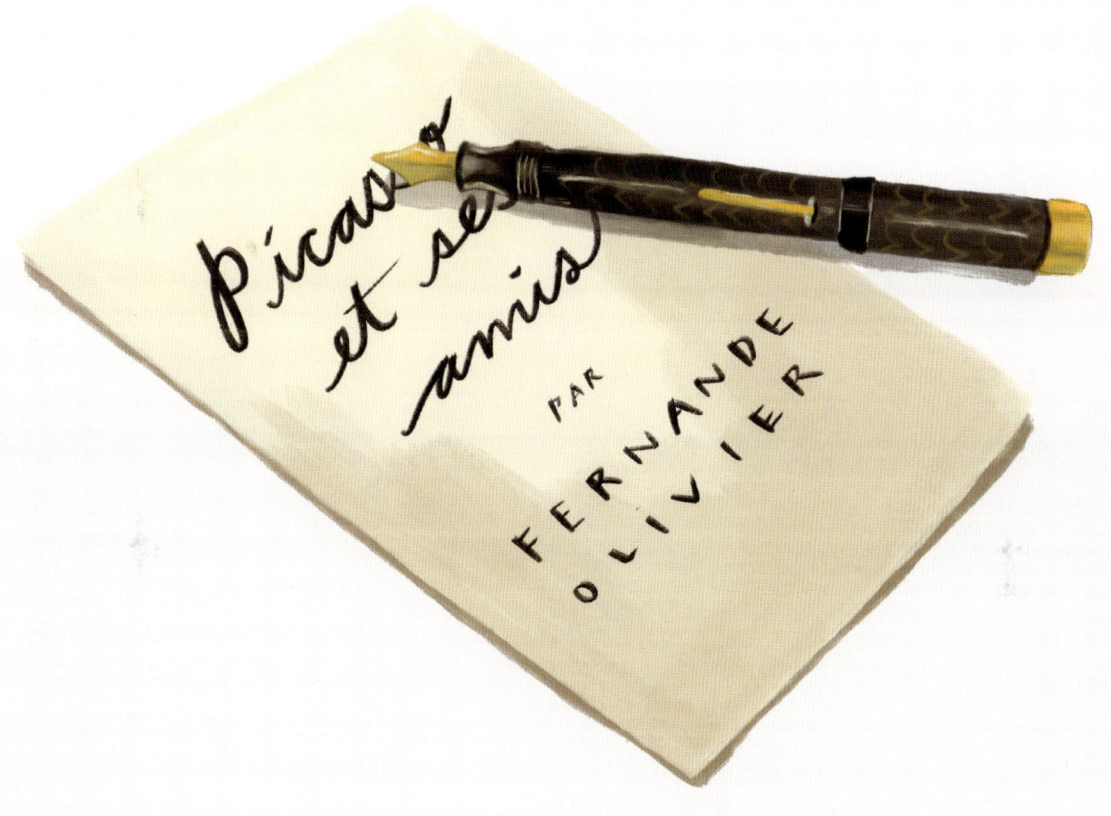

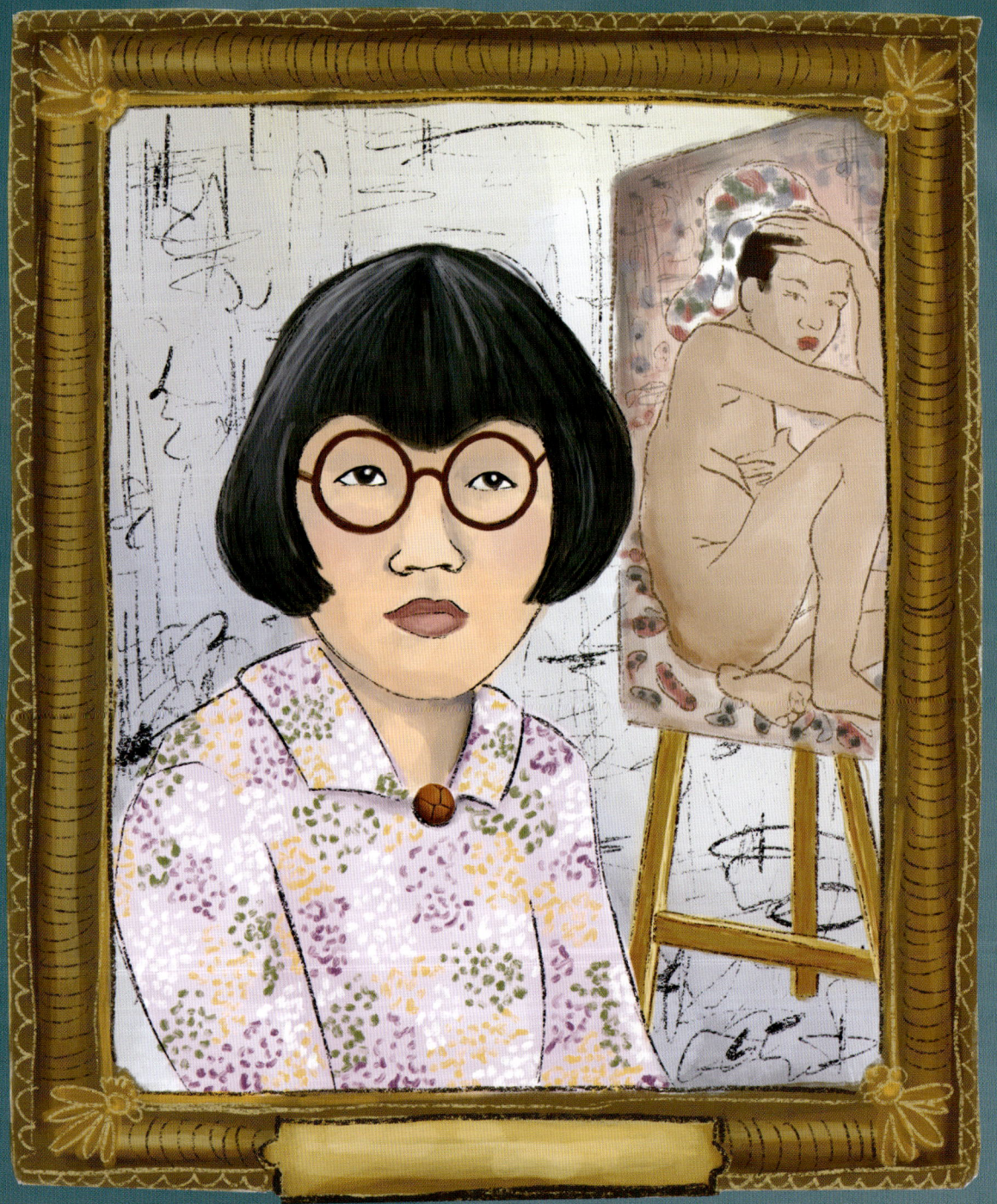

PAN YULIANG

THE FIRST CHINESE WOMAN TO PAINT IN THE WESTERN STYLE

JUNE 14, 1895–JULY 22, 1977

While female artists in turn-of-the-twentieth-century China were relegated to painting traditional flowers, birds, and nature scenes, Pan Yuliang painted what she knew best—her own body. In the years after the People's Republic was formed in 1912, Pan was captivated with the "Western ideas" and modern art ideals that swirled among Chinese universities, which inspired her to defy centuries of conservative art expectations imposed on her gender and Chinese culture as a whole. She was permanently impacted by the deliberate markings of the Impressionists during her studies at Shanghai Art Academy in the early 1920s and later won the title of the first woman in China to paint in the Western style. At the same time, she lost the support of the Chinese art world by painting thousands of then-taboo female nudes and maintained a lifelong art practice of depicting whatever she wanted regardless of whether anything sold or not. Her proclivity for and challenge of the female nude—reserved for so long by men who painted for the male gaze—should have earned her extensive study by the budding feminist scholars of the last century. Yet her name is largely left out of art history books, perhaps because of her unceasing determination to play by her own rules.

To say Pan's beginnings were humble is an understatement. Born Chen Xiuqing in Yangzhou in 1895, she suffered the unimaginable at an early age. When she was a young teen, both of her parents died, leaving her in the custody of an uncle. Unwilling to serve as her guardian, her uncle sold her to a brothel in Wuhu in the Anhui province after inexplicably changing her name to Zhang Yuliang, perhaps to shield the family name from the shame of such an association. As if the trauma of being sold into child prostitution were not enough for one person to bear, the unfair stigma of forced sex work left an indelible mark on her life and art career, even after death. During Pan's lifetime, critics and colleagues regularly judged her for her "unclean"—yet completely unchosen—past, seeing her as a harlot rather than a sex-trafficked child. Even more disheartening is the way her abuse has been characterized by writers to this day. You'll find many clickbait articles about Pan across the internet, which use clichéd terms and egregious quips like "From Brothel to Beaux-Arts" and "From Prostitute to Post-impressionist." Each one is worse than the last. This exploitation of a child victim has come to define Pan for some people, both during her life and afterward. And it is exceptionally unfair.

Pan spent most of her teen years indentured at the brothel. But when she was eighteen, a regular customer fell in love with her and bought her "freedom." Pan Zanhua was a well-to-do customs official, who was already married and had a family. Since she could not be his wife, Pan became his concubine—which was common in China until 1949. She changed her surname once again from Zhang to Pan and moved with the family to Shanghai. Despite essentially buying her, Zanhua was allegedly good to Pan and is responsible for fostering her artistic education. The scenario feels a bit fantastical, like a darker version of the Hollywood blockbuster *Pretty Woman*, but Pan maintained loyalty to Zanhua throughout her lifetime, so I'd like to assume this was true.

As a concubine, Pan was spared the brunt of domestic duties and was encouraged to explore creative hobbies. She began painting under the tutelage of a neighbor, studying guó huà, the national Chinese painting style—similar to calligraphy—that used brush, colored pigments, and black ink. In 1920, Zanhua paid for Pan to enroll in the Shanghai Art Academy, where professors focused on the Western painting style, called xiyanghua, which was still a new concept in the quickly changing country. The Shanghai Art Academy was the first in China to bring in nude models for live drawing classes, which radically deviated from the traditional genres of landscapes, historical figures, and birds or flowers. Pan thrived, but her education and career were limited. Studying art was seen as an elite form of learning, and many of Pan's classmates were unwilling to overlook her traumatic past. They would not and could not accept a victim of child prostitution as a member of their artistic circles. Undaunted, she turned her eye to Europe to immerse herself in the xiyanghua greats she had learned about in school—Paul Cézanne, Henri Matisse, and Georges Seurat.

When Pan first arrived in France in the early 1920s, she did not know she would spend most of her life there. The young painter joined a wave of Chinese artists who visited the country to study Western art techniques, and she was one of sixty students to study at the Sino-French Institute in Lyon between the 1920s and 1940s. She continued at the École National Supérieure des Beaux-Arts in Paris, where she immersed herself in the new styles of painting and thrived on the freedom that many artists and intellectuals experienced in Paris in the 1920s. Pan soaked in the art movements that were developing around her, like Expressionism, Surrealism, and Cubism, while studying the movements of the past that hung in the museum halls—Impressionism, Romanticism, Fauvism, and Symbolism. She expanded her use of materials to incorporate both old and new, creating a style that felt fresh and modern. She began using colorful oil paints and calligraphy inks together, in a unique combination that further cemented her Western approach to her Eastern upbringing. With a head full of new ideas, Pan readdressed her favorite subject: the female nude.

Artists have depicted nudes since the beginning of time, to represent fertility, physical perfection, allegorical tales, and the like. The practice waned around the Middle Ages, because images of the uncovered human body did not mesh with the ideals of modesty and chastity that strictly observant Christian leaders were pushing. During the Renaissance, the female nude reappeared, though largely at the hands of male painters. Hundreds of nude masterpieces were painted over the centuries that followed, though under the modern lens, most have been revealed to be strictly from the male perspective. In these paintings—many of which are gorgeous treasures of art history—the eyes of the female subject meet the viewer, presumed to be male, with a sultry, sensuous look. Bodies are idealized, sensual, and sometimes overtly sexual, with the subjects often seeming to offer themselves up to the viewer. There was no question of what audience these paintings were for.

Pan was, of course, not the first to challenge this paradigm. Édouard Manet and Gustave Courbet had already made waves painting nudes in contemporary settings the century before. But Pan had a complex perspective that her male counterparts did not. For one, she used herself as a model, as well as women she met in Shanghai, a departure from the "beauty ideals" in Western art and culture in which models were almost always white. Unlike her contemporaries, as a woman the naked body had different meanings to her. It was natural; it was home. To her, a nude did not just have to show submission. It could also show strength, pride, comfort, motherhood, tenderness, or vulnerability. The body could present intimate, private moments of solitude or friendship, unsullied by eroticism or sexualization. Her approach to painting nudes, often featuring herself or other women she knew, was to borrow from her past and fuse it with her present. The resulting paintings were as innovative as they were beautiful, with the curves of her figures rounded with the brush of a calligraphic line, Fauvist-inspired colors, and

pointillist marks that filled in the shadows of the flesh and the backgrounds. The women in her paintings look comfortable, confident, and content, unbothered by the gaze of the viewer.

Pan's nudes did something else that those of her male contemporaries did not. She was painting women in a Western style but from an Asian woman's perspective. Europeans had been enamored with Orientalism since the late eighteenth century, clinging to an aesthetic fascination from a Eurocentric point of view. Orientalism was essentially a fantasized impression of the distant "Orient," illustrated with the pens and brushes of European men who had traveled the world or sometimes just read about it. Many of these creators only experienced the cultures they were allegedly depicting as tourists. Their "inspired" views bordered on exploitative, leaning into the perceived exoticism of the East. In fact, even the geography in question was fantastical, as it lumped together the Middle East, North Africa, and the whole of Asia, despite this array encompassing an area with cultures so different from one another that a perceived sameness could only be attributed to rampant stereotypes. People of these countries were largely painted as caricatures, with women mostly portrayed as concubines and harem girls. The favored subject known as the odalisque showed women as possessions instead of people, and can be found in works by Jean Auguste Dominique Ingres, Eugène Delacroix, and Matisse. These paintings are undeniably beautiful, but they also offer only a superficial interpretation of a world outside of Europe. Pan's paintings are the antithesis of these works, humanizing the women from these cultures in art.

With her challenge to the heaviness of historical and sexist stereotypes, Pan's work had the potential to turn the modern art world of Paris on its head. At the same time, she just wanted to go home. After a semester studying in Rome in 1929, she was offered a job as an art professor at her alma mater, the Shanghai Art Academy. She took the opportunity to get back to Zanhua. Over the next eight years she continued teaching and mounted several exhibitions at galleries across China, showing off her body of modernist paintings, including her celebrated nudes. But China was not Europe.

At the time, China was going through extensive changes. The Republic of China invented and reinvented itself during her years there. Although the nation was modernizing, women were still relegated to painting nature scenes, so Pan's nudes came under the scrutiny of government officials.

Unfazed, she continued her work, turning to bathhouses to find subjects when she couldn't otherwise hire a nude model. When this strategy failed, she painted herself. She found fans and supporters in some corners of the Chinese art world, but her past kept coming back to haunt her.

By 1937, nationalism and feminism were rising in China, as was tension with Japan. The New Culture Movement introduced the New Woman ideal, which advocated for women's rights in the country and pushed the notion that women could be seen as so much more than wives and mothers. Only, somehow, this did not apply to Pan. Even the most progressive individuals could not forgive her for the abuse she had faced as a teenager. Pan even came under scrutiny at the university when someone complained that a former prostitute should not be teaching life drawing. Government officials continued to criticize the fact that she painted nudes. Not long after these complaints, one of her paintings was defaced at a gallery exhibition, with the vandal scrawling "A prostitute's tribute to her patron" across its surface. After war was declared with Japan, she decided to return to Paris, leaving Zanhua and his family behind.

Pan's Paris sojourn ended up being permanent. For the next forty years, she continued to paint and occasionally sculpt, building up a body of thousands of works. She started teaching at the École des Beaux-Arts and was elected chairperson of the Chinese Art Association of France. She held exhibitions in Paris and other parts of Europe, yet she lived on the edge of poverty. Some say this was because she was sending money home to Zanhua to help his family survive the tumultuous times in China. Others say it was because she refused to sign with an art dealer in Europe, choosing her freedom over a paycheck. (I'd like to think it was the latter.)

Her poverty may have also been a reason that she never returned to China. Letters and journals reveal that she wished to return several times, but she never did. The Cultural Revolution also had made it unsafe for a female modern artist to continue her work inside China, and she was unwilling to change her art practices. In Paris, even her financial hardships couldn't stop her productivity. When she was too poor to buy art materials, she simply painted on the backs of used canvases or sometimes even painted over them. When she couldn't afford oils, she watered down her inks. In lean times, when she couldn't afford to hire artists' models, she turned to painting herself, as she had done so many times before. With a catalog of thousands of works left

after her death, Pan was clearly a woman determined to create.

Despite her contributions to art in Paris and China, Pan was mostly outcast from the art worlds of both. France saw her as a foreign painter, and her lack of alignment with an art dealer meant her works remained largely unsold. Her story is absent from the artistic lore of Paris in the 1920s. Meanwhile, China characterized her as a rebel, with the Communist government seeing her as a dissident who chose herself over the good of the people.

In 1977, at the age of eighty-two, Pan died alone in her attic flat in Montparnasse. In death, she finally found herself among the artists she so admired during her lifetime. Pan is interred alongside the likes of Constantin Brâncuşi, Chaïm Soutine, and Man Ray in Montparnasse Cemetery. She left behind 4,000 paintings and one wish—to have her works returned to China. They were transported to the basement of the Chinese Embassy in Paris, where they were stored until 1984, when the Chinese government finally accepted them back. Most of her work is now in the collections of the National Art Museum of China in Beijing and the Anhui Provincial Museum in Hefei, but a few remain in her adopted home of Paris at the Cernuschi Museum.

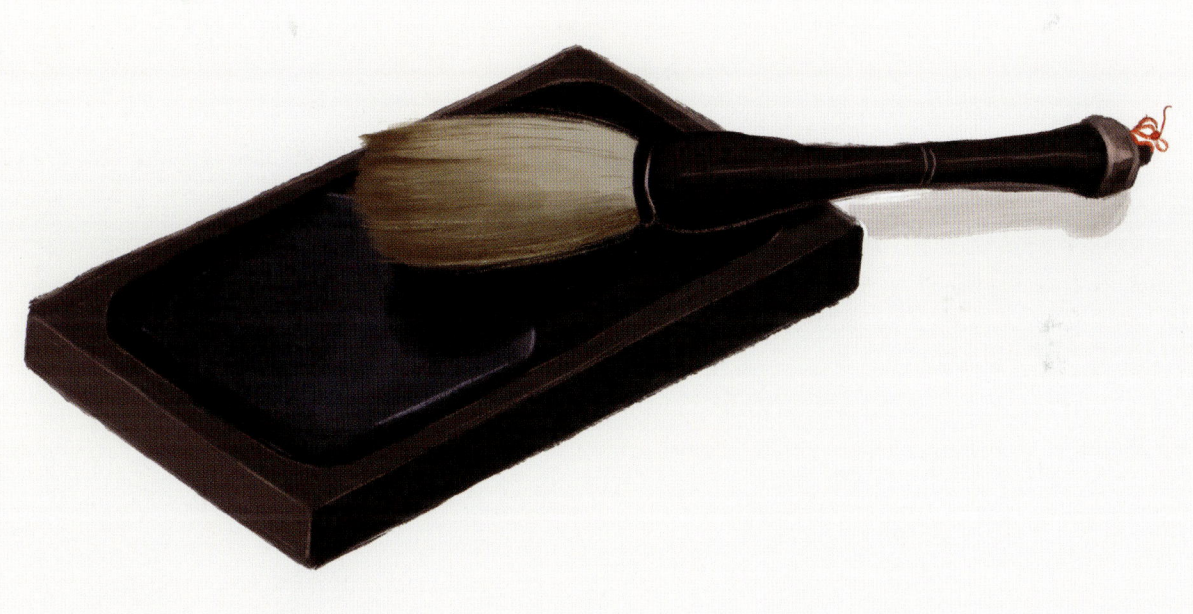

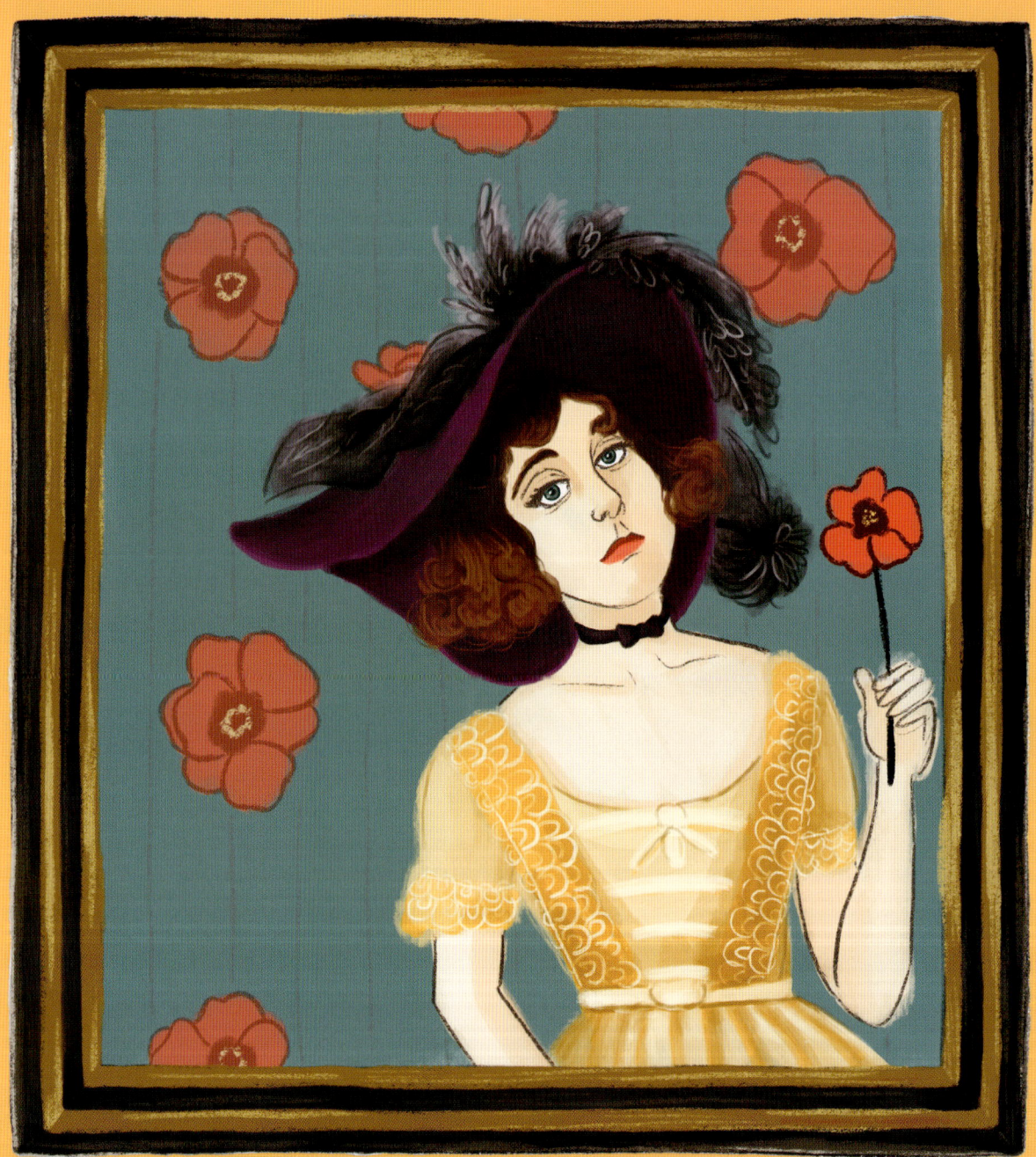

ETHEL REED

MISADVENTURES OF
THE POSTER MOVEMENT

MARCH 13, 1874–MARCH 1, 1912

For three short but spectacular years at the tail end of nineteenth century, Ethel Reed was *the* queen of the poster craze that swept North America and Europe. Reed was a mysterious young woman who caught as much fame for her wild beauty as she did for her illustrations of languidly elegant women. She became the toast of Boston in 1895, when the *Sunday Herald* published one of her drawings on its cover. At just twenty years old, her overnight success led to a prolific, albeit ridiculously short, career during which she became the most in-demand female graphic artist in the United States. Because of her success, Reed lived as an exceedingly modern woman, joining the New Woman movement that pushed against the repressive Victorian expectations of the day. She lived as she liked: indulging in opium, entertaining as many lovers as she pleased, and aspiring to a bohemian lifestyle. Then suddenly, when she was seemingly at the top of her game, Reed disappeared from the public eye, turning up in London briefly before she vanished for good. Her haunting beauty and dark illustrations, deeply coded with references to sex and drugs, made Reed and her sudden exodus legendary. She was an enticing, unsolved mystery, who continued to enrapture creative society after her disappearance until inevitably it moved on as new legends emerged. After Reed vanished, her work remained known among experts and auctioneers of the poster art world, but in popular culture she was eclipsed by artists like Jules Chéret and Alphonse Mucha, whose careers lasted well into the twentieth century.

Posters born from the crisp and curvy lines of Art Nouveau became the ultimate equalizers in the art world, as they toed the line between fine art and advertising in a most elegant way. Suddenly, illustrations used to sell perfume, alcohol, or magazines were being enlarged, framed, and hung on walls in parlors and living rooms. Posters were affordable and easily reproduced, making them available to those who, for financial or social reasons, might not have owned art otherwise. With this rise in demand came the need for more artists who understood that their work could serve dual purposes—art and commerce. Reed entered the scene just as the popularity of posters hit its apex in the 1890s.

For the most part, Reed's artistic skills were self-taught. As a child, she had modeled for a local artist named Laura Coombs Hills in Newburyport, Massachusetts, where she gained her first exposure to the world of art and artists. Hills took Reed under her wing for a time, and at one point gave her a handful of informal drawing lessons. Reed was also briefly a student at Cowles Art School in Boston in 1893, but quit rather quickly out of boredom. Apart from Hills's lessons and the few classes at Cowles, Reed drew inspiration for her illustrations entirely from within. Her body of work, which can be found in magazines, posters, and books, showed elegant and aloof women. Her figures were dressed in billowing gowns, looking dramatically at the viewer, often with bright red flowers—almost always poppies. At first glance, Reed's illustrations look like typical, albeit a bit subdued, Art Nouveau works with simple, graphic lines and blocks of color. But to anyone who knew her, they were mostly obvious self-portraits, peppered with double meanings that gave hints at her private life.

That first illustration published on February 24, 1895, in the Boston *Sunday Herald*—which Reed submitted on a whim on the suggestion of a friend—was perhaps a hint at what was to come. A woman with a neckline considered plunging at a time when a flash of an ankle was thought scandalous reads a newspaper in front of a row of poppies, with text exclaiming "Ladies Want It" emblazoned across the bottom of the page. To the *Herald*, this was no doubt in reference to the Sunday magazine—a special addendum for "ladies" all about domesticity, tips for housework, recipes, beauty product reviews, and adverts for hats and stockings. But the jaunty little slogan was also a reference to Reed's favorite drug: opium. In the nineteenth and early twentieth centuries, opium was used as a creative stimulant for artists, musicians, and writers, as well as a medical treatment for pain and insomnia. It should come as no surprise that Reed may have heard of it or even taken it. But an emphatic proclamation that ladies wanted it was so scandalous that it was hardly believable. Such a statement would be so improper that we must surmise that Boston *Sunday Herald* readers were oblivious—or intrigued. Either way, the provocation worked to Reed's advantage.

The *Herald* launched her artistic career to new heights. The poppies stayed, becoming both Reed's style signature and a lifelong habit. In 1895, new clients, collectors, and lovers began to pour in. In addition to the gigs Reed had illustrating for children's magazines, she was now highly sought after for better-paying assignments that included national magazines, book covers, short

story illustrations, and even art prints arranged by Chéret himself. The poppies appeared in her new projects as background patterns, details on dresses, or as bouquets held by figures—who looked hauntingly like Reed. Sometimes the flowers morphed into the figures themselves. Whatever the poppies and the pretty ladies were doing, people wanted them. Reed's fan base was beginning to grow, and people wanted to know more about the elusive illustrator who looked like her drawings.

Reed was becoming a true Boston bohemian during this time. She moved into a studio in the art enclave on Boylston Street, where she fell in with the well-to-do artistic crowd that included architects Bertram Goodhue and Ralph Adams Cram, artist Philip Leslie Hale, and photographers

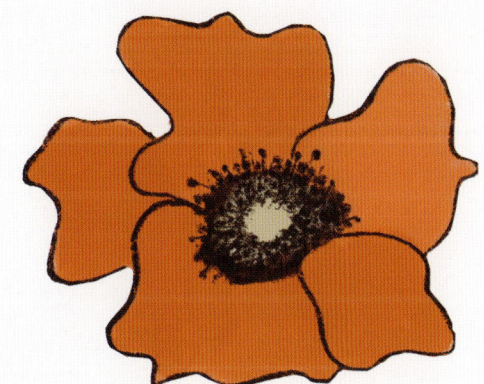

Frances Benjamin Johnston and Fred Holland Day. Her friendship with Johnston and Day would increase her star power, as the photographs each made of Reed captured her wild beauty and charisma so perfectly that copies were widely circulated. Johnston, an important photographer and self-proclaimed New Woman herself, took a series of glamorous studio portraits of Reed looking intensely at the camera, with her signature poppies pinned in her hair. The intoxicating portraits by Day look as if they could have been taken at any American art school in the 1990s or in Bushwick today. At a time when women were taught to be restrained, Reed's bluntness was captivating. It was this spirit, the rousing charisma that exuded from the photographs and through her illustrations, that tantalized the press and the public.

Reed was open about who she was, but when the press inquired about her past, she would clam up. The truth was that she was born in Newburyport in 1874 to a failed photographer father and an Irish immigrant mother who could barely keep a roof over their heads. The family bounced from boardinghouse to boardinghouse until her father eventually became estranged. He died when Reed was sixteen, leaving a mountain of debt. Mother and daughter moved to Boston, where there

were better opportunities. Though Reed was very open, and perhaps proud, about her lack of schooling (she loved to say her work was "untutored, instinctive, and spontaneous"), she was not at all proud of her humble beginnings. She took great pains to obscure any details about her past, telling the press she liked to remain a mystery.

By 1896, Reed's career was at its apex. At twenty-two, she had produced dozens of illustrations for popular posters and books, had a solo exhibition in Washington, DC (where she was a guest at the White House!), developed an adoring public, and . . . hooked a rich fiancé. When Philip Leslie Hale, a fellow artist from a *very* prominent Boston family, proposed to Reed, it became instant national news due to both her fame and his family's money. Hale's family did not appreciate the spectacle. Despite Reed's best efforts to conceal her past, Hale's family did not approve of the beautiful and wild artist who drew beautiful and wild women.

Reed and Hale's breakup threw a sudden bend in her path. Hurt and embarrassed by the whole ordeal, Reed's first impulse was to run. She and her mother boarded the ship *Pavonia* for Europe, leaving behind both Hale and Reed's art studio. They wandered from Ireland to Germany to Italy, then finally settled in London in the Rossetti Garden Mansions, named for Pre-Raphaelite painter Dante Rossetti, who had once lived at number 16. Reed revived her career by replacing Aubrey Beardsley—whose work she was more than inspired by, which she freely admitted—as an illustrator at *The Yellow Book*. She also illustrated book covers for writers like Richard Le Gallienne, with whom she had a doomed affair. He was married. She got pregnant. And his wife wouldn't let him leave. Reed gave birth to their son on November 28, 1900, when she was twenty-six. She named the boy Antony, after the protagonist in La Gallienne's *The Worshipper of the Image*. The series of events crushed Reed. After another affair with a married man, which led to another pregnancy and a daughter, Reed withdrew from society at twenty-eight. Everyone thought she had vanished without a trace.

In reality, Reed never left London. She married a man named Arthur Whiteley, who abandoned her for another woman, leaving Reed and her children penniless. All the while, her eyesight was failing, which prevented her from working. Reed descended further into drugs and alcohol.

It is no wonder she wished for her disappearance to remain a mystery. The internet is rife with articles playing into the legend that Reed vanished into thin air, her whereabouts forever unknown. But, as discovered by Reed's biographer William S. Peterson, records show that Reed spent the second half of her life mostly in boardinghouses in London with her two children. She lived in abject poverty, and what little money she had she spent on alcohol, sedatives, and opium, which she claimed she used to treat her chronic insomnia. Reed was found dead in her rented room in 1912 with a half-empty bottle of the narcotic sulfonal on her nightstand, as well as several empty handles of whiskey. She was almost thirty-eight years old. The coroner's official ruling was "death from misadventure."

One hundred ten years later, Ethel Reed was finally properly introduced to the art world. The exhibition *Ethel Reed: I Am My Own Property* opened at the Poster House Museum in Manhattan on February 25, 2022. Those charismatic photographs by Day and Johnston stared down visitors while they took in her gorgeous work.

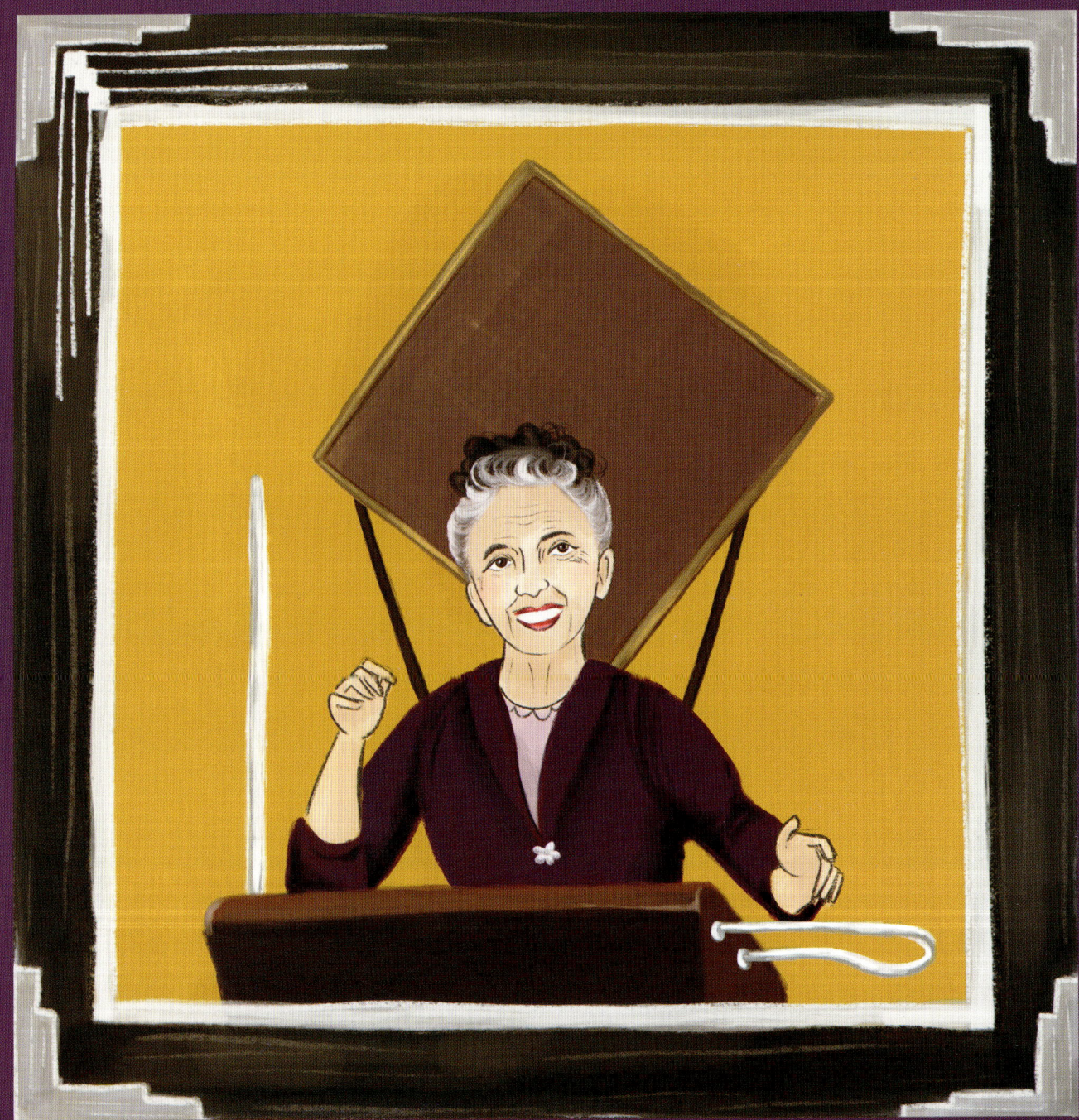

CLARA ROCKMORE

ELECTRONIC MUSIC PIONEER

MARCH 9, 1911–MAY 10, 1998

As a small child, Clara Rockmore (then Reisenberg) showed early promise as a violinist. Born to Jewish parents in Vilnius, Lithuania, Rockmore and her sister were both musically talented, and the nurturing of those gifts was generally put above the other needs of the family. Early on, she demonstrated perfect pitch, which she refined as she learned to read music. In 1915, at age four, she became the youngest person to ever study under Leopold Auer at the prestigious Saint Petersburg Conservatory—where Pyotr Tchaikovsky was an alum. But after more than a decade of performing professionally, often with her older sister Nadia on piano, the teenager's classical music career came to a screaming halt. One day, her bow arm seized, leaving her unable to perform the nuanced movements required for her violin. A diagnosis of early onset tendinitis, likely a result of childhood malnutrition and excessive violin performance at a young age, would end her momentum as a violinist. Years later, a chance encounter at the Plaza Hotel thrust her beyond her classically trained past and into the future of music. Rockmore would indeed travel to the great stages of the world, but trading her violin for a new instrument that straddled the line between science and music—the theremin. With her exquisite talent and glamor, Rockmore commanded audiences and became the greatest theremin player the world would ever see. Along the way, she was able to legitimize and influence the development of electronic music.

Russian scientist Lev Termen—known as Leon Theremin outside Russia—*was* technically the inventor of the mysterious oblong box that allowed a player to seemingly pull musical notes from thin air. (That's why the creation bears his name.) However, the instrument's true commander was a young woman Termen met by chance. The inventor and the virtuoso were brought together in 1928, when Rockmore tagged along with a friend to a party at the Plaza Hotel in Manhattan, where Termen was demonstrating his new musical invention. Termen had just come off of a successful tour during which he had shown audiences across Europe the magical instrument that played notes without physical touch and had settled in New York to work with RCA to produce theremins commercially. At the party, most guests struggled to control the unusual sounds made by plucking the air surrounding the strange box, which emitted a squeal when a finger or other body part entered the electromagnetic field suspended between two antennae. When it was Rockmore's turn, she approached the antennae

confidently, lifting her arms in a way that made the air seem to dissolve into a melody.

The party guests and the instrument's inventor were awed. With her rigorous classical training and perfect pitch, Rockmore could intuitively command the theremin almost instantly. It was love at first sight—for Rockmore, with Termen's instrument, while for Termen, with the beautiful musician. His romantic interest would go unrequited, but creatively, the two would form a powerful partnership.

After being given an RCA theremin by Termen, Rockmore set to the work of mastering it. After enduring arm strain with the violin, she threw herself into the theremin, which was more forgiving physically but presented a thrilling technical challenge. The theremin is a fickle beast, without a fingerboard that lets players distinguish between traditional notes. Instead, the player is faced with an infinite range of pitches and sounds. They must learn to play in-between notes, carving out melodies using subtle movements near the vertical antenna, which controls pitch, and the looping antenna, which controls volume. The margin of error is vast, and a slight breath or even the length of a fingernail can completely alter the intended note.

Rockmore gave herself completely over to the theremin, even with all of its attendant difficulties. Her immediate and innate understanding of the complicated instrument was nothing short of magical. Termen turned to Rockmore for recommendations on design improvements. As a musician, she saw issues that he did not as a scientist. Together, they developed a more precise and responsive machine, allowing Rockmore to create music that elevated the theremin from novelty to serious instrument. Soon, she found herself playing alongside orchestras in concert halls. Rockmore charted a path for the future of electronic music and in turn found an outlet for her musical talent and ambition.

It was Rockmore's idea to increase the looped antenna's sensitivity—to allow for short, punctuated notes—and to increase the theremin's octave range from three to five, among other technical adjustments that enabled the player to perform complicated classical compositions. She also changed the positioning of the instrument to a height akin to a podium, which allowed the

performer to be seen more easily by the audience. Rockmore herself was a glamorous beauty, and when she performed, she positioned the instrument's diamond-shaped speaker behind her like a halo, creating a striking scene that entranced audiences. Just as captivating were her dramatic movements, which established a harmony between her body and the instrument. This bewitching grace is evident in gorgeous historical photographs of Rockmore performing.

Termen and Rockmore worked together for four years, pushing the limits of the theremin's ability. But when she married entertainment lawyer Robert Rockmore in 1933, Termen abruptly, and unfairly, cut all ties with her. It seems his unrequited love was acceptable to him only so long as she was not requiting with anyone else. Despite the falling out with Termen, Rockmore would continue to play the theremin, touring with an orchestra and alongside performer Paul Robeson, a dear friend and client of her husband's, before retiring in 1963 after Robert passed away.

The theremin, and specifically Rockmore's playing, inspired a young Bob Moog, who made his own theremin in his father's basement workshop as a teenager. He would sell models of his version until he was later inspired to develop the

Moog synthesizer. It was also Moog who pushed Rockmore to record her first album, released in 1977 when she was sixty-six years old. Though there are many singular recordings from over the years, only a few videos exist of Rockmore playing, taken by Moog from a performance in her home and accompanied on piano by her sister Nadia (now readily available on YouTube and worth watching). These videos were also filmed in the late 1970s, and they show a woman in total, glorious command of her instrument—*the* original, made for her by Termen. With poise and control, Rockmore, ever elegant in a silver head wrap, slices through the air in a trancelike state, conjuring melodies of familiar works in clear notes that could be mistaken for a variation of a cello. Forty-some-odd years later, her performance still captivates and her skill still impresses, though she is only known to a very niche audience.

Today, the theremin is mostly associated with kitsch—the eerie sound effects of campy sci-fi movies, the famous hook of the *Dr. Who* theme, and the trippy soundscape of the Beach Boys' hit "Good Vibrations." Lev Termen is of course remembered, at the very least as the namesake for the mysterious machine, but without Clara Rockmore's intuitive talent, guts, and gusto, electronic music may not have had its start a century ago. Rockmore saw the theremin's potential to rise from gimmick to serious instrument and elevated electronic music into the realm of concert halls.

After their estrangement, Rockmore only saw Termen once in the 1960s, after he had allegedly been kidnapped from his 54th Street apartment in 1938 by Russian authorities and taken back to his home country. (There are other theories, but this story isn't about him.) They were unexpectedly reunited in 1991, when filmmaker Steven M. Martin (not *that* Steve Martin) brought Termen to New York as part of his documentary *Theremin: An Electronic Odyssey*. Rockmore, then eighty and still glamorous, told her ninety-seven-year-old friend, "I may have inspired you, but you get all the credit as the genius who invented it. That's enough." And it truly is.

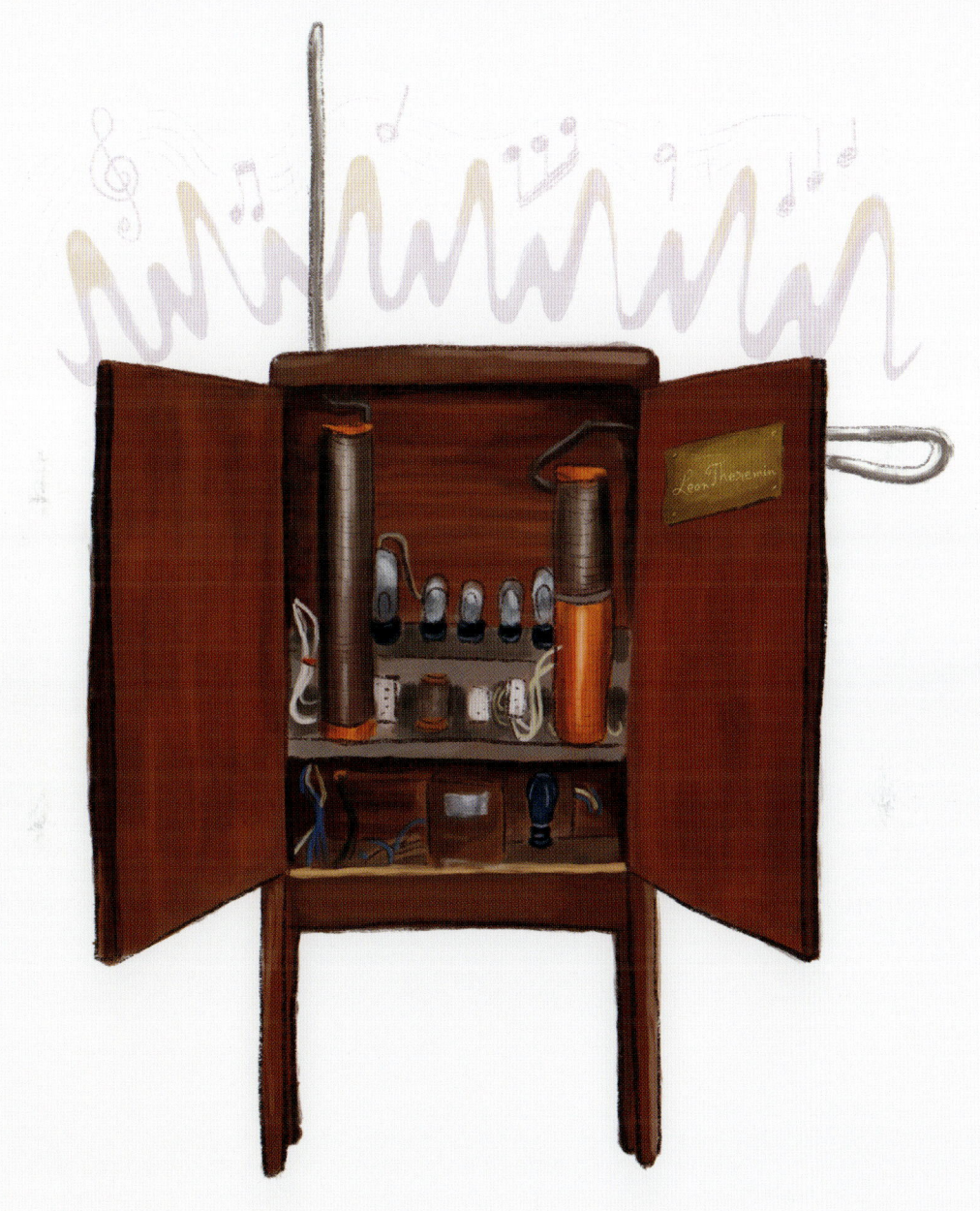

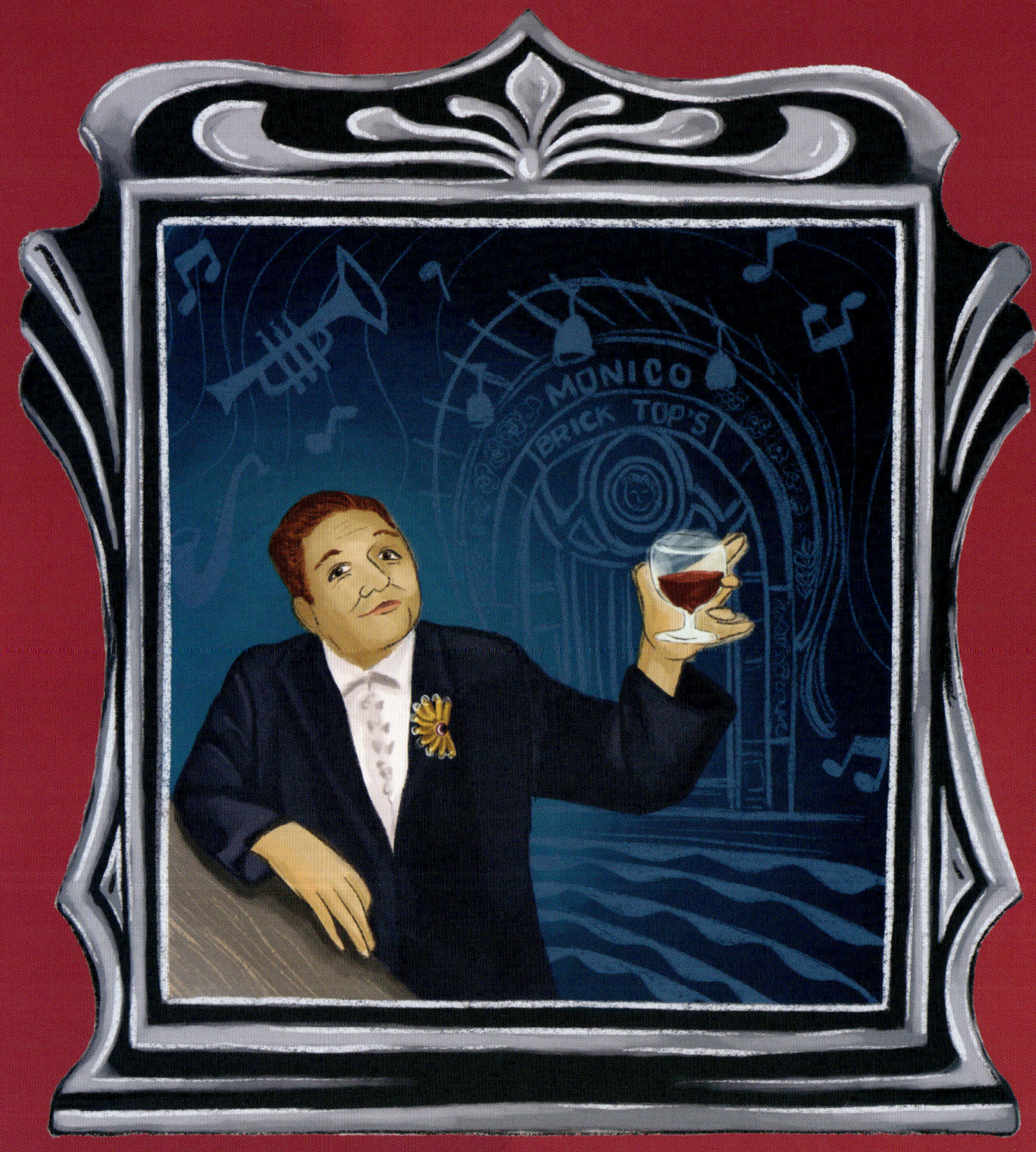

ADA BRICKTOP SMITH

THE CULTURE CATALYST

AUGUST 14, 1894–FEBRUARY 1, 1984

With her signature shock of red hair and no-nonsense attitude, Ada "Bricktop" Smith lit up the nightclub circuit of Paris during the storied Jazz Age. In the late 1920s and '30s, her namesake club in Pigalle was a cultural pilgrimage. There the Années Folles—a decade of rich cultural and artistic collaboration—unfolded around her night after night. Celebrities, royals, writers, and musicians flocked to her, tantalized by her brash American charisma and her storied discretion regarding their private lives. She called Cole Porter, F. Scott Fitzgerald, and the future King Edward VIII lifelong friends and parlayed her network of connections to foster the early careers of greats like Duke Ellington, Josephine Baker, and Langston Hughes. Her Paris club became a home base for expats, particularly Black performers, whom she encouraged to tour the more progressive nightclub circuits of Europe. The self-described "saloonkeeper" was so much more than a nightlife hostess. She was a tastemaker and innovator whose efforts and influence helped shape the rich cultural landscape of the Lost Generation and beyond.

Born Ada Beatrice Queen Victoria Louise Virginia Smith, Bricktop was an internationally celebrated entertainer for most of her life, though she came from modest beginnings. Her mother Hattie was enslaved at birth, just two years before the signing of the Emancipation Proclamation.

(Hattie's daughter's red hair was believed to be attributed to enslavers who forced themselves into her lineage.) When Hattie's father Henry died in 1898, she moved, with her children, to the South Side of Chicago to run a boardinghouse. That's where Bricktop got her first taste of vaudeville. She came up during the era of ragtime and spent her early teenage years lingering outside of clubs and saloons to hear the exuberant music. Finally, when she was sixteen, her mother allowed Bricktop to drop out of high school to join the vaudeville circuit. She toured as part of a singing and dancing trio with the Theater Owners Booking Association (TOBA), a segregated vaudeville circuit that went up and down the East Coast of the United States. When her trio arrived in New York, they found an explosion of inspiring cultural activity, now known as the Harlem Renaissance. Bricktop quickly became a headliner at the famous Connie's Inn, whose proprietor Connie Immerman is responsible for her enduring nickname. Prior to her time in New York, she had gone by variations of Ada, but "Bricktop" made her feel like the star she was.

Even with the protective cocoon of the Harlem Renaissance, Bricktop became frustrated with the systemic racism she faced in the United States. She was a star who commanded a large audience, but she was still subject to the rules of segregation when she performed. And the treatment she endured was even worse when she went on tour. The apparent cultural freedom Black performers could enjoy in Paris began to call to her, and in 1924 she moved to the City of Light. Once there, she landed at Le Grand Duc, a modest club in Montmartre that was barely big enough for a band and a couple of tables—which were usually empty. For the first few weeks, she cried after her set nearly every night to the busboy (a young Langston Hughes!), until one evening F. Scott Fitzgerald, already a bit of a literary star, wandered in. They bonded over their mutual American habits, and shortly after, Fitzgerald would drive her home every morning after the club closed. Cole Porter came next. He arrived late one evening in 1925, alone, and ordered a club sandwich, which he ate while Bricktop performed. He came back the next night, then again later in the week with friends. Fitzgerald loved to brag that he knew Bricktop first, but her relationship with Porter sent her career to new levels. Porter had been living a very lavish lifestyle in Paris since 1917 and had become known for his music, among other things. His parties were among the most coveted invites in Paris, with an excitingly scandalous mix of celebrities, musicians, and nobility and an atmosphere fueled by endless champagne and other recreational refreshments. Enamored with Bricktop's exuberant act, he convinced her to teach dance lessons at his shindigs, while paying her handsomely—as any supportive friend of means should!

At Porter's parties, Bricktop taught the Charleston and the Black Bottom to his celebrity guests, who in turn came to Le Grand Duc where she continued to perform and run day-to-day operations. Porter understood the allure of Bricktop's celebrity before she did, quietly observing as his famous friends fawned over her—just as their fans did to them. She attributed this attention to her perfect manners, but Porter knew she had a certain sparkle others couldn't match. When she decided to open a club of her own, Porter was the one to insist she name it after herself, ensuring the crowds would come.

Chez Bricktop opened at 66 Pigalle in 1929 and remained an unrivaled fixture of avant-garde Paris until World War II forced its closure. She hired future cabaret legend Mabel Mercer as her assistant and headlining act, as well as Josephine Baker, Maya Angelou (who was a singer at

the time), and her friend Duke Ellington. The big names poured in. Pablo Picasso came in when Bricktop herself performed. Fitzgerald brought the literary set. (She was thoroughly unimpressed with Ernest Hemingway, but loved John Steinbeck after he sent her a taxi full of roses as an apology for a night of belligerence.) Porter brought the well-heeled socialites who could really rack up a tab. Every person who passed through the door considered Bricktop to be a close friend—and therein lay her true talent. She had an innate understanding of what it meant to be a legendary host. Inside Chez Bricktop, they were all friends. She was gracious, polite, and above all discreet. She never gossiped about a client to anyone. (She kept this fierce loyalty throughout her life, much to the chagrin of publishers, who expected her to reveal the juiciest secrets in her memoirs since she had outlived most of her clients. She never did.) However, Bricktop did not continue these friendships outside of the club, nor would she date clients. She understood that her privacy was as important as that of her patrons. Bricktop did get married, though most of her associates were unaware of it. Peter DuCongé, her husband, was a saxophonist for Louis Armstrong's band. Though they wed in 1929, their actual relationship was short-lived. As an observant Catholic, however, Bricktop never legally divorced.

Jazz Age Paris convened night after night at the club, with Bricktop at the helm. She was often found with a cigar between her lips, glamorously clad in couture and feather boas made especially for her by Edward Molyneux or Elsa Schiaparelli. But in the daytime, she treated her club as her living room and welcomed her guests to do the same. It became a comfortable hub for the entertainment industry, where leading performers could relax and be themselves without fanfare. During the day, she allowed these friends to use the club as a practice space. In the early 1930s, Fred and Adele Astaire worked on dance routines; Django Reinhardt played guitar; and socialites like Lady Mendl and Wallis Simpson and her beau, Edward, the Prince of Wales, came in for Bricktop's famous dance lessons off-hours. The club helped other expats by functioning as a makeshift post office where they could leave letters to be sent abroad and a bank, usually with Bricktop as the lender. She also kept a running list of employment opportunities, largely reserved for Black performers seeking the same magical opportunity she had found in Paris. Some even say Bricktop is responsible for encouraging a wave of African American acts to relocate to Paris, where she said they would find appreciation rather than racial discrimination.

With the onset of World War II, Bricktop begrudgingly closed shop and headed back to New York, which she found to be shockingly unwelcoming. She followed friends who had also fled the Nazis to open a Bricktop's in Mexico City, but later returned to Europe once Rome had been crowned the new expat hot spot. The Roman Chez Bricktop opened in 1950 on Via Veneto and attracted a wave of Hollywood clients. For fifteen years, she catered to legends of the silver screen like Elizabeth Taylor, Richard Burton, Ava Gardner, and Frank Sinatra. She kept their secrets too.

This time, her club would be shuttered by disco rather than war. Sadly, Bricktop's brand of old-style entertainment fell out of vogue. In 1965, at age seventy-one, Bricktop returned to New York, where she remained until her death in 1984 at eighty-nine. Five boxes of her correspondence, spanning from 1926 to 1983, can be checked out from the Schomburg Center for Research in Black Culture in Harlem. Leafing through the folders of calendars, diaries, address books, newspaper clippings, and cards, I felt like I was dropping in on a life well-lived. Her early notebooks are pocket-size and leather bound, with pages of inventory and tallies of champagne bottles interspersed with celebrity names and phone numbers. Both her rich social glamor and fervent business acumen are contained together in these tiny volumes. "Porter owes 78.90 francs," "meet Prince of Wales October 29, 7pm," "Party at Schiaparelli," are all written casually in pencil, without pretension, as Ms. Bricktop always did.

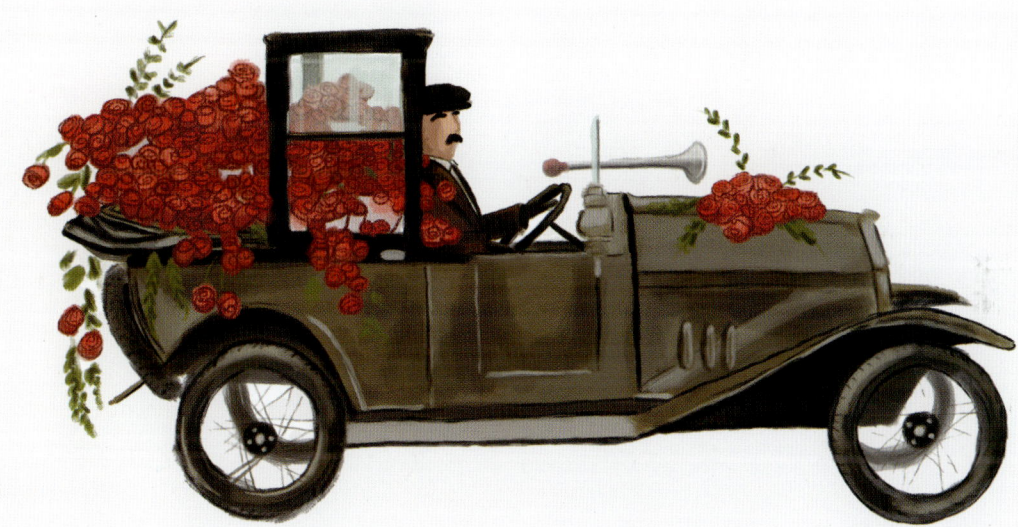

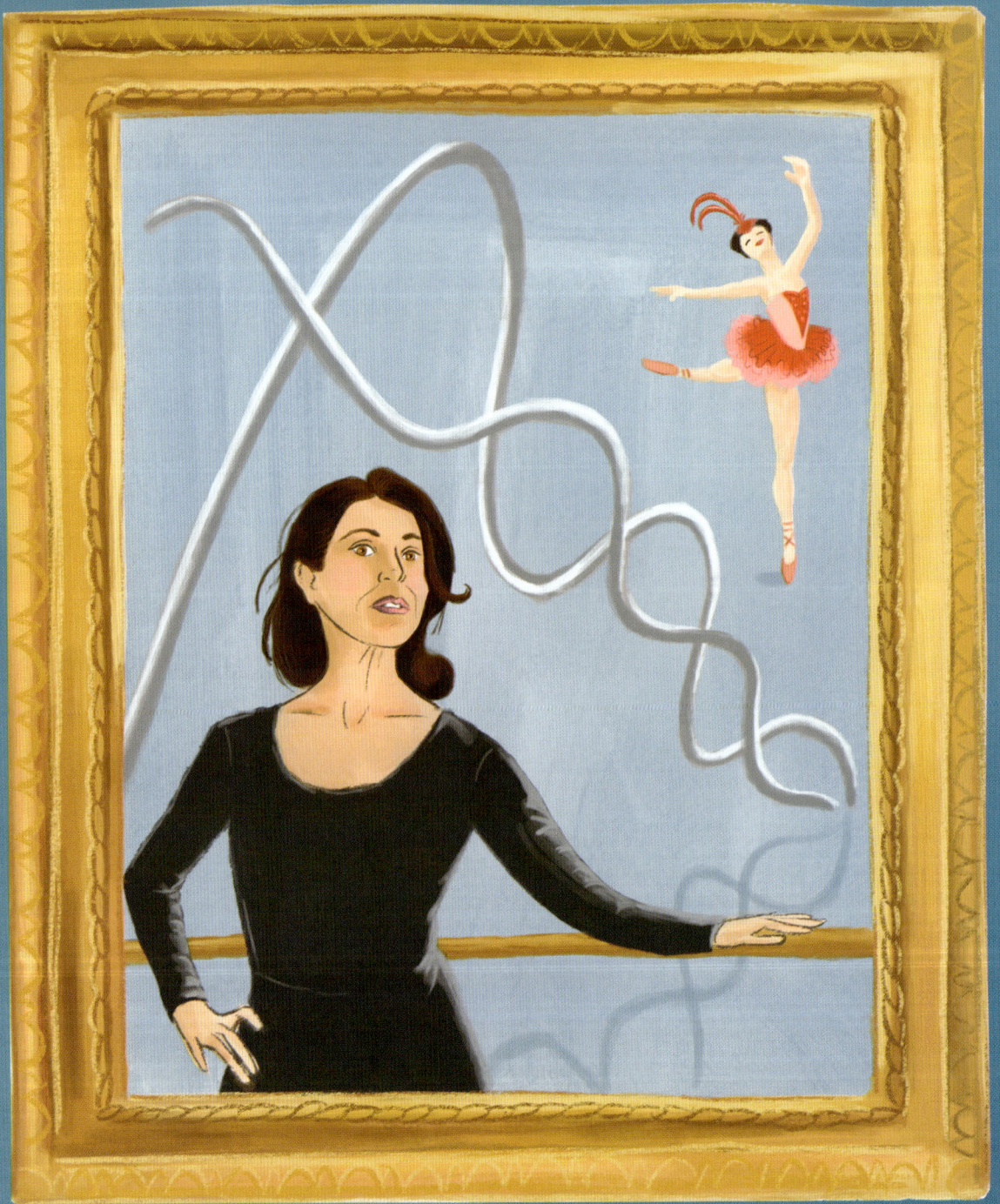

MARIA TALLCHIEF

AMERICA'S PRIMA BALLERINA

JANUARY 24, 1925–APRIL 11, 2013

When Maria Tallchief jetéd off the stage after performing the lead role in George Balanchine's rendition of *Firebird* on November 27, 1949, the audience at New York's City Center didn't know what had hit them. Between Balanchine's fresh take on the choreography, Marc Chagall's exquisite sets and costumes, and Tallchief's energetically precise movements, ballet was revolutionized right then and there. "American ballet" was born, and the United States got its first prima ballerina in a dancer more American than the nation itself. Hailing from an Osage reservation in Oklahoma, Tallchief was a dancer who changed the face of ballet: in heritage, race, and movement. Her electrifying talent was so powerful it silenced bigoted critics, translated the genius of Balanchine, and, in turn, made the country fall in love with a ballet all their own.

Despite its extensive reach through culture both high and low, American ballet had a late start. The first ballet troupes from Western Europe and Russia were introduced to North American society in the mid-nineteenth century, to mixed reviews. The democratic ideals held by U.S. audiences did not exactly gel with the heavily aristocratic overtones of European ballet. The nascent American culture was simply too new to relate to the staunch historical traditions that had been woven into European cultures for centuries. In the 1930s, though, choreographer

George Balanchine introduced a fresh, neoclassical style of ballet to New York City with seemingly light but vigorous movements that broke with tradition just enough to feel modern. Balanchine's aggressive adaptations with pared-down costuming that accentuated the lines of a dancer's body ushered in his reign as the "father of American ballet." When his innovative choreography met the dynamic dancing style of Maria Tallchief, the chemistry was off the charts. The planets aligned, the stars crossed, and the magic made with Tallchief's footwork and Balanchine's moves propelled ballet to the forefront of American culture. Together, the two would found the New York City Ballet, eventually weaving Balanchine's production of the *Nutcracker* into the very fabric of American life, with Tallchief as the Sugar Plum Fairy bordering on celebrity.

Tallchief was one of those otherworldly talents who comes around once in a generation. (Well, for the Tallchiefs, perhaps twice, as Maria's sister Marjorie was a ballet star in her own right.) Though Tallchief did not share the European pedigree of the best ballerinas of the time, she had trained vigorously since age three. Born Elizabeth Marie Tall Chief (nicknamed Betty Marie as a child) in 1925, she was a member of one of the Osage Nation families who had grown wealthy from the vast oil reserve discovered on their Oklahoma land at the tail end of the nineteenth century. Tallchief's family was able to lead a comfortable life, thanks to her great-grandfather Peter Greatheart's negotiation of mineral rights for the Osage people at the turn of the twentieth century. Tallchief's mother Ruth, who was of Scottish-Irish descent, enthusiastically enrolled her daughters in dance and piano lessons. The girls immediately excelled, and when Maria was eight, the family moved to Los Angeles so the girls could audition for Hollywood musicals. At twelve, Maria began to study with Bronislava Nijinska and narrowed her focus solely to dance.

As an American ballerina, Tallchief faced adversity in the Russian and Eurocentric field. Most high-level dancers of the time saw Americans as laughably inferior. And as a dancer from an underrepresented demographic, she was met with discrimination and further ridicule. When she joined the Ballet Russe de Monte Carlo in New York at age seventeen, she was largely ostracized by fellow dancers due to her heritage. When she dazzled audiences as the first American to dance in the Paris Ballet in 1947, her achievement was met with a racist headline. She had already adopted what she though was a more professional-sounding first name with Maria and had joined the Tall and Chief in her Indigenous surname, but her colleagues pressured her to change it further to the Russianized Tallchieva to combat future bigoted comments. But Tallchief wouldn't acquiesce, refusing to turn her back on her Osage heritage and demanding the world judge her for her dancing alone.

(It is rare that a woman has the opportunity to be judged solely for her talent. There is an often relentless cloud of preconceived judgments and misconceptions that swirl around the things we do: how we look, the way we dress, our background and heritage, with whom we are romantically entwined. These, among many other factors, weigh on our talents with biases often superseding our accomplishments. This is another reason why Tallchief was so extraordinary—her raw, undeniable talent eclipsed the haters.)

Tallchief's star rose even further when the Ballet Russe hired Balanchine in the spring of 1944. Their creative chemistry was almost instantaneous. Tallchief was inspired by the elegant simplicity of Balanchine's moves, and he, in turn, was dazzled by her vigorously graceful interpretations. Her radiant dancing inspired Balanchine to create roles specifically for her, which thrust otherwise obscure ballets to the forefront of public discourse. With Balanchine's choreography, Tallchief made the then-sleepy roles of the Sugar Plum Fairy in the *Nutcracker* and the Swan Queen in *Swan Lake* into cultural icons that continue to resonate today. They worked together harmoniously for sixteen years, founding the New York City Ballet, where Tallchief was prima ballerina, in 1948. Together, they were sort of a magical yin and yang, with Tallchief as the physical instrument that translated Balanchine's mental compositions. Their creative chemistry could not be snuffed out by their failed marriage—which was annulled in 1952 after six years. And their artistic dedication to each other was interrupted only briefly in 1958, when Tallchief took a short leave of absence to have her daughter Elise with second husband Henry Paschen Jr., though not before creating the lead for Balanchine's *Gounod Symphony*. In 1960, she bid the New York City Ballet a final farewell to work with other companies and perform on the still-novel medium of television. She retired from professional dance in 1966, moved to Chicago to teach the Balanchine method, and finally founded the Chicago City Ballet with her sister Marjorie. She continued to advocate for the Osage Nation and Native Americans until her death in 2013.

Balanchine is deserving of every inch of the titles and accolades he earned for his innovative approach to choreography and staging, which made the United States fall in love with ballet. I can't help but wonder, however, if his work would have had the same impact without the magical symbiosis he shared with Maria Tallchief. Her fiery, energetic, "electrifying passion" not only brought Balanchine's visions to life, but pushed them into the fabric of American culture.

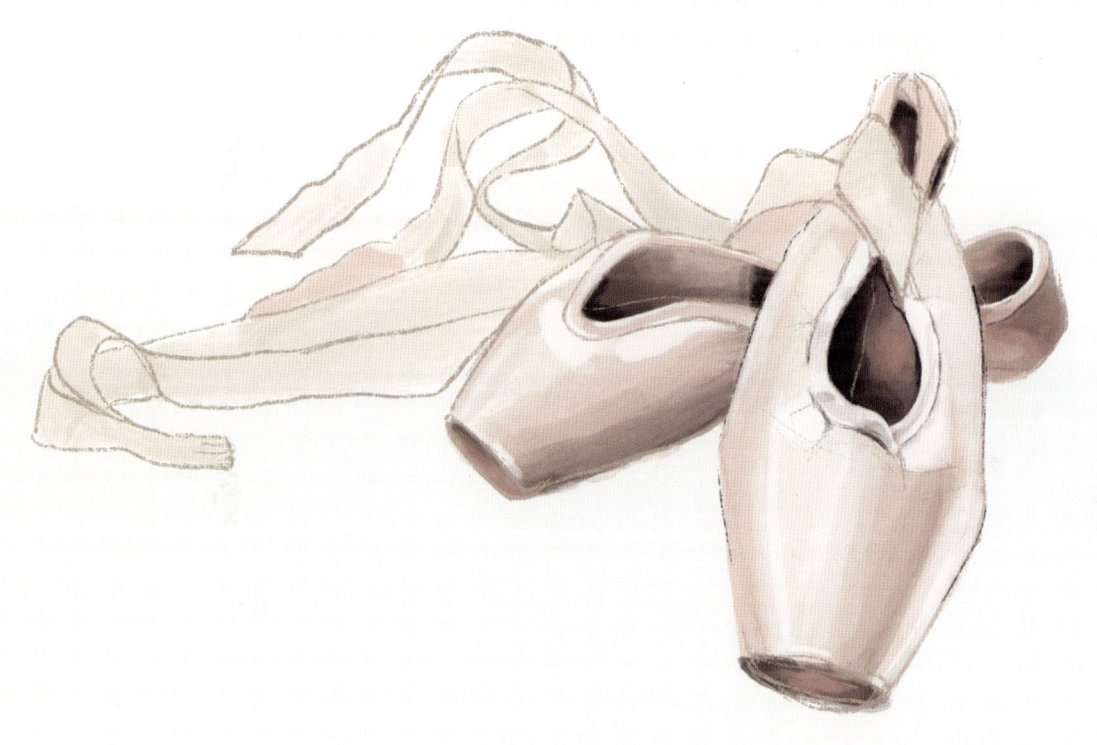

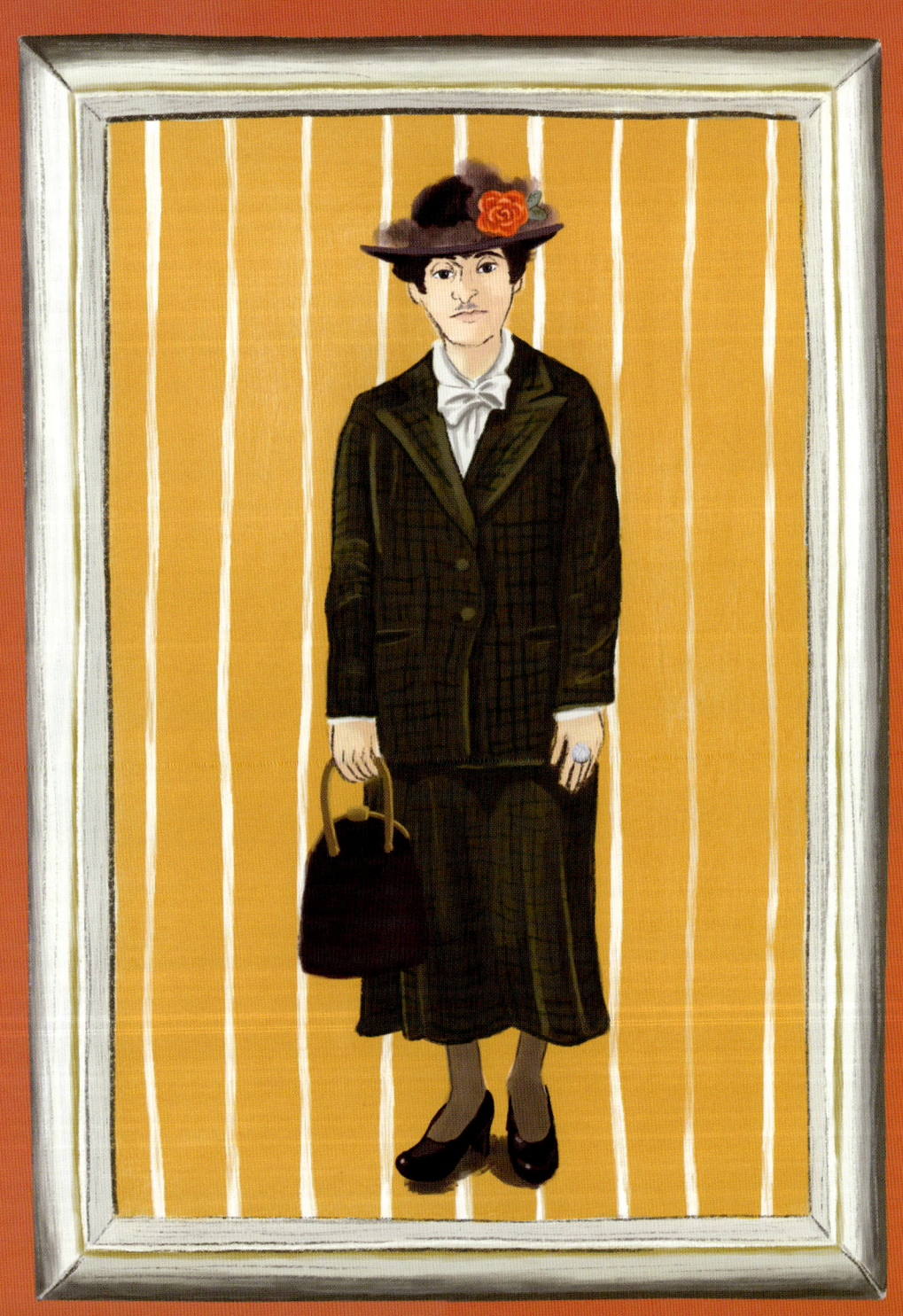

ALICE B. TOKLAS

THE COOKBOOK OF LIFE

APRIL 30, 1877–MARCH 7, 1967

For almost forty years, Alice B. Toklas lived a life of complete devotion to Gertrude Stein, both personally and professionally. Her roles in the relationship were varied, but they were all in support of what she believed to be Stein's genius. Toklas excelled at the organizational and managerial, and had an innate love for the domestic pleasures that avant-garde Paris allowed a lesbian couple in the early twentieth century. Almost instantly after they met in 1908, Toklas became Stein's well-respected secretary, editor, adviser, housekeeper, manager, faithful companion, and doting life partner. Without Toklas, Stein may not have been a historically lauded art and literary figure unencumbered by the duties of daily life. But after Stein's death, Toklas revealed a talent that had remained dormant while her partner was alive: she was a gifted writer herself. While Stein continues to receive literary and cultural accolades, Toklas was both an integral part of her success and a creator with a legacy of her own.

I came upon this legacy by chance. A few years ago I was rifling through the stacks at Mercer Street Books, a fantastic used bookstore on the cusp of SoHo and Greenwich Village in New York City. On a sale shelf, I found an aged, small paperback called *The Alice B. Toklas Cook Book*. From my time studying Gertrude Stein—mostly for her art historical significance rather than her prose—I knew that Toklas was, among many things, an extraordinary cook. So for two bucks I picked up the book with the intention of channeling a sort of romantic connection to the past. I would make a recipe exactly as it was once made for Stein. I also hoped the book might contain the instructions for Toklas's fabled "hashish fudge," which she said was great to "whip up on a rainy day." While I didn't find that cheeky recipe—which sadly was only included in British printings before 1960—I was pleasantly surprised to discover that Toklas's legendary dishes were interwoven with richly poetic writing that told the story of her life with Stein. That worn paperback was a very well-written memoir masquerading as a book of recipes, and I could not put it down.

My own interest in Stein has always centered on her involvement with art and artists, rather than her writing—something I struggle to connect with. To my surprise, my experience with Toklas was quite the opposite. As I read the *Cook Book*, I felt myself standing beside her as she creamed hazelnuts or watching as she changed the water in the turtle meat she was soaking, even though I didn't truly understand what either of those things meant. Each recipe was written like a time capsule, taking the reader from an afternoon

spent with Picasso (in which she made a wine-poached bass decorated with red mayonnaise) to the French countryside and a bouillabaisse enjoyed in a small town with Stein on one of their jaunts in the car named Auntie. The book even brought me to the bleak days of the German occupation of France in World War II, when provisions were scarce, though Toklas's culinary creativity was not. Each anecdote led seamlessly into a recipe and then back to another anecdote, utilizing exquisitely prepared food to link points in time. Toklas's articles—mostly book reviews and narratives of her life and travels with Stein written for the *New York Times* and other publications—carry the same inclusivity that welcomes readers into her storied life with vivid and singular detail.

With such talent, one wonders why Toklas waited until Stein passed in 1946 to begin writing. (The *Cook Book* was published in 1954, when Toklas was already seventy-seven years old. She had begun writing articles around 1950, released a straightforward cookbook in 1958, and published her memoir *What Is Remembered* in 1963.) One reason might be money. After Stein's death, Toklas was left largely destitute, as their lesbian relationship had no legal standing at the time. Stein's relatives also challenged her will and claimed many of the paintings that had been left to Toklas. Perhaps just as likely is the explanation that Toklas believed the literary realm belonged to Stein—a notion reinforced by Stein's 1933 publication of *The Autobiography of Alice B. Toklas*, a bestseller that could be read as Stein's assertion of her literary primacy in the relationship.

But, in all likelihood, Toklas relished the duties of domesticity while Stein was alive. As a lesbian in the early twentieth century, her ability to live in such an arrangement was unique. And it would not have been available to her outside of Paris. Paris, at the time, was an anomaly for expats and served as an escape from the confines of post-Victorian societal norms. There, avant-garde artists and writers could push boundaries, live unburdened by racial prejudices (to an extent), and love whom they wished quietly. Though Stein's own description of her partnership with Toklas used traditional gendered sig-

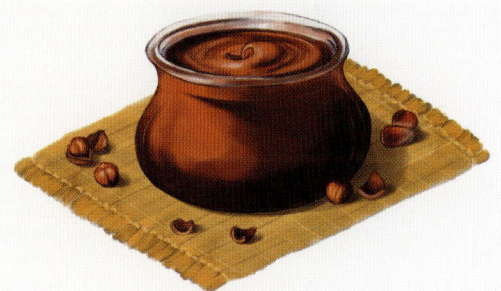

nifiers—with herself in the role of husband and Toklas as wife—they lived outside of the conventional gender roles that weighed upon women of the first half of the twentieth century. And, crucially, in their partnership Toklas *chose* the supporting role; it was not thrust upon her by societal expectations. In point of fact, she relished it. In Paris, Toklas could assume the role of wife to someone she loved. In the United States, she would have been forced to marry or else deemed a "spinster" and reliant upon her family, never knowing independence.

While Stein met with the great minds of the art and literary worlds in their Parisian living room, Toklas entertained their wives and girlfriends separately. After a night spent by Stein scribbling away at her writing desk beneath her favorite Cézanne, there was always a morning spent by Toklas, typing up Stein's scrawls and adding editing notes and corrections in the margins. No matter where Stein was, Toklas was not far behind, dotting *i*'s, crossing *t*'s, and generally keeping their lives together. She was Stein's lover, but also her caretaker, her gatekeeper, and the shadow that kept her manuscripts typed, her books promoted, her stomach fed (exquisitely), and her household running. When publishers rejected Stein's submissions, Toklas managed the

Plain Edition Press so that the pair could privately print Stein's work. She knew she was an integral part of Gertrude Stein's legacy.

When Stein died, Toklas was truly lost. For nearly forty years, she had found freedom and joy in domesticity. As "modern" people, we tend to look down on a woman who acquiesces to playing a supporting role for a man. But with patriarchal connotations removed, we can see the power in Toklas's choice. She challenged the hetero norm by choosing to act as an early twentieth-century wife in a same-sex relationship, living a full life during a time when homosexuality was illegal in much of the world. When she died in 1967, they were reunited. She is buried next to Stein at Père-Lachaise Cemetery in Paris.

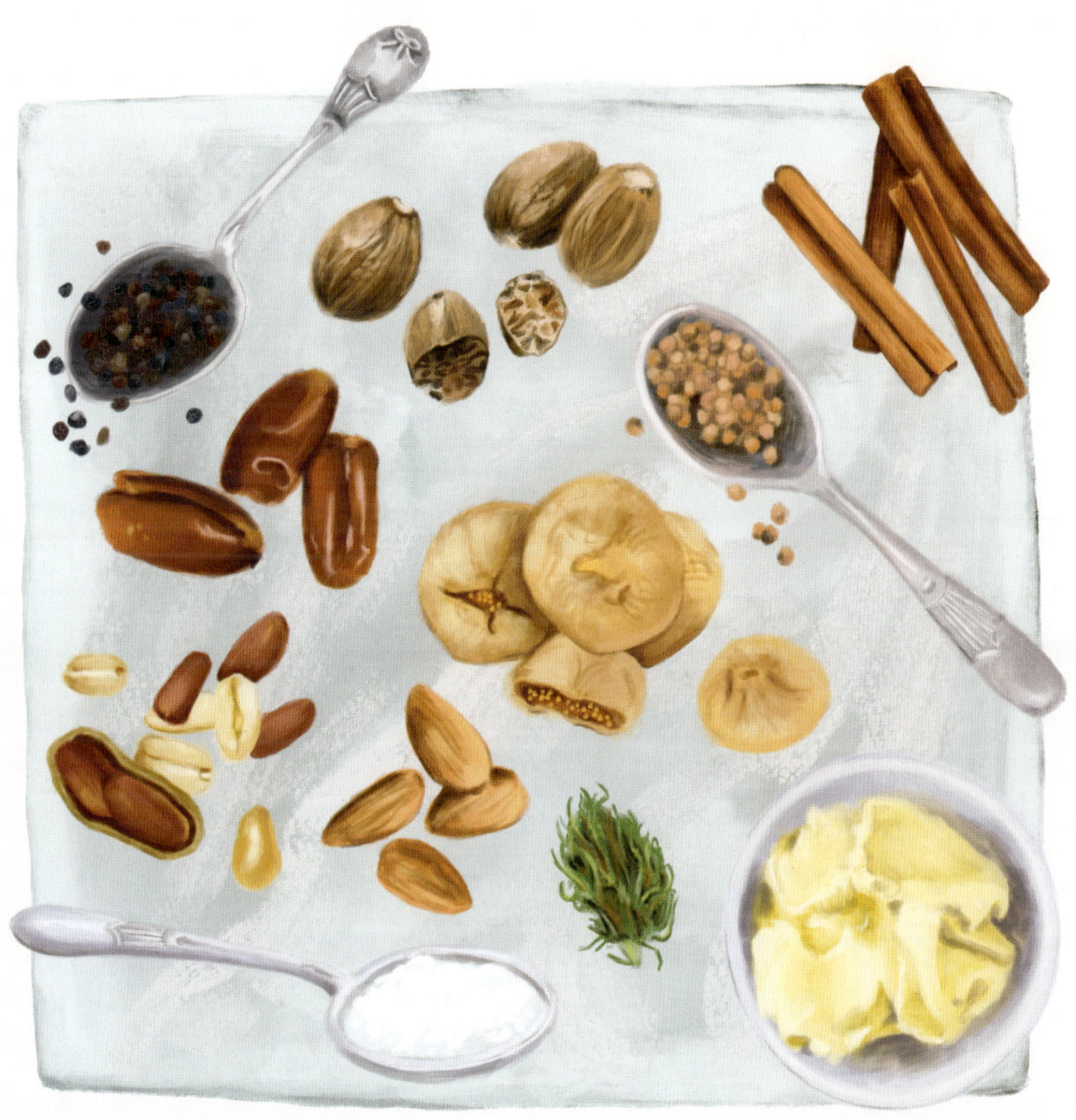

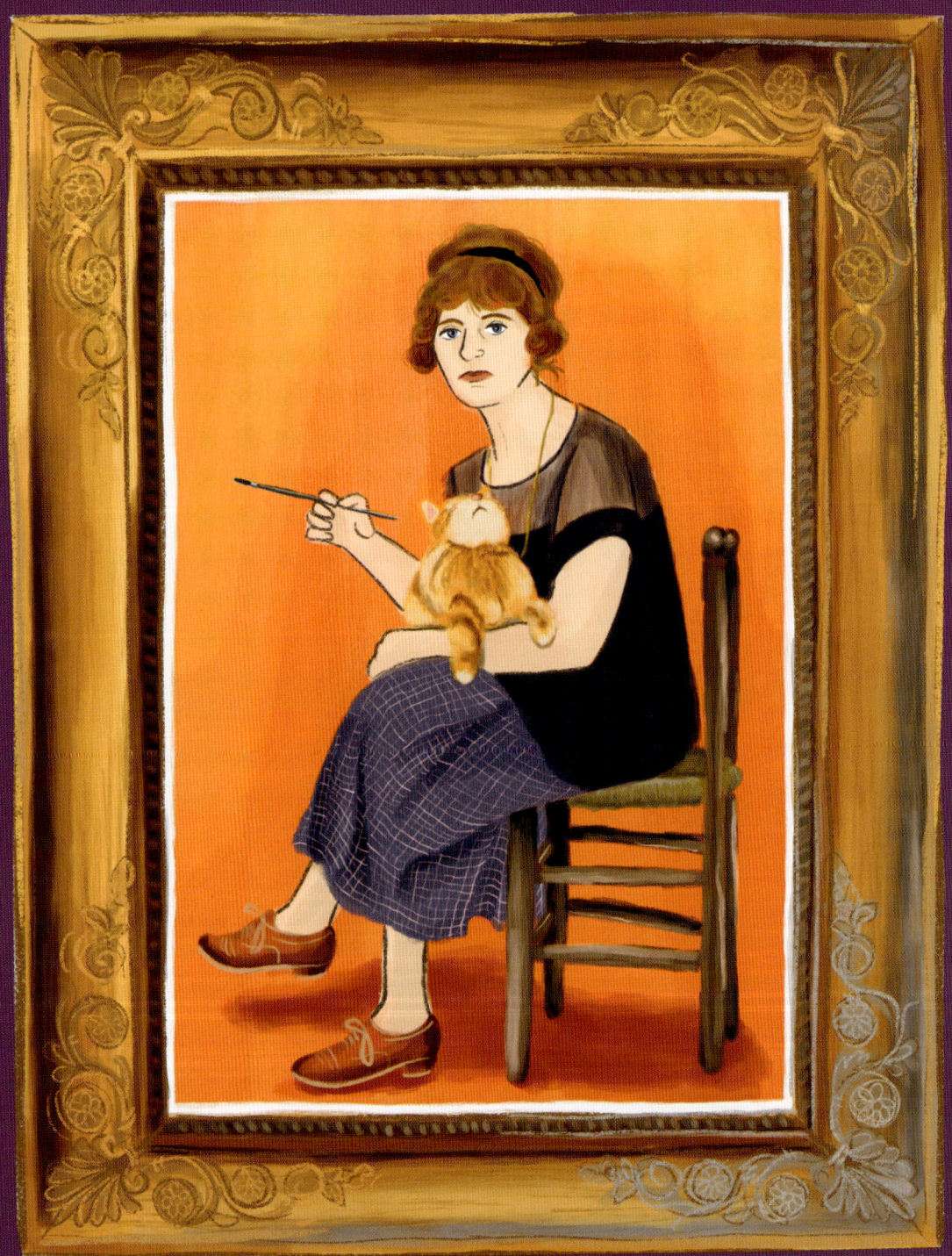

SUZANNE VALADON

THE MARVEL OF MONTMARTRE

SEPTEMBER 23, 1865–APRIL 7, 1938

At the end of the nineteenth century, Paris was a hotbed of creative activity. It was in the full swing of what would later be called the Belle Époque—the thirty-year period of prolific advancement in architecture, science, invention, and the arts. At the very epicenter of this cultural production was a new arrondissement on the northern edge of Paris. Perched on a hill overlooking the city, Montmartre was an unlikely place for artistic innovation. The neighborhood, annexed to Paris in 1860, still very much appeared to be a country village, untouched by Baron Haussmann's renovations that had reconstructed Paris into the series of opulent boulevards we know today. It was for this very reason that artists of all persuasions flocked to Montmartre in search of cheap accommodations among the hardworking class and the impoverished. Along with their creative spirit came cabarets, dance halls, and cafés, which became constant inspiration for the artists and writers who patronized them into the early hours of each day. Suddenly, a working-class neighborhood was the center of Parisian culture, populated by a laundry list of artists whose works are coveted by today's museums and auction houses. Claude Monet, Édouard Manet, Paul Cézanne, Edgar Degas, Vincent van Gogh, Henri de Toulouse-Lautrec, and Pierre-Auguste Renoir—a veritable who's who of men in art history came together in Montmartre, where they shaped the future of art by breaking with the confines of tradition and forming movements like Impressionism, Symbolism, Art Nouveau, and Postimpressionism. Alongside these famous men, in the cafés, salons, studios, and on gallery walls, was Suzanne Valadon, a fiery, talented painter who rose from poverty to artistic fame through sheer determination. Valadon found her way into Montmartre's inner circle as a popular artists' model and remained there as a celebrated artist who painted women honestly—including herself. Her contrasting perspective challenged the idealized male gaze of her day. Throughout her forty-year art career, the rebellious Valadon did as she pleased and found success doing so, as she refused to adhere to the societal expectations and restrictions placed on women at the turn of the twentieth century. The fact that an impoverished, unwed teenage mother rose to artistic prominence during her own lifetime is a testament to Valadon's talent and tenacity.

Although she was technically from the southwestern town of Bessines-sur-Gartempe, Valadon epitomized the spirit that made Montmartre legendary. She was born Marie-Clémentine to an unwed seamstress named Madeleine Valadon. Mother and daughter, along with an older sister, moved to Montmartre in 1869 in pursuit of a better life in the city. As a child, the rebellious and confident Valadon independently roamed the streets of her beloved neighborhood, collecting pieces of coal that had fallen from carts so she could sketch and doodle on any surface she could find. She was uninterested in school and, at eleven, joined the ranks of her hardworking neighbors and got a series of jobs to help support her mother. Dismayed by the hard labor required to work the positions available to women—seamstress, laundress, or a waitress—she became intrigued by the promises of the bohemian life, which valued freedom and creativity over money or social status. Her first foray into a life less ordinary was in 1880, at age fifteen, as a circus performer. But a back injury sustained from a fall from the trapeze cut her circus career short and led her to a job even more suited for the bohemian life: as a model for the hordes of artists who enlivened Montmartre.

Beautiful, voluptuous, and, most important, able to hold poses for long periods of time, Valadon, who went by Maria, became a popular model whose charisma and wit made her all the more interesting to those for whom she worked. By day, she posed for artists whose output defined the era, including Berthe Morisot, Pierre Puvis de Chavannes, Renoir, and Toulouse-Lautrec, who became a close friend, sometimes lover, and the person responsible for her lasting nickname of "Suzanne" (after the biblical Susanna and the Elders, meant as a jab at her penchant for posing for and possibly becoming a lover of aging artists). At night, she joined the raucous fray at the dance halls or the intellectual discourse at the cafés. When she became pregnant at eighteen and grew too large to model, she suddenly found herself with time to spare and spent her days experimenting with her own drawings, using tips and tricks she had gleaned from watching the artists who watched her. After her son, the artist Maurice Utrillo, was born in 1883, rumors swirled that

Renoir or Chavannes might be the father. But her pal, painter Miguel Utrillo, signed the birth certificate to remove any stigma associated with Valadon's unmarried status—not that she was the least bit concerned what anyone thought, then or ever. She was an advocate of free love and was entirely disinterested in societal norms. With her mother's help, Valadon remained a single mother and raised Maurice just as she was, in the thick of the wilds of Montmartre.

Valadon worked tirelessly as a model for more than ten years as she continued to create her own art privately. With the unique perspective of being both model and artist, she developed a style that was raw and honest, painting figures with bold colors and hard-edged lines. While other women worked with the soft, feminine idealism favored by the era, she painted figures and self-portraits with a straightforward honesty that would shock audiences as much as it enticed them. When Renoir and Toulouse-Lautrec came across her drawings, they were mystified, impressed that she had developed such a style and skill entirely without formal training. Degas, an early collector of Valadon's work, encouraged her art career and introduced her to other collectors and art dealers. By 1894, she had been accepted into the prestigious Salon de la Nationale, an incredible feat for a woman artist from the lower class, who was entirely self-taught to boot.

There were several other prominent female painters hovering around Impressionist circles. Her friend Morisot and the American painter Mary Cassatt received accolades during their day, but Valadon had little in common with them other than her gender. Morisot and Cassatt both came from wealthy, upper-class families and were well-traveled and well-educated. Unlike Valadon, they painted subjects and styles deemed acceptable for women. Valadon's work was a reflection of her lifestyle—gritty, sexy, and unafraid. Her unidealized depictions of the female nude were as impolite as they were real. She painted self-portraits throughout her life that showed honest signs of aging, and she painted the male nude as an object of desire, challenging the dominant male gaze. Her work was personal and subversive, but by the 1920s, it was also extremely popular.

Although she was an advocate for free love, Valadon married twice. She shocked her bohemian friends in 1896 by tying the knot with a businessman, although the record of their marriage is lost. Paul Mousis was a well-to-do businessman who was tired of Montmartre and moved the family to a bourgeois suburb. Although life with Mousis meant she could paint without worrying about money, the rebel in her was bored, and the artist in her was left uninspired. By 1909, she engaged in a very bohemian affair with her son's best friend, the twenty-three-year-old painter André Utter, who was twenty-four years her junior. Valadon eventually got around to divorcing Mousis in 1913 and married Utter the following year. Utter, Utrillo, and Valadon became inseparable and moved into a lovely house on Rue Cortot together (where her studio is still preserved as part of the wonderful Musée de Montmartre). Perhaps unsurprisingly, the three became known as the "Unholy Trio" among their neighbors for their irreverent relationship, drunken antics, eccentric styles, and Utrillo's crippling alcoholism.

Reinvigorated by her beloved arrondissement, Valadon began the most prolific era of her life, including a series of rich oil paintings for the Salon d'Automne and the Salon des Indépendants. Much of this series, painted between 1909 and 1911, was sensual and sexy, including a depiction of herself and Utter as *Adam and Eve*—a tongue-in-cheek comment on her controversial relationship with a younger man and forbidden fruit. Oddly, it was also the first known painting of a nude couple painted by a woman. Utter gave up his art practice to help Utrillo and Valadon, serving as their manager until he and Valadon divorced in 1934, when she was almost seventy years old. With Utter's help, Valadon had had fourteen solo exhibitions and thirteen group exhibitions during her lifetime.

Valadon died of a stroke on April 7, 1938, leaving behind 478 paintings, 273 drawings, and 31 etchings, many of which are in permanent collections in museums around the world. Sadly, six paintings of her likeness by her male contemporaries have long overshadowed her own impressive legacy. An asteroid (6937 Valadon) and a crater on Venus are named after her. (I bet she would have thought that was fantastic.)

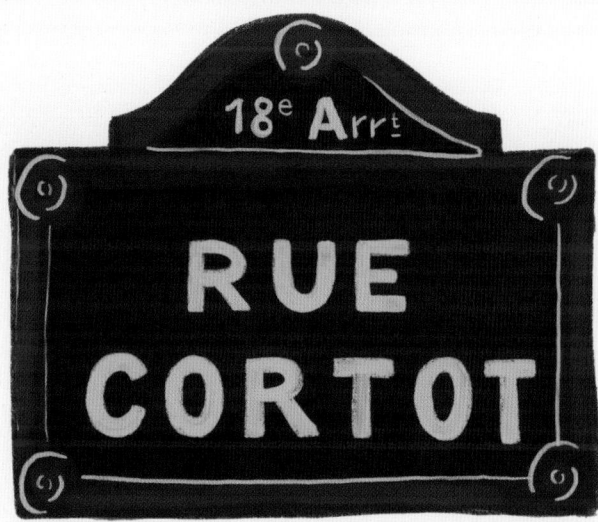

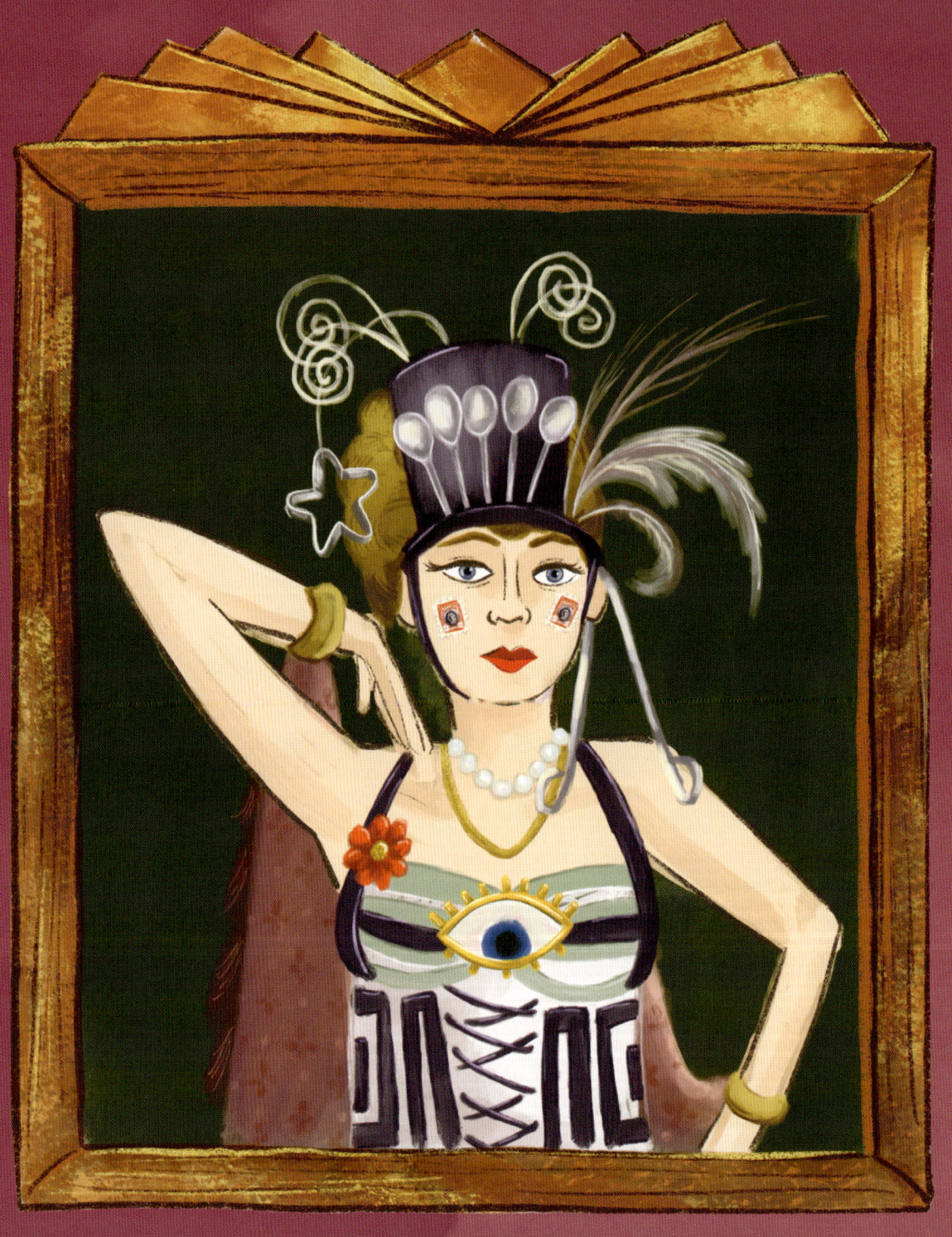

BARONESS ELSA VON FREYTAG-LORINGHOVEN

DADA PERSONIFIED

JULY 12, 1874–DECEMBER 14, 1927

With the onset of World War I, the modern art movement relocated from Europe to New York, as many artists sought safer ground across the ocean. Without the albatross of centuries of art history hanging over them, these artists were inspired to challenge the academic ideals of art that had begun to feel dusty and antiquated in the wake of global industrialization with a new vigor. In the 1910s, those who would eventually form the anti-art Dada movement settled in Greenwich Village, an enclave for artists, writers, and bohemians. As the controversial paintings of Paul Cézanne, Marcel Duchamp, Henri Matisse, and Pablo Picasso were introduced on the walls of Manhattan's 69th Regiment Armory at the esteemed International Exhibition for Modern Art (now known simply as the 1913 Armory Show), Baroness Elsa von Freytag-Loringhoven spread the controversial anti-art message of Dada to the streets of New York. On any given day, the Baroness, as she was known, could be found wandering the Village clad in an array of everyday objects, with curtain rods as bracelets, spoons hanging from her ears, postage stamps as rouge, and rusted pipes tied around her waist. Her head was sometimes shaved and shellacked in brilliant colors, and she was often devoid of any clothing apart from the accoutrements she hung from her body. Her assemblages for these outlandish costumes were walking collages, making her an embodiment of Dada who roamed Greenwich Village reciting witty poetry and collecting found objects to transform into works that Duchamp would soon call "readymades." A Village fixture, the Baroness—who also made paintings and published her writings—was anything but forgettable.

The Baroness, originally from Germany, landed in Greenwich Village in 1913, just a few months after the Armory Show that changed modern art and mere weeks after her second husband, writer Frederick Philip Grove, deserted her on a farm in Kentucky. (Previously, she had divorced her first husband, architect and founder of the Jugendstil art movement August Endell, after their "open marriage," in which Grove was entwined, became closed.) After the dissolution of her marriage to Grove, she supported herself by working in a cigarette factory and as an artists' model, then quickly met her third husband, an impoverished German baron named Leopold von Freytag-Loringhoven who was working as a busboy. Freytag-Loringhoven bestowed a title on her, but gave her little else. (Shortly after their wedding he returned to Germany to join the army and then shot himself.) Left alone in their loft in New York, the Baroness began to fill the empty space with "interesting" objects she'd scavenged, like dirty ribbons picked up from flooded gutters, rusted pieces of ironwork, old tires that had been worn bald, coal buckets, doorknobs, unmatched silverware, feathers fallen from a society woman's hat, and nearly anything else she came across on her daily walks around the city. The collection became her source for making sculptural pieces and assemblages. The materials she used were both random (scavenged) and extremely specific. She would often request that friends bring her tin cans flattened by trucks or specific articles to make into a sculpture.

Up until this movement, sculptures had always been produced out of sanctioned fine materials—carved with purpose from wood and stone or molded from clay. But Dada said that anything—even trash—could become art and have meaning. Because of that, the Baroness's scavenged objects became some of the first Dada sculptures.

The sculptures soon merged with the Baroness herself, as she took the daring leap to become the first person in the West to truly explore the body as canvas. Her assemblages, which only a few photographs document, look alien and otherworldly, especially in an era when corsets were only beginning to be phased out and showing an ankle was still a bit taboo. In each photo, she poses defiantly and in character as the Baroness, looking regal while fanning out her limbs to show her costume. She would parade through the streets in each look, reciting her Dadaist poetry and occasionally getting arrested for indecent exposure. She was unafraid of nudity and of using her body in ways that would be considered unfeminine. Her body sculpture acted as a sort of precursor to performance art. She wanted to disassemble decency,

disrupt, and provoke. She was so futurist, she was the future.

At least, that's what Duchamp said. The pair were friends and sometimes collaborators—though the Baroness did occasionally attempt further seductions, which Duchamp did not respond to. He was the subject of one of her Dada portraits, and they made a film together with Man Ray called *The Baroness Shaves Her Pubic Hair*, in which she allegedly does just that, though only a few film stills survive. Together, Duchamp and the Baroness explored what would become known as readymades—sculptures comprised of existing manufactured objects that are changed through either modification or simply the process of the artist's choosing them. In 1913, the Baroness placed a rusted iron ring she found lying on a sidewalk on a plinth, as if it were a totem to her impending marriage, and called it *Enduring Ornament*. The ring, along with Duchamp's *Bicycle Wheel*, is considered by some one of the first examples of readymades.

The Baroness stayed in Greenwich Village for ten years and became part of the Arensberg circle, where she befriended photographer Berenice Abbott and writer Djuna Barnes, who got her a writing gig for *The Little Review* and would serve as her biographer after her death. In 1923 she went back to Berlin, thinking she would find better opportunities, but all she found was a war-ravaged country. She moved to Paris and died in her apartment on December 14, 1927, of gas suffocation.

Even with such an outsized life, the Baroness's legacy lay dormant for many years. Indeed, despite being an undeniable fixture of American Dada, the Baroness's name would not pass the lips of art critics or art historians until her very existence was brought into question in the origin story for *Fountain*, the "most influential artwork of the 20th century." *Fountain*, an ordinary urinal placed on its side with "R. Mutt" written on it, has historically been attributed to Duchamp. But in 2002 a letter written by Duchamp to his sister came to light that alluded to a woman who brought the urinal to the 1917 Society of Independents exhibition in New York. This, in turn, cast doubt on the piece's origin and whether Duchamp meant that the unnamed woman was then the author. This revelation spurred hot debate among historians about the woman's identity, and the otherwise unknown Baroness was put forth as a candidate by biographer Irene Gammel, who had written about her similar piece *God*, a plumbing pipe she affixed to a wooden miter box.

Overnight, the Baroness became a media sensation and the subject of art historical fascination. The historic photos of her posing in elaborate costume were dubbed "revolutionary," appearing in dozens of articles and art publications. Fashion houses styled Baroness looks on the runway and creations inspired by her Dadaist assemblages appeared in magazine editorials and fashion spreads. In 2022, London's Mimosa House staged a massive group show dedicated to the Baroness, and the Venice Biennale paid tribute to the Baroness in its exhibition, calling her "audacious creativity" a "beacon of artistic revolution." Nearly every facet of the art and fashion world claimed the previously unknown Baroness as their inspiration.

Would they feel the same if she had been dismissed from the *Fountain* debate and Duchamp definitely proven to be the work's author? It's hard to say. But does the authenticity of the urinal, or even its origin story, matter anyway? I don't think the Baroness would think so. The art she made, wore, and lived was meant for the moment. It was meant to be experienced and contended with, to provoke the culture of that moment—her moment. She could not be replicated.

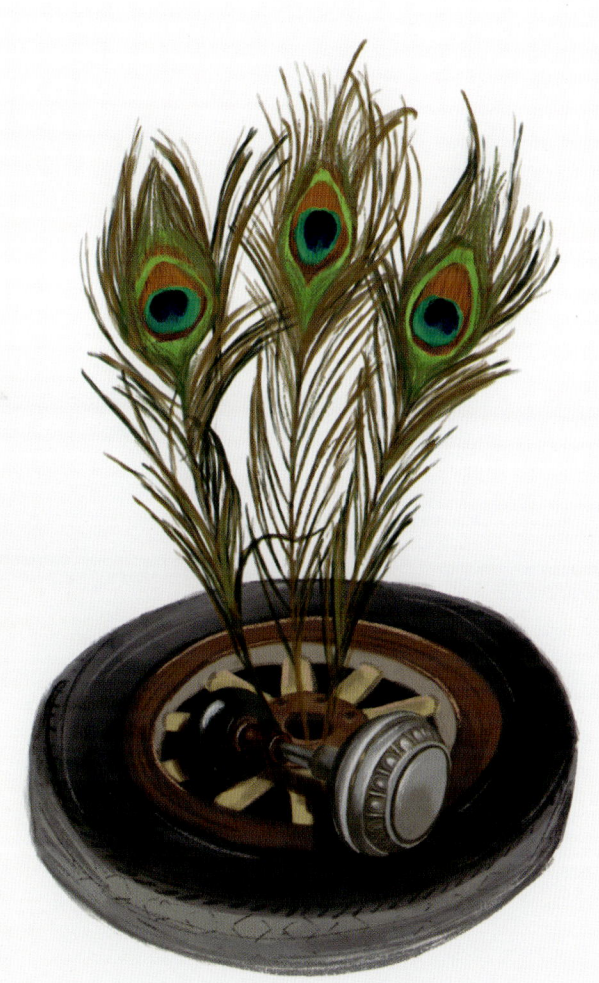

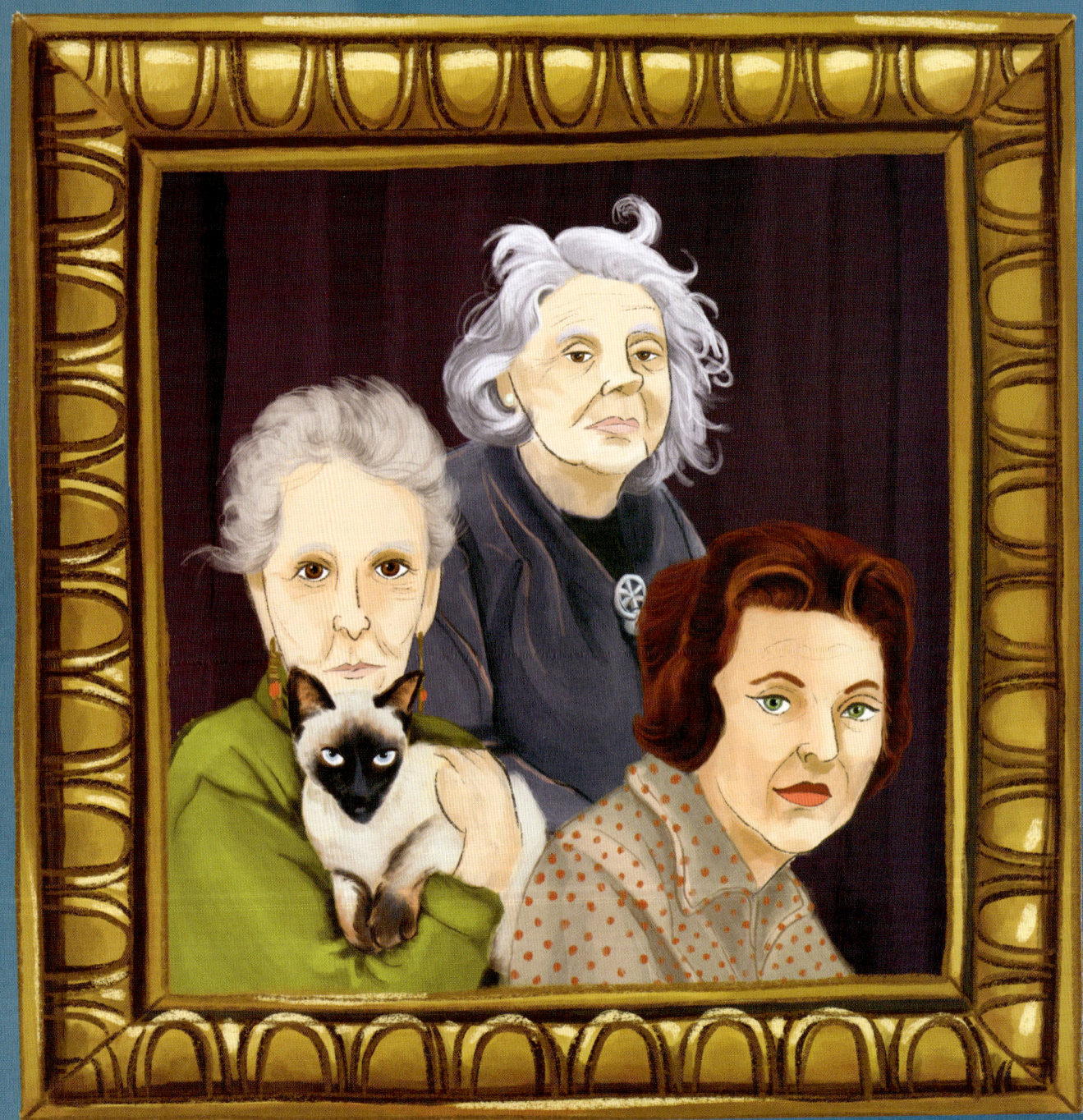

CODA:
WE SHOULD ALL
BE WITCHES

LEONORA CARRINGTON

APRIL 6, 1917–MAY 25, 2011

REMEDIOS VARO

DECEMBER 16, 1908–OCTOBER 8, 1963

KATI HORNA

MAY 19, 1912–OCTOBER 19, 2000

Occasionally, life creates a moment when utter, inimitable magic rises from absolute, brutal tragedy. Somehow, in these instances, we end up exactly where we are supposed to be, arriving at a heaven we would not have found if we had not passed through the gates of hell. As I have mentioned many, many times in this book, World War II was a soul-crushing period that upended millions of lives, while mercilessly claiming so many more (as if you didn't know this already). But sometimes, the cruel catalyst leads to a fortuitous future. Rising from the ashes of the Second Great War, three Surrealist women found a home in a new country, and more important, in each other. Before the war, Leonora Carrington, Remedios Varo, and Kati Horna each faced their own difficult paths through the misogyny of the Surrealist circle and unspeakable traumas, both personally and because of war. By some mystical act—and more realistically, being forced to flee their homes and comfort zones—the three women serendipitously ended up a stone's throw from one another in sprawling Mexico City. As each was finding their footing in a new country, they would cross paths in the Colonia Roma neighborhood and begin a life of art, creativity, magic, and deep female friendship. With the absolute horror of the years leading up to World War II at their backs, the Three Witches—as they would soon be called—unexpectedly began living their best lives. And they were never going back.

Surrealism rose from the ashes of the First Great War, as artists looked to psychology and the unconscious mind to try to make sense of the atrocities they had experienced across Europe. That war had triggered an approach to art that explored the subconscious, dreams, fantasy, and irony through experimental imagery and absurdist prose. Though Surrealism spread across Europe in the 1920s, the main group headquartered itself in Paris. Before the war, Carrington, Varo, and Horna had each orbited this famed Surrealist circle in Paris. Still, while they each had a seat at the table, they were not permitted to speak. The Surrealists were a notorious boys' club where women were seen as impossible paradoxes who combined the erotic temptress and femme-enfant, a "woman-child" who was beautiful, young, and certainly not to be taken seriously as an artist. She was a muse, a vessel whose beauty and youth were used to inspire, and little else. Salvador Dalí himself excluded women from the Surrealist conversation when he said, "Talent was in the balls," and André Breton put them in their place in his second Surrealist manifesto, saying "the problem of woman is the most marvelous and disturbing problem in the world." Translation? Women are only good for male creativity.

Kati Horna began as a student of political science at a university in Berlin, but returned to her native Budapest when Hitler gained power in the early 1930s. As a radical and a Marxist, she would need to outrun fascism several times before landing in Mexico City in 1939. Back in Budapest, she had begun to study photography under József Pécsi. Robert Capa was a fellow student and would be a lifelong friend. When Capa decided to move to Paris in 1933, Horna tagged along (with her first husband, a Hungarian activist named Paul Partos, whom she was married to briefly). In Paris, Horna worked as a freelance photographer, taking photos of Parisian street life, and stretched her wings as an artist. The presence of the Surrealists inspired her first foray into experimental photography—a series of eggs painted as a cartoon Hitler, in collaboration with cartoonist Wolfgang Burger, which were published in anarchist magazines.

Four years later, Horna moved to Barcelona to photograph the Spanish Civil War for the Spanish Republic government in opposition to fascist Francisco Franco. Here she met José Horna, a sculptor who would become her second husband. While her friend Capa captured the gore of the front lines, Horna focused on the civilian communities near the front, a subject largely ignored in war. Her strategy of "gender witnessing" showed the women, children, and elderly who were living amid an active war front, as well as the devastation in the villages. Aside from civilians, some of her most powerful images from the war show bombed-out schools, shops, and abandoned children's toys— among them dolls, a theme that would show up in her later work. Her photos showed the human side of war and were published widely across Europe.

In 1939, as Franco's troops advanced, Horna's work made her a target, so she and José escaped back to Paris for a brief time before it, too, became unsafe. Unable to get an American visa due to her radical political leanings (just thinking the word *communism* immediately blew any chance of getting one), she and José married and fled to Mexico City.

Carrington's entry into Surrealism was a result of her own personal backlash against British social hierarchy. She was born to a British nouveau riche family, with a father who was obsessed with social climbing into the upper echelons of "proper society." Carrington was not. After her parents forced her to be presented to the king at a debutante ball—at which she sat at a table reading a copy of Huxley's *Eyeless in Gaza* rather than participate in the choreographed dances—she was done. She studied art and fell in love with Max Ernst through his artwork. They met coincidentally in 1937 at a party in London and immediately clicked. She was twenty, and he was forty-six. By the next year, the couple had moved to France, at the protestation of her strict father, and Carrington began creating her incredible oeuvre of Surrealist sculptures and paintings. With Ernst, she was welcome among the Paris Surrealists, but as someone gorgeous and barely out of her teenage years, she epitomized the femme-enfant the Surrealists fetishized. No matter how often she reminded the group that she herself was an artist, she was not taken seriously.

The couple then moved to the South of France. When the war ramped up in 1939, Ernst, being both German and a modern artist—and therefore "degenerate"—was sent to an internment camp. Carrington received no news of whether Ernst was alive or dead, which caused the young woman to suffer a nervous breakdown. Her parents committed her to a mental asylum in Spain,

where she was often strapped down, tortured with electroconvulsive therapy, and drugged with powerful convulsants and barbiturates in tandem. These intense abuses were set against the backdrop of a raging war and the imprisonment of her lover by the Nazis. These and other traumatic events would show up in Carrington's paintings throughout her life. After *three years* in the institution, her parents sent to have her transferred to a sanitorium in South Africa, but Carrington, ever the rebel, managed to escape in Portugal.

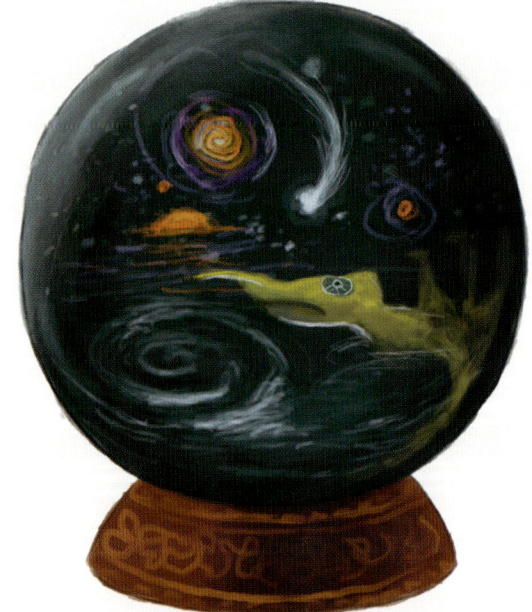

She fled to the Mexican Embassy to find Renato Leduc, a friend and Mexican ambassador she had met through Pablo Picasso. They got married (as friends) so that Carrington could have political immunity as a diplomat's wife. She moved to New York for a year and then to Leduc's home in Mexico City. They divorced once Carrington was safe.

Varo was destined for the Surrealist life. When she was a child, her father, a hydraulic engineer, emphasized a life of free thought and knowledge to her. Through his work, the family traveled around Spain and North Africa, which exposed the young Varo to new locales, religions, and beliefs. Her father taught her technical drawing and gave her volumes to read by Alexandre Dumas, Jules Verne, and Edgar Allan Poe, as well as books on mysticism, philosophy, and science, which made her voracious for knowledge and curious about the world. Once the family returned to Madrid, she fell in love with the brilliant and haunting sixteenth-century paintings of Hieronymus Bosch that hung at the Prado Museum. With a head full of fantastical ideas, she quietly experimented with art as a private hobby.

Like her future best friends, Varo moved to Paris in 1930 (with her first husband, Gerardo Lizárraga) to immerse herself in the artistic avant-garde. But after a year, the couple returned to Spain, where her husband had taken a job in Barcelona. The move proved to be fantastic for Varo. In the 1930s, Barcelona had an avant-garde art scene to rival that of Paris, and it was one in which women were welcome at the table. She was invited into the Spanish Surrealist sect by Marcel Jean, then joined the Grupo Logicofobista, which was made up of artists and writers who combined Surrealism with metaphysics. For six years, Varo cavorted with fellow artists in Barcelona and exhibited her paintings alongside theirs, until she, too, fled as Franco took control of Madrid. She landed back in Paris, this time with her new love, Surrealist poet Benjamin Péret. But, much as before, she was welcome to the party, but only as an observer.

We know the progress of the war by now, and that Varo's time in Paris would be cut short by the advance of the Germans. She and Péret, also extreme leftists, were briefly imprisoned by the Vichy French before making it to safety in Mexico City in 1942, where Varo was about to enter the most productive period of her career.

In Mexico City what started as a temporary stopover to wait out war became a fever dream of

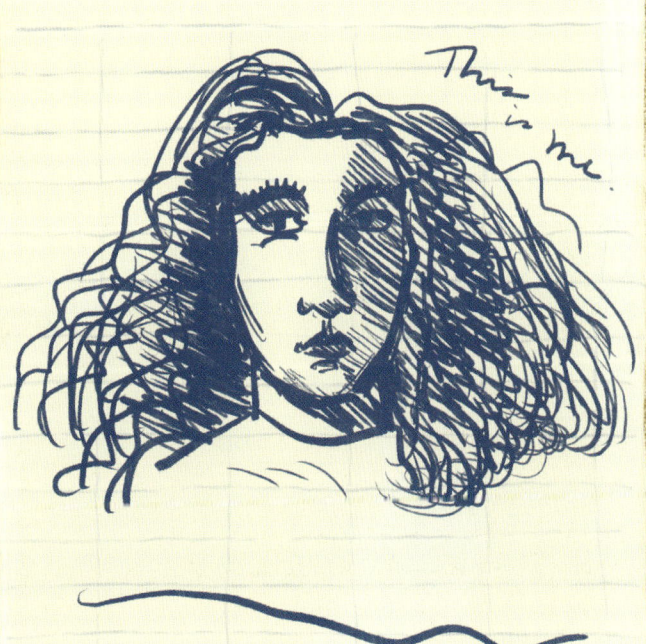

This is me.

I didn't have time to be anyone's muse.

I was too busy rebelling against my family and learning to be an artist.

— Leonora

inspiration, productivity, and deep connection. It would become the home that Horna, Carrington, and Varo had never known was possible. Though fate had put them within blocks of one another in the Colonia Roma, the three women were also somewhat familiar with one another from their past lives. Varo and Carrington had met briefly in Paris, where they were acquaintances at best, but all three were familiar with one another's work. The European expat community that had formed in Mexico City was a close-knit one, as nothing bonds like the trauma of a world war. As neighbors, their meeting was inevitable, but it felt more like destiny than the result of simple circumstance.

In general, the term *soulmates* is reserved for romantic love, but it shouldn't be. What Carrington, Horna, and Varo found in one another was perhaps a step beyond even that. They formed a deep, loving relationship in which each was friend, family, critic, and collaborator. They felt a complete affinity for one another—three weird sisters who unconditionally supported one another, both personally and artistically. From the outset, Carrington, Varo, and Horna bonded over their shared war stories, but also their love of magic, mysticism, the

occult, tarot, and, of course, art making. It was this laundry list of shared passions that gained them the nickname the "Three Witches." They liked it. As refugees, they felt an unexpected artistic freedom that served as a powerful inspiration. In Mexico City, they could start anew, without the unspoken rules put in place by the gatekept version of Surrealism in Paris. Finally, they were free from the male institution that had frustrated them so. They were suddenly able to explore the movement's ideologies in their own ways. Rather than basing their works on Freudian thought and other philosophies like the Parisian circle had, they turned inward. They drew upon elements from their pasts, personal traumas, emotions, and memories, which they transformed into inspiration for their artworks. Carrington drew on a repressed childhood in English society and her painful time in the asylum, all of which appeared in her paintings and writings. The broken dolls Horna came across on the streets of war-torn Spanish villages resurfaced in her photographs, as did her strong political beliefs. Varo combined her studies of math and mysticism with her father and her formal education in art history to make fantastical paintings that echoed the structure of the great masters with a Surrealist twist.

As the Three Witches, they created a world of magic and the occult, spirituality and spells, inspired by the lore of the cultures they brought with them entwined with those of their adopted country. Mexico was rife with its own traditions and tales, which the women drank in. Though each created work that was distinctly their own, it was all born of their same invented language, with subtle crossovers and not so subtle collaboration. They often modeled for one another, with Varo and Carrington appearing in many of Horna's Surrealist photographs—as did sculptures and masks produced by one or the other. In Mexico, the Three Witches made Surrealism their own and allowed the movement to thrive well into the 1950s.

Perhaps more important—to me at least—the Three Witches eschewed the confines of the societal expectations they had felt as women in Europe. There is a feeling of "otherism" that comes with being an expat, of not totally belonging to an adopted society for better or worse. In this way, the women were able to live somewhat outside of the existing expectations of Mexican society. In this separate, liberated space, Carrington, Horna, and Varo had the unique opportunity to flip the script on domesticity and

motherhood. Instead of being expected—or forced—to take care of the home or children, they chose it. Their kitchens became the center of their homes, where they would gather, cook together, make art together, and talk until the sun came up. They raised Carrington's two sons together (she married Horna's friend Chiki Weisz, a Hungarian photographer whom she would be with until his death in 2007) in their self-made utopia where women did not have to apologize for their greatness. Their spoils of war were finding each other.

Sadly, Varo died in 1963 of a sudden heart attack at just fifty-four years old. Horna and Carrington stayed in Mexico City for most of the rest of their lives, continuing to make art. Carrington was also active in the women's liberation movement in Mexico in the 1970s, which I would like to think was inspired by the life she, Varo, and Horna had made for themselves. Horna died in 2000 at eighty-eight and Carrington in 2011 at ninety-four.

The Three Witches left behind incredible bodies of work that have happily gained attention in recent years, in museum and gallery exhibitions round the world. But the beauty of their friendship is just as important—and a lesson to us all. In a society when women still struggle for equality a quarter of the way into the twenty-first century, we should look to Carrington, Varo, and Horna, who chose to uplift each other, to collaborate rather than compete, to celebrate one another instead of letting society put them against each other. We should all be witches.

ACKNOWLEDGMENTS

FROM LORI

This book would not be possible without Jess Zak, who dutifully read every sentence, almost entirely over iMessage at all hours of the night. It has been a gift to work on a third book with an incredibly inspiring team: Maria (whom I met in fourth grade!), our agent Lindsay Edgecombe at Levine Greenberg Rostan, editor Shannon Connors Fabricant, designer Amanda Richmond, and the rest of the Running Press team. Thanks to my other half Logan Hicks, my perfect child Sailor Hicks, and Cindy and Shelby for understanding that I had to write through the holidays. I would also like to thank the Morgan Library, the New York Public Library (especially the Schomburg Center for Research in Black Culture), the International Hildreth Meière Association, the University of Buffalo Libraries, the New York Historical Society, filmmaker Sandra Osawa, filmmaker Barbara Hammer, and the Musée de Montmartre, whose exhibitions about the important women making art in Montmartre helped to inspire this book.

FROM MARIA

In a book about brilliant artists and visionaries, foremost thanks go to the dream team: my partner in art and dog memes Lori Zimmer, our agent Lindsay Edgecombe, editor Shannon Connors Fabricant, and designer Amanda Richmond. And further thanks go to the American Library in Paris, whose collections and archives provided endless visual inspiration; the innumerable women I am forever awed and uplifted by: Vanessa, Kelli, Anja, Michel, Rachel, Massiel, Kaye, Karen, Tiko, Nino, Marci, Elodie, so many more . . .; my mom and AB and Aunt Dar, my magical guardians who hold up more than their share of the sky; my grandmothers, whose lived experiences live on in me; Abel and Babu, whose motivation and care (and Photoshop support) got me through; and my brother Gary. Still having fun.

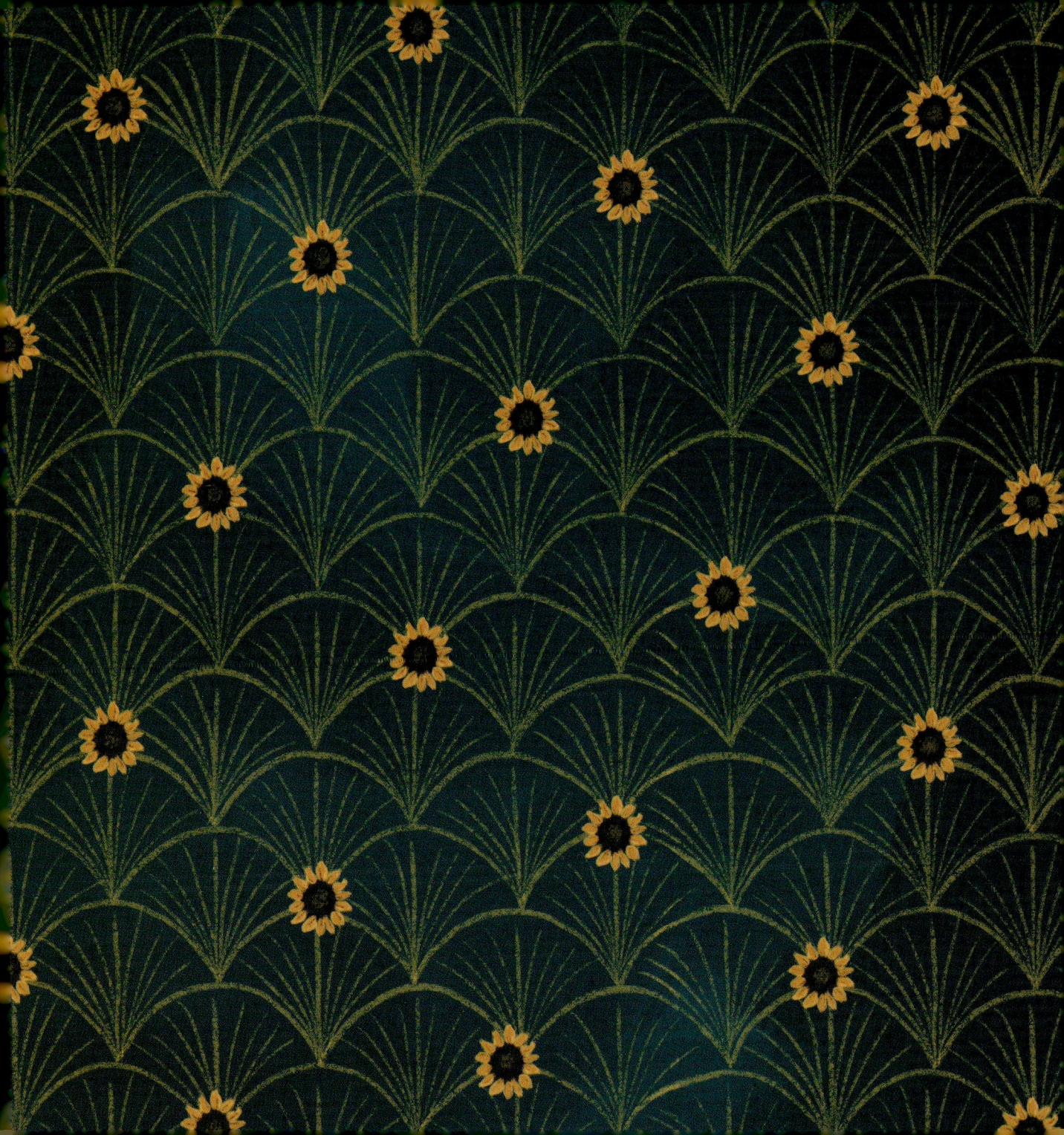

FURTHER READING

I read dozens of books during the long research process for writing this one. I found that the only existing biographies for several of the women featured here were either out of print and impossible to find or very old and very dry. I hope that these vignettes inspire someone to pen the exquisitely fascinating biographies these women deserve.

The following are some of my favorite books I read along the way.

Benedict, Marie, and Victoria Christopher Murray. *The Personal Librarian, A Novel.* New York: Berkley (reprint), 2022.

Bricktop, with Jim Haskins. *Bricktop.* New York: Welcome Rain Publishers, 1999.

Chadwick, Whitney. *Farewell to the Muse: Love, War, and the Women of Surrealism.* London: Thames & Hudson (reprint), 2021.

Elkin, Lauren. *Art Monsters: Unruly Bodies in Feminist Art.* New York: Farrar, Straus and Giroux, 2023.

Hewitt, Catherine. *Renoir's Dancer: The Secret Life of Suzanne Valadon.* New York: St. Martin's Press, 2018.

Jackson, Jeffrey. *Paper Bullets: Two Artists Who Risked Their Lives to Defy the Nazis.* Chapel Hill, NC: Algonquin Books, 2020.

Krysa, Danielle. *A Big Important Art Book (Now with Women): Profiles of Unstoppable Female Artists—and Projects to Help You Become One.* Philadelphia: Running Press, 2018.

Moorhead, Joanna. *Surreal Life of Leonora Carrington.* London: Virago, 2019.

Quinn, Bridget. *Broad Strokes: 15 Women Who Made Art and Made History (In That Order).* San Francisco: Chronicle Books, 2017.

Sullivan, Rosemary. *Villa Air-Bel: World War II, Escape, and a House in Marseille.* New York: Harper, 2006.

Toklas, Alice B. *The Alice B. Toklas Cook Book.* New York: HarperCollins (reprint), 1984.

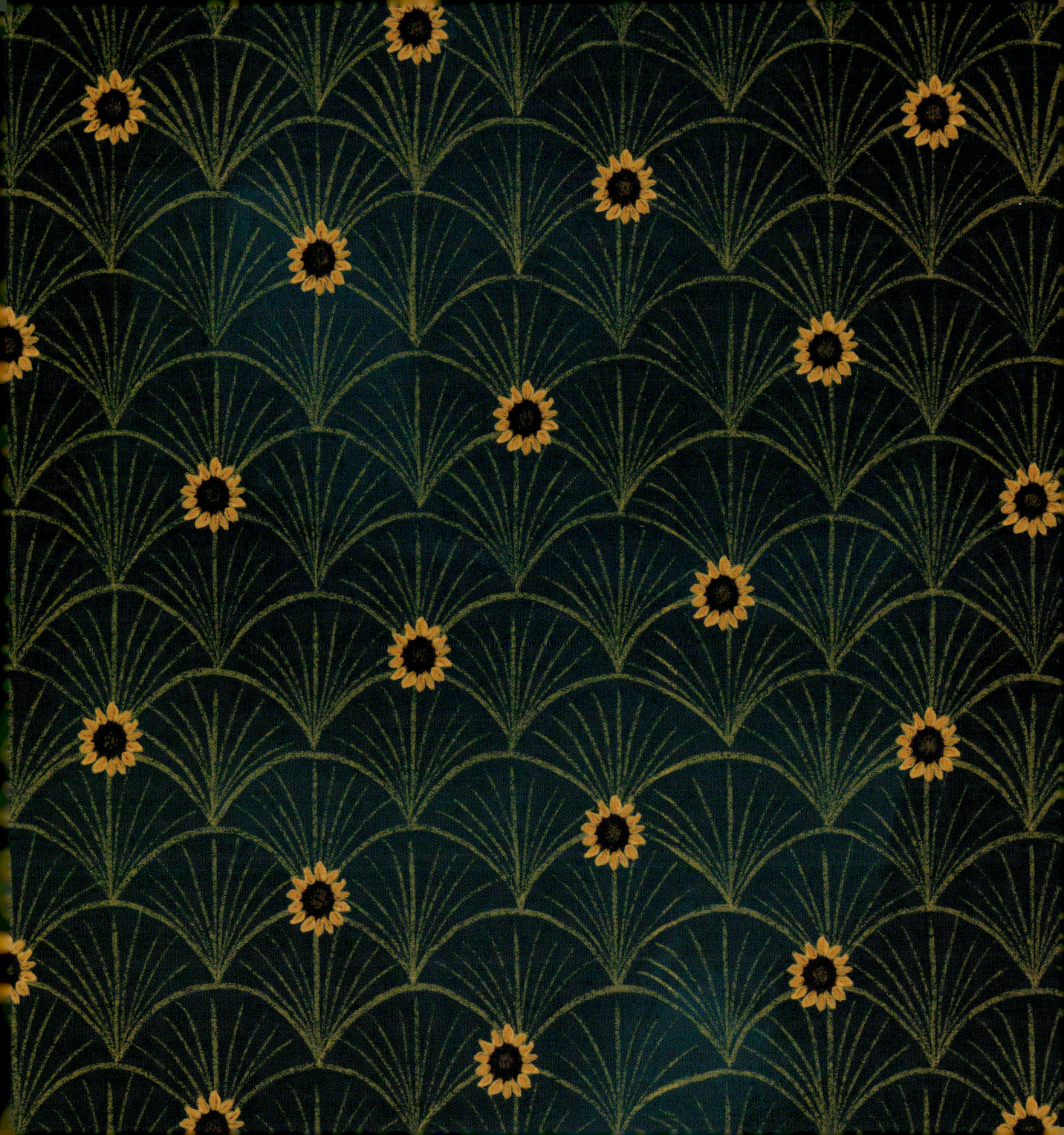

INDEX

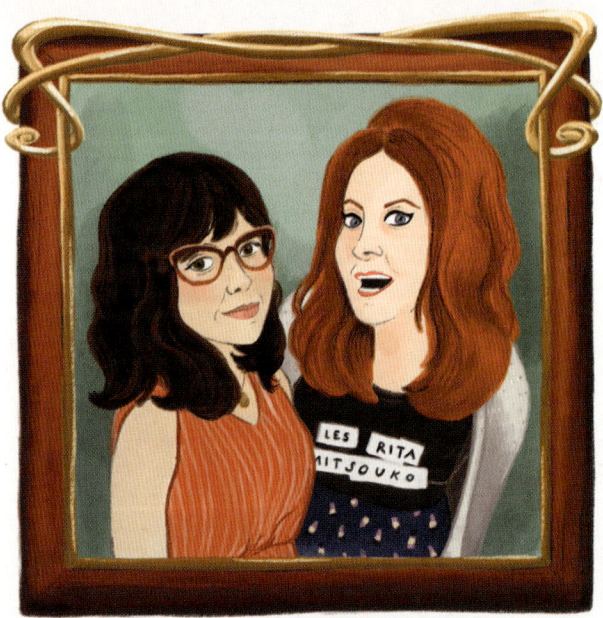

ABOUT THE AUTHOR

LORI ZIMMER is the author of four other books, including *Art Hiding in Paris: An Illustrated Guide to the City of Light* and *Art Hiding in New York: An Illustrated Guide to the City's Secret Masterpieces* with Maria. A longtime New Yorker, she has served on the Board of Directors & Advisers for the Historic Districts Council of New York since 2022.

ABOUT THE ILLUSTRATOR

MARIA KRASINSKI is an artist, educator, and illustrator of the *Art Hiding* series with Lori Zimmer. By day, she works with a global media platform for young people that amplifies overlooked stories. A former Peace Corps volunteer and *Jeopardy!* runner-up, she lives in Paris.

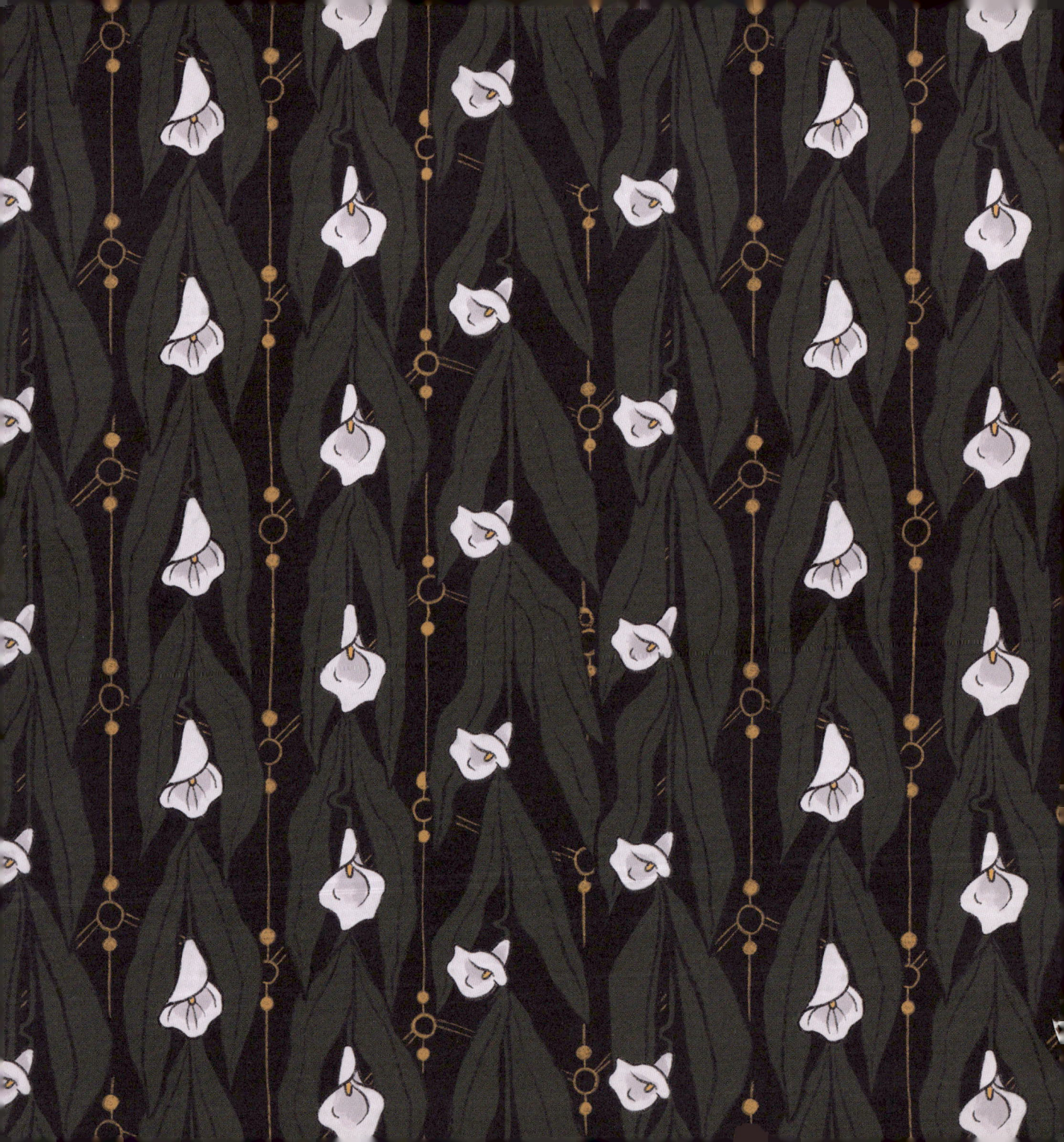